SANTA ANA PUBLIC LIBRARY

LION *of* LIBERTY

*Clay bust of Patrick Henry by
"itinerant Italian sculptor" in 1788.*
(Red Hill Museum Collection, Patrick Henry
Memorial Foundation, Brookneal, VA)

LION *of* LIBERTY

PATRICK HENRY
AND THE CALL TO A NEW NATION

HARLOW GILES UNGER

DA CAPO PRESS
A Member of the Perseus Books Group

Designed by Trish Wilkinson
Set in 11.5 point Adobe Garamond Pro

Cataloging-in-Publication Data is available from the Library of Congress
ISBN: 978-0-306-81886-8

First Da Capo Press edition 2010

Published by Da Capo Press
A Member of the Perseus Books Group
www.dacapopress.com

Da Capo Press books are available at special discounts for bulk purchases in the U.S. by corporations, institutions, and other organizations. For more information, please contact the Special Markets Department at the Perseus Books Group, 2300 Chestnut Street, Suite 200, Philadelphia, PA 19103, or call (800) 810-4145, ext. 5000, or e-mail special .markets@perseusbooks.com.

10 9 8 7 6 5 4 3 2 1

To my friend and mentor
John P. Kaminski

Contents

Illustrations · ix

Acknowledgments · xi

Chronology · xiii

Introduction · 1

CHAPTER 1
Tongue-tied . . . · 5

CHAPTER 2
Tongue Untied · 19

CHAPTER 3
The Flame Is Spread · 27

CHAPTER 4
We Are Slaves! · 47

CHAPTER 5
To Recover Our Just Rights · 65

CHAPTER 6
We Must Fight! · 83

CHAPTER 7
"Give Me Liberty . . . "   93

CHAPTER 8
"Don't Tread on Me"   107

CHAPTER 9
Hastening to Ruin   127

CHAPTER 10
Obliged to Fly   141

CHAPTER 11
A Belgian Hare   161

CHAPTER 12
Seeds of Discontent   183

CHAPTER 13
On the Wings of the Tempest   197

CHAPTER 14
A Bane of Sedition   215

CHAPTER 15
Beef! Beef! Beef!   233

CHAPTER 16
The Sun Has Set in All Its Glory   257

Afterword   275

Appendix A. The Speech   279
Appendix B. Henry on Slavery   283
Appendix C. Henry's Heirs   285
Notes   287
Bibliography   305
Index   311

Illustrations

Maps

1. British Colonies, 1763   8
2. Confederation of American States, 1783   176

Illustrations

1. Hanover County Courthouse   6
2. Virginia Capitol at Williamsburg   29
3. Patrick Henry Condemns the Stamp Act   39
4. Richard Henry Lee   48
5. Patrick Henry as a Virginia Burgess   56
6. Raleigh Tavern   63
7. Boston Massacre   68
8. Henry's Home at "Scotchtown"   70
9. John Adams   77
10. George Washington   86
11. Site of "Liberty or Death" Speech   96
12. Interior of St. John's Church   99
13. Virginia's Rattlesnake Flag   109

14. George Mason   117
15. Dorothea Henry   144
16. Benedict Arnold   155
17. Thomas Jefferson   159
18. James Madison   168
19. Virginia State Capitol in Richmond   172
20. Edmund Randolph   190
21. Patrick Henry at the ratification   231
22. Sketches of Patrick Henry   250
23. Henry's Home at Red Hill   262

Acknowledgments

My deepest thanks to Karen Gorham and Edith C. Poindexter of the Patrick Henry Memorial Foundation at Patrick Henry's Red Hill home, in Brookneal, Virginia. Karen Gorham is director at Red Hill, and Edith Poindexter was, until her recent retirement, curator and genealogist there for many years. Both are superb historians and were generous in sharing their encyclopedic knowledge of Henry, his family, and his times. In addition, both ladies were gracious enough to vet the final manuscript to ensure its accuracy. Ms. Poindexter also shared important research materials that shed new light on Patrick Henry's life and family, while Ms. Gorham provided me with several key illustrations and a number of essential research materials. I must add, as well, that both ladies deserve the thanks of all Americans for their important work at the Patrick Henry Memorial Foundation in Brookneal, Virginia.

I am also most grateful to John P. Kaminski, one of America's premier (and busiest) scholars, who, with his usual generosity, was kind enough to vet this manuscript. Historian, author, educator, lecturer, documentary editor, and patriot, John P. Kaminski is founder and director of the Center for the Study of the American Constitution. He is also responsible for producing one of the nation's most important historical treasures: *The*

Documentary History of the Ratification of the Constitution, and I am honored by his friendship.

I want to express my deepest thanks as well to the many gracious folks at my publisher, Da Capo Press of the Perseus Books Group, who work so hard and expertly behind the scenes and seldom receive public acknowledgment for the beautiful books they help produce and market. Among them are Lissa Warren, Director of Publicity; Kevin Hanover, Director of Marketing and the wonderful sales force for the Perseus Books Group; Sean Maher in marketing; assistant editor Jonathan Crowe; project editors Renee Caputo and Cisca Schreefel; copy editor Anais Scott; proofreader Laura Keenan; indexer Robie Grant; and designer Trish Wilkinson.

Finally, my deepest thanks to my editor, Robert Pigeon, executive editor at Da Capo Press, for the time and effort he put into improving this manuscript, and to my friend and literary agent, Edward W. Knappman, of New England Publishing Associates.

Author's Note: Spellings and grammar in the eighteenth-century letters and manuscripts cited in this book have, where appropriate, been modernized to clarify syntax without altering the intent of the original authors. Readers may find the original spellings in works cited in the endnotes and bibliography at the back of the book. Regarding the depictions of Patrick Henry, the wide and sometimes incongruous differences in the portraits and sculptures result in part from the degenerating effects of malaria as he aged. A second reason, however, is that Henry only sat for four portraits during his lifetime—two miniatures, the sketches by Latrobe on page 250, and the clay bust on the frontispiece. Subsequent portraits shown in this book were made long after his death from the two miniatures and include distortions by artists who never actually saw Henry. The clay bust, however, "was considered a perfect likeness [at the time]," according to Patrick Henry's friend, Judge John Tyler.

Chronology

May 29, 1736. Patrick Henry born in Hanover County, Virginia.

1752. Opens store with brother William; fails one year later.

1754. Marries Sarah Shelton; begins farming.

1757. House burns down; farm fails; he opens a new store.

1759. Economic depression closes store; he moves into tavern; tends bar, studies law.

1760. Passes law exams; begins practice.

1763. Gains fame in "Parsons' Cause" case.

1765. Elected to House of Burgesses; Stamp Act Speech, May 29.

1767. Moves to "Scotchtown" plantation; wife Sarah suffers depression.

1774. Delegate to Continental Congress.

1775. "Liberty or Death" speech, March 23; Virginia's commander in chief; wife Sarah dies.

1776. Resigns military command; returns to state assembly; Virginia declares independence; helps write state constitution; champions religious liberty and end to slave trade; elected Virginia's first governor; leads war effort.

1777. Elected to second term as governor; organizes Virginia Navy; sends troops against British in Illinois, Indiana, the Carolinas; marries Dorothea Dandridge.

1778. Elected to third term; exposes plot to oust Washington; uncovers corruption behind Valley Forge miseries.

1779–1784. Leader, Virginia Assembly; champions restoration of British trade, return of Tories; intermarriage of whites and Indians.

1784. Elected governor a fourth time.

1785. Threatens secession over Mississippi River navigation rights; re-elected governor; rejects stronger confederation; supports farmer tax protests; nation faces anarchy.

1786. Daughters marry; his views on women, marriage, slavery; declines another term as governor.

1787. Refuses to attend Constitutional Convention; prophesies tyranny under national government.

1788. Leads fight against ratification; demands Bill of Rights and limits on federal powers; resumes law practice.

1791. Quits politics for full-time private law practice; landmark British Debts Case.

1792. Land speculations; Yazoo scandal.

1794–1796. Declines appointments as U.S. Senator, Secretary of State, Chief Justice of the U.S. Supreme Court, and other federal posts.

1799. Returns to politics; recaptures Assembly seat; Dorothea gives birth to her eleventh child—his seventeenth—lives four days.

June 6, 1799. Patrick Henry dies at sixty-three. Buried at Red Hill, Charlotte County, Virginia.

Introduction

"As this government stands," Patrick Henry thundered, "I despise and abhor it. . . . I speak as one poor individual—but when I speak, I speak the language of thousands. If I am asked what is to be done when a people feel themselves intolerably oppressed, my answer is . . . 'overturn the government!'"

Henry's roar of exhortation was not aimed at Britain; it was aimed at the United States, as the thirteen former British colonies considered whether to adopt a new constitution. As he had done a decade earlier in his famed cry for "liberty or death," Henry once again roared for the rights of free men to govern themselves with as few restrictions from government as possible. His roar would reverberate through the ages of American history to this very day.

Known to generations of Americans for his stirring call to arms, "Give me liberty or give me death," Patrick Henry is all but forgotten as the *first* of the Founding Fathers to call for independence, for revolution against Britain, for a bill of rights, and for as much freedom as possible from government—American as well as British. If Washington was the "Sword of the Revolution" and Jefferson "the Pen," Patrick Henry more than earned his epithet as "the Trumpet" of the Revolution for rousing Americans to arms in the Revolutionary War.[1]

1

As first governor of Virginia—then the most important colony in America—Henry became the most important civilian leader of the Revolutionary War, ensuring troops and supplies for Washington's Continental Army and engineering the American victory over British and Indian forces in the West that brought present-day Illinois, Indiana, Ohio, and Kentucky into the Union. Without Patrick Henry, there might never have been a revolution, independence, or United States of America.

A champion of religious freedom, Henry fought to end slave importation and was the true father of the Bill of Rights. Recognized in his day as America's greatest orator and lawyer, Henry bitterly opposed big national governments—American as well as British. He sought, instead, to unite American states in an "amicable" confederation that left each state free to govern itself as it saw fit, but ready to unite with its neighbors in defense against a common enemy. A bitter foe of the Constitution, he predicted that its failure to limit federal government powers would restore the very tyranny that had provoked the revolution against Britain. He warned that the Constitution as written failed to include a bill of rights to guarantee freedom of speech, freedom of religion, freedom of the press, trial by jury, redress of grievances, and other basic individual rights.

Although the First Congress passed some of Henry's amendments to protect individual liberties, it rejected his demands to impose strict limits on federal powers and safeguard state sovereignty. His struggle for the rights of states to govern themselves sowed the seeds of secession in the South and subsequent growth of the large intrusive federal government that Henry so despised. Within months of taking office, Congress enacted a national tax without the consent of state legislatures—as Parliament had with the Stamp Act in 1765. In 1794, President Washington fulfilled Henry's prophesy of presidential tyranny by sending troops into Pennsylvania to suppress protests against federal taxation—as Britain's Lord North had done in Boston in 1774.

To this day, many Americans misunderstand what Patrick Henry's cry for "liberty or death" meant to him and to his tens of thousands of devoted followers in Virginia's Piedmont hills—then and now. A prototype of the eighteenth- and nineteenth-century American frontiersman, Henry claimed that free men had a "natural right" to live free of "the tyranny of rulers"—American, as well as British. A student of the French political philosopher Montesquieu, Henry believed that individual rights were more secure in small republics, where governors live among the governed, than in large republics where "the public good is sacrificed to a thousand views." Rather than the big government created by the Constitution, Henry sought to create an alliance of independent, sovereign states in America—similar to Switzerland, whose confederation, he said, had "stood upwards of four hundred years . . . braved all the power of . . . ambitious monarchs . . . [and] retained their independence, republican simplicity, and valor."[2]

The son of a superbly educated Scotsman from Aberdeen, Henry grew up in Virginia's frontier hill country—free to hunt, fish, swim, and roam the fields and forests at will. Far from government constraints and urban crowding, everyday life in the Piedmont was an adventure with wild animals, Indian marauders, and fierce frontiersmen. Unable at times—or unwilling—to distinguish between license and liberty, they viewed government with suspicion and hostility—and tax collectors as fit for nothing better than a bath in hot tar and a coat of chicken feathers. The results were often conflict, gunfire, bloodshed, death, and quasi-civil war. For backcountry farmers and frontiersmen, the business end of a musket was the best way to preserve individual liberty from government intrusion. And Patrick Henry was one of them—their man, their hero. George Washington viewed frontier life as anarchy; Henry called it liberty!

Neither saint nor villain, Henry was one of the towering figures of the nation's formative years and perhaps the greatest orator in American history. Lord Byron, who could only read what Henry had said, called him "the forest-born Demosthenes," and John Adams, who did hear him, hailed him as America's "Demosthenes of the age."[3] George Washington "respected and esteemed" him enough to ask him to serve as secretary of state, then Chief Justice of the United States. Virginia Patriot George Mason called Henry "the first man upon this continent in abilities as well as public virtues" and the Founding Father most responsible for "the preservation of our rights and liberties."[4]

Unlike Washington and Jefferson, who tied their fortunes to Virginia's landed aristocracy, Henry achieved greatness and wealth on his own, among ordinary, hard-working farmers in Virginia's wild Piedmont hills west of Richmond, where independence, self-reliance, and a quick, sharp tongue were as essential to survival as a musket.

A charming storyteller who regaled family and friends with bawdy songs and lively reels on his fiddle, Henry was as quick with a rifle as he was with his tongue—and he fathered so many children (eighteen) and grandchildren (seventy-seven at last count) that friends insisted he, not Washington, was the real father of his country. His direct descendants may well number more than 100,000 today—enough to populate the entire city of Gary, Indiana.

Remembered only for his cry for "liberty or death," Henry was one of the most important and most colorful of our Founding Fathers—a driving force behind three of the most important events in American history: the War of Independence, the enactment of the Bill of Rights, and, tragically, the Civil War.

Chapter 1

Tongue-tied . . .

Eloquence had flowed from his family's lips for generations. The echoes of his kinsmen's voices resounded from the pulpits in Midlothian and Edinburgh to the halls of London's Houses of Parliament. Even in the far-off hills of central Virginia, the dazzling voice of his uncle and namesake, the Reverend Patrick Henry, drew worshipers from miles around for the rapture of his wondrous words each Sunday—words, it seemed, from God himself.

It was quite natural, then, that spectators flocked to Hanover County Courthouse on December 1, 1763, for the inaugural courtroom appearance of the Reverend Henry's nephew, Patrick Henry Jr., as defense lawyer in a major case. Although he had spent three years practicing mostly "paper law" (deeds, wills, and such) and defending petty thieves, this was his first appearance in the theatrical setting of a major courtroom case. Headlined in the press as the "Parsons' Cause," the case had far-reaching religious and political implications for both Virginia and Mother England, where the official Church of England supported itself by taxing landowners in each parish, regardless of whether they were Anglicans or not. In the Parsons' Cause, a Church of England priest sued the vestrymen and landowners of his parish—almost all of them small farmers—for failure to pay all their taxes in 1758. If Henry lost the case, many would lose their homes and lands.

The Hanover County Courthouse, where Patrick Henry began practicing law and won fame in the Parsons' Cause case. (FROM A NINETEENTH-CENTURY PHOTOGRAPH)

Henry had started well enough, shooting to his feet to object when appropriate, and successfully countering his opponents' objections during jury selection, and he'd done well enough during the main trial. But now it was time for his closing argument, and, as an eerie stillness settled over the courtroom, he moved to center stage, bowed his head, and stared at the floor. Seconds went by . . . a minute . . . then another. . . . He seemed at a loss for words. Inquietude spread across the room; spectators exchanged puzzled looks with one another, shifting in their seats uncomfortably. The plaintiff's attorney broke into a snide grin; defendants groaned, and Patrick Henry's father—the presiding judge—slumped in his chair in embarrassment—his expectations for his son all but crushed.

Judge John Henry finally shook his head in despair and prepared to pound his gavel and end his son's travail with a summary judgment for the plaintiff. It was a difficult moment. . . .

Neither he nor the rest of Henry's family could understand why twenty-seven-year-old Patrick was flirting with failure again—as he had in three previous careers—twice as a storekeeper and once as a farmer. He was intelligent, hard-working, cheerful, personable, learned, extremely talented in innumerable ways and, above all, he came from solid, well-educated, hard-working, and successful Scottish and Welsh stock.

The judge, his father, had been born in Aberdeen, Scotland, to a devoutly Anglican family "more respected for their good sense and superior education than for their riches."[1] At fifteen, John Henry had won a Latin composition prize and a scholarship to Aberdeen University, where he spent four years before emigrating to the United States at the behest of John Syme, a boyhood friend and Aberdeen schoolmate. Young Syme had sailed to America three years earlier and grew rich growing tobacco and speculating in land. His education, erudition, and wealth propelled him into Virginia's highest social and political circles—and such sinecures as a militia colonelcy and membership in the House of Burgesses, the colonial legislature. At Syme's urging, John Henry followed his friend to America in 1727, learned surveying and, in partnership with Syme, began speculating in land. Surveying skills were essential in Virginia, where tobacco crops consumed soil nutrients after four to six years and forced planters to find virgin lands in which to plant new crops. Speculators joined the search, of course, and those who were first to claim virgin lands reaped the most profits reselling claims to planters.

Within four years, John Henry had accumulated more than 15,000 acres in three counties, including a 1,200-acre plantation in Hanover County, about sixty miles upriver from Virginia's capital at Williamsburg. In 1731, John Syme died, and after letting two years elapse in the interest of decency, Henry married Syme's "most attractive" widow, Sarah. Of Welsh descent, she was a devout Presbyterian, and brought a dowry of 6,000 acres to the marriage, along with a step-son, John Syme, Jr. Although John Henry scorned her religion, he tolerated his wife's heresy in silence, given all the other benefits she brought to their marriage.

"A person of a lively and cheerful conversation," with "remarkable intellectual gifts" and "an unusual command of language," Sarah traced her

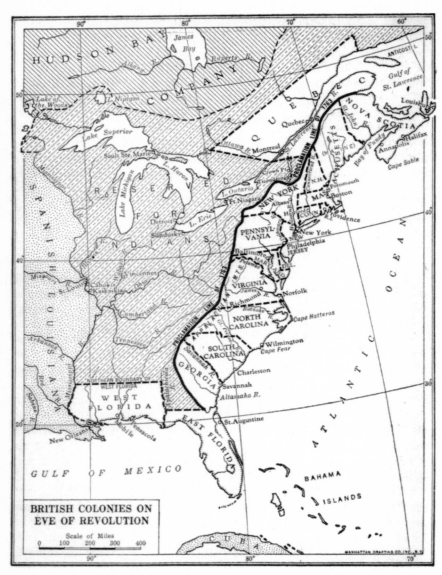

British Colonies in 1763.

lineage to two of Virginia's oldest, most accomplished families—the Winstons and Dabneys—who welcomed John Henry into Hanover County's ruling circle by arranging his appointments as a vestryman of the Church of England, chief justice of the county court, and colonel of the militia. As a vestryman *and* chief justice, John Henry became one of Hanover County's most powerful figures—only nine years after his arrival in America. To reinforce his authority he maneuvered relatives into six of the twelve county judgeships and his older brother, Reverend Patrick Henry, into the pulpit of St. Paul's Anglican church. With his brother governing its spiritual life and John Henry its political life, Hanover County evolved into nothing less than a Henry family fiefdom.

John and Sarah Henry had nine children—two sons and seven daughters—of whom the oldest was William, born in 1735 and named for Sarah Henry's father William Winston. Patrick Henry—named for his priestly uncle—followed a year later, on May 29, 1736. In 1750, with a third child on the way, the Henry family moved from what had been the Syme home into a larger house twenty-two miles from Richmond on an elevation—"Mount Brilliant"—by the South Anna River, where Patrick Henry, the future lawyer, would spend his formative years.

Prominence, power, and wealth in the Hanover County hills, however, did not mimic Virginia's eastern Tidewater region, where such legendary names as Lee, Fairfax, and Carter reigned over 20,000-, 30,000-, and 40,000-acre plantations from palatial mansions that mirrored their ancestral seats in Georgian England. As hundreds of slaves worked the fields, Virginia's Tidewater aristocracy rode to the hounds and sipped tea by marble-mantled fireplaces that filled each room with aromatic warmth. In contrast, Patrick Henry's childhood home was pure "country"—a two-story, forty-by-thirty-foot rectangular box covered with whitewashed clapboards and topped by a half-story dormered attic. Like most Virginia farmhouses, front and rear doors opened on opposite sides of a large central hall on the ground floor to let breezes flow through and cool the house in summer. Although they spent idle moments on the porch, the hall was the center of family life—a combined living room, dining room, and kitchen. A slow wood fire kept meats crackling on a spit in the open hearth, while stews bubbled in kettles dangling from wrought-iron cranes. Two bedrooms lay off the central room, and a staircase to the second floor led to sleeping areas for children.

Patrick Henry grew up "an indolent, dreamy, frolicsome creature," according to William Wirt, a family friend, who said the boy harbored

> a mortal enmity to books, supplemented by a passionate regard for fishing rods and shotguns; disorderly in dress, slouching, unambitious; a roamer in woods, a loiterer on river-banks; having more tastes in common with trappers and frontiersmen than with the toilers of civilized life; giving no hint or token, by word or act, of the possession of any intellectual gift that could raise him above mediocrity, or even up to it.[2]

Although Wirt called Henry's "aversions to study . . . invincible, and his faculties benumbed by indolence,"[3] one of Henry's boyhood friends portrays him as simply a normal country boy. "He was remarkably fond of fun . . . but his fun was innocent, and I never discovered in any one action of his childhood or youth the least spice of ill-nature or malevolence; he was remarkably fond of hunting, fishing, and playing on the violin."[4]

Henry's future brother-in-law, Samuel Meredith, who was four years older and lived nearby, remembered him as

> mild, benevolent, humane . . . quiet, thoughtful, but fond of society. . . . He was fond of reading, but indulged in innocent amusements. He was remarkably fond of his gun. He interested himself much in the happiness of others, particularly his sisters . . . His father often said he was one of the most dutiful sons that ever lived . . . He had a nice ear for music . . . was an excellent performer on the violin.[5]

Fiddling, of course, was one of the most popular pastimes in early America. Fiddlers such as Henry seldom read music, relying instead on memory and improvisational skills to learn the tunes they played. He also learned to play the flute, English guitar, and harpsichord.

Like most country boys, he learned to fish in his early years, and, by the time he was ten, his father had taught him to shoot a muzzle-loading musket with unfailing accuracy—and add tasty small game to the family fare. Like most literate parents in the colonies, the Henrys taught their two boys to read, write, and calculate, using the Scriptures and a variety of literature and periodicals. John Henry taught his sons Latin, Greek, French, mathematics, and science—and the histories of Rome, England, and the American colonies. Sarah improved their skills in reading and writing and exposed them to English literature. "He was delighted with *The Life and Opinions of Tristram Shandy*," one friend recalled. "I have known him to read several hours together, lying with his back upon a bed. He had a most retentive memory, making whatever he read his own."[6]

By the time Patrick Henry was fifteen, he and his brother had read the *Odyssey* in Greek, mastered Horace, Virgil, and Livy in Latin, and conversed well enough in colloquial Latin to chat with educated Europeans who could not speak English.

Despite his fine education, Patrick Henry grew up with the coarse mountain accent of the wild country boys that lived nearby. "Mr. Henry was remarkably well acquainted with mankind," his son-in-law Judge Spencer Roane explained. "This faculty arose from mingling freely with mankind and from a keen sense of observation. . . . Nothing escaped his attention."[7]

Unlike Tidewater Virginians, Piedmonters were a secular lot, chafing under taxes they had to pay to the Anglican Church, resenting restrictions on non-Anglican religious practices, hating government agents, and mocking both royalty and nobility in the bawdy folk tunes they sang at local taverns. Although baptized in the Anglican Church of his father and uncle, Patrick Henry also attended his mother's Presbyterian services, where he learned the differences between autocracy and democracy. Anglicans pledged unquestioned allegiance to the king and the Bishop of London, who appointed all parish priests; Presbyterians governed their own churches and elected their own ministers. It was the Presbyterian Church that "nourished . . . his partiality for the dissenters of the Established Church," according to Edmund Randolph, a cousin of Thomas Jefferson and scion of one of Virginia's oldest and most powerful families. "From a repetition of . . . the history of their sufferings," Randolph said, Henry began "descanting . . . on the martyrs in the cause of liberty."[8] By attending two churches, Henry received a broad-based religious education, learning of the infallibility of King and Church in his father's Anglican church and the fallibility of King and Church in his mother's Presbyterian church.

When Patrick Henry turned fifteen, John Henry lacked the money to send his son to an English or Scottish university, but reasoned that a university education would be of little practical use in the West. He sent young Patrick to work in a country store to learn how to run a business. A year later he helped Patrick and William open a store of their own, where Virginia's complex barter economy put the boys at an immediate disadvantage. Ninety-five percent of Americans lived on farms and bought what they needed with a jug of whiskey, a bag of grain, a piglet, a chicken, a land certificate, or a personal note. By the end of their first year, the Henry boys had accumulated a stack of IOUs, but no liquid assets to replenish their merchandise, and they went out of business.

In the fall of 1754, Patrick Henry, now eighteen, married sixteen-year-old Sarah Shelton, a girl he had known since early childhood. Sarah's grandfather was a bookseller and the first publisher of the *Virginia Gazette*. Her father was not only a successful Hanover County planter, he owned the thriving inn and tavern opposite the Hanover County Courthouse, on the Stage Road from Fredericksburg to Williamsburg. After Patrick Henry's uncle married them, Sarah's father gave the newlyweds a 300-acre farm adjoining his own, along with six slaves. From the beginning, however, their lives on the farm seemed destined for disaster. Years of successive tobacco crops had depleted soil nutrients and left the land yielding low-quality weed. In 1757, Henry harvested only 6.5 bushels of tobacco, for which he received just over £10 pounds ($610 today) at market. Making matters worse, their six slaves were mere boys—children of recently imported slaves. Unskilled and unable to speak English, they were of little use to Patrick, who nonetheless had to feed, clothe, and house them—while he himself performed the "labor on his farm with his own hands," according to his grandson.[9]

Nor was Sarah's life any easier. Within a year, their first child, Martha, was born. A boy, John, followed the next year, and a third—another boy, William—was on his way in 1757 when fire consumed their farmhouse and its contents. Patrick, Sarah, and the children moved into an empty cabin and tried to halt their financial free fall. Patrick sold his slaves to furnish the cabin and buy a stock of goods to open another store, then hired a clerk to tend the store while he worked the fields and Sarah tended the children and kitchen garden.

He could not have picked a worse time to open a store: A drought had devastated the area's harvest and left farmers without means to buy necessities, let alone extras or luxuries. At the end of his first year, Patrick Henry had collected a mere £10. During the first half of his second year, only twenty-six customers set foot in the store. In debt himself, without capital to buy more inventory, with a wife, a newborn, and two other children to feed, he closed the store and moved his family into the attic of his father-in-law's inn, across the road from the Hanover County Courthouse. In exchange for room and board, Henry tended bar and entertained customers with his fiddle, hiring an overseer to continue wringing whatever he could out of the farmland.

In the winter of 1759–1760, Patrick went by himself to several Christmas celebrations to search for job opportunities, leaving Sarah alone at home to mind the children—a lonely, isolated role she would play almost without variation the rest of her life.

"My acquaintance with Mr. Henry commenced in the winter of 1759–1760," Thomas Jefferson recalled. On his way to enroll at the College of William and Mary, Jefferson was spending his Christmas holidays on the 6,000-acre Hanover plantation of the wealthy shipbuilder Nathaniel West Dandridge, a son-in-law of the colonial governor and a cousin of George Washington's fiancée, Martha Dandridge Custis. A neighbor of John Henry, Dandridge was a close friend of the judge, and young Patrick "was at home as one of the family," according to Jefferson.

> During the festivity of the season I met Mr. Henry in society every day. His manners had something of coarseness in them; his passion was music, dancing, and pleasantry. He excelled in the latter, and it attached everyone to him. Mr. Henry had, a little before, broken up his store—or, rather, it had broken him up; but his misfortunes were not traced, either in his countenance or conduct.[10]

Hanover County was entirely rural, with only about 10,000 people scattered across the land—more than half of them slaves. Hanover town—the county seat and largest community—had fewer than fifty houses. Court days, though, turned the town into a fairground. A procession of vendors peddled horses, quilts, "white lightning," and patent medicines often more potent than white lightning. In the yard before the courthouse, burly sheriffs and fierce-looking deputies dispensed justice—often dragging sobbing women or somnambulant drunks into the stocks or flogging runaway slaves, as spectators hallooed at the agony.

Across the road from the courthouse, the Shelton tavern was aswarm with lawyers and their clients, debating virtually every written, unwritten, and should've-been-written law. Henry's cousin William Winston recalled that Patrick dressed like most hill folk—in coarse work clothes, "very often barefooted. . . . He was very active and attentive to his guests and very frequently amused them with his violin on which he performed very well."[11] Reels were popular, setting the men to dancing—and tripping over themselves. Patrick Henry sang Scottish ballads—some bawdier than others, but all of them enlivened with facial expressions that sent drinkers doubling over with laughter:

> *"Go get me some of your father's gold*
> *And some of your mother's too,*
> *And two of the finest horses he has in his stable*
> *For he has ten and thirty and two."*

> *She got him some of her father's gold*
> *And some of her mother's too,*
> *And two of the finest horses he has in his stable*
> *For he had ten and thirty and two.*

> *Then she jumped on the noble brown,*
> *And he on the dappled gray,*
> *And they rode till they came to the side of the sea,*
> *Two long hours before it was day.*

"Let me help you down, my Pretty Polly;
Let me help you down," said he.
"For it's six king's daughters I have drowned here,
And the seventh you shall be."

"Now strip yourself, my Pretty Polly;
Now strip yourself," said he.
"Your clothing is too fine and over-costly
To rot in the sand of the sea."

"You turn your back to the leaves of the trees,
And your face to the sand of the sea;
'Tis a pity such a false-hearted man as you
A naked woman should see."

He turned his back to the leaves of the trees,
And his face to the sand of the sea;
And with all the strength Pretty Polly had
She pushed him into the sea. . . .[12]

Between the laughter, singing, and dancing, Patrick Henry listened intently to the legal arguments in the tavern and attended trials at the courthouse when he could. As his interest peaked, he bought copies of a *Digest of Virginia Acts* and Sir Edward Coke's *First Part of the Institutes of the Lawes of England, or, A Commentarie upon Littleton.*[13] Using a fragmented grasp of the law, he debated lawyers in the tavern and practiced a crude but entertaining form of law, offering free legal counsel for every drink his client bought and revealing a spell-binding gift for "talking a long string of learning." Warned that practicing without a license carried the risk of personal liability—and even a musket ball from a disgruntled client—he went to the colonial capital to get a license.

On April 1, 1760, Patrick Henry arrived in Williamsburg for oral examinations, each to be administered by a renowned legal scholar. In contrast to the impeccably tailored, bewigged examiners, Henry appeared in drab homespun—his mountain drawl all but unintelligible as he spoke of his country learning, which he feared was scarcely up to Williamsburg standards.

Truth was, Henry knew next to nothing about the law, but he needed to pass only two of four examinations to obtain a license. The first examiner, law professor George Wythe, refused to receive the ill-dressed young man at first, but relented—as did the second, the illustrious attorney Robert Carter Nicholas—after Henry made a dramatic plea defending his right to be heard. Even then, he resisted arbitrary rule by authorities. Henry entertained both Wythe and Nicholas with dramatic gestures and effusive praise for the "righteousness of the law," the "natural rights of man," and "the blessings which a gracious God hath bestowed upon us" in Virginia. He had heard the phrases in his father's courtroom, his father-in-law's tavern, and his uncle's church, and he assumed they were relevant to the law.[14] He spoke of honest, hard-working farmers in Virginia's hill country, beset by savage Indians and vicious squatters. He talked of scalpings, murders, and cries of orphaned children—and the need for lawyers to defend their interests. "The music of his voice" and "natural elegance of his style and manner" all but transfixed Nicholas, and, after eliciting Henry's promise to continue studying the law, he signed the young man's license.

Deciding to obtain a third, but unnecessary signature, Henry foolishly chose to challenge Williamsburg's legal establishment by approaching Attorney General John Randolph, who boasted the best legal training and legal mind in the colony. Randolph was affronted by Henry's farm clothes and set about humiliating the arrogant farm boy with an examination that "continued for several hours," according to one of Henry's friends, "interrogating him, not on . . . law, in which he no doubt soon discovered his deficiencies, but . . . on the laws of nature and of nations, on the policy of the feudal system, and on general history, which last he found to be his stronghold."

"'You defend your opinions well, sir,' Randolph conceded. 'I will never trust to appearances again. Mr. Henry, if your industry be only half equal to your genius, I augur that you will do well and become an ornament and an honor to your profession.'"[15] And so, with almost no knowledge of law,

Henry returned to his native hill country and, on April 15, 1760, took an oath and gained admission to the bar.

In fact, Henry's legal training was no less than that of most country lawyers—and more than many. America had no law schools, and only a handful of wealthy young men could afford to travel to London to study law at the Inns of Court. The rest learned their trade through a combination of self-study and apprenticeships with "master lawyers." Once in practice, most lawyers did little more than draw up bills of sale, deeds, contracts, and wills, leaving serious disputes in small towns and rural areas to mediation by sheriffs and ministers. For court cases, jury pools were so small that jurors, lawyers, and defendants were on a first-name basis and defense lawyers routinely packed juries with friends and neighbors.

With his father, step brother, and five other family members presiding in the Hanover County Court, it was not surprising that Patrick Henry proved phenomenally successful—so much so that he attracted clients from the farthest points of neighboring counties to appear with him in his father's court. In the closing months of 1760 after receiving his license, Patrick Henry handled 197 cases; by 1763 his caseload had climbed to 374 and his income had reached more than £600, or about $42,500 in today's currency—an enormous sum in eighteenth-century rural Virginia. In the first three years of practice, he handled 1,185 suits, in addition to preparing legal documents and dispensing legal advice in his father-in-law's tavern.

To his credit, Henry kept his word to Nicholas and studied the full range of legal texts, including Sir William Blackstone's *Commentaries on the Laws of England*, William Bohun's *Declarations and Pleadings*, Giles Jacob's *The Compleat Chancery-Practiser*, Samuel Pufendorf's *The Law of Nature and Nations*, and other tomes. Little by little, he acquired as much knowledge of British law as any lawyer in Virginia, and on December 1, 1763, after three years of practicing mostly "paper law," he stepped onto center stage for his inaugural appearance in a major courtroom drama—the Parsons' Cause.

But as his father the judge and the rest of the packed courtroom awaited his closing argument, Patrick Henry stood silent, his head bowed, staring at the floor, apparently at a loss for words. His clients could only fear the worst for their case.

Chapter 2

Tongue Untied

Patrick Henry's clients had good reason to despair. Depending on his summation, many could lose their properties and all their assets. In an earlier trial, the court had already found them guilty of failure to pay their taxes to the Anglican Church, as required by law—regardless of their religion. This was their second trial to determine how much they owed—a far more complex calculation than it might seem.

In the absence of currency, Virginia required each parish to pay the Anglican minister 16,000 pounds of tobacco a year, which the minister then sold in the open market. Parish landowners paid into the total in proportion to the acreage they had under cultivation. Ministers earned more when tobacco prices rose and absorbed losses when they fell, but over the years they earned an average of about two pence per pound. In 1758, however, a catastrophic drought devastated Virginia's tobacco crop, sending tobacco prices to record highs but reducing tobacco stocks to levels that would have left many planters bankrupt, without any tobacco left to sell if they delivered the required 16,000 pounds of tobacco to each parish priest. Virginia's legislature—the House of Burgesses—passed the Twopenny Act, to permit each parish to pay its minister in cash instead of tobacco at the average rate that ministers had earned in the sixty years the tobacco tax had been in effect—namely, two pence a pound, or a total of about V£133 (Virginia currency), instead of 16,000 pounds of tobacco.

The drought, however, had sent the actual market value of tobacco soaring to more than three times that amount, and each minister would have earned about V£400 had he been paid in tobacco and sold it on the open market. With the richest planters profiting most from high tobacco prices, the outraged ministers protested, saying that the House of Burgesses had no authority to alter what was "the king's law" on church taxes. They sent lawyers to London, where the British government agreed—and voided the Twopenny Act. The ministers then sued their respective parishes for payment of the difference between the two pennies per pound they received in 1758 and the market value of the 16,000 pounds of tobacco that they should have received. The Reverend James Maury, a renowned scholar who had tutored young Thomas Jefferson and prepared him for the College of William and Mary, filed his suit in the County Court of Hanover before the devout Anglican Justice John Henry. Henry declared the Twopenny Act to have been "no law," ruled in favor of Reverend Maury, and ordered a second trial to determine damages.

Believing that Justice Henry's decision had made the amount of damages a mere formality, the lawyer for parishioners quit the case, telling his clients to await the inevitable jury determination and pay Reverend Maury his due. Refusing to face trial without counsel, however, the vestrymen turned to young Patrick Henry, with hopes that, given his uncle's ties to the church, he might persuade Reverend Maury to reduce his monetary demands enough to permit local farmers to avoid bankruptcy.

Reverend Maury's renown drew a larger than normal crowd to the Hanover County Courthouse. Anxiety and anger tinged the usual holiday mood, as prosperous planters mixed with ordinary farmers and their relatives from Maury's parish—all of them stern-faced over the prospect of paying the minister his pound of flesh. Adding to the agitation was a large group of dissenters—Presbyterians and the like—who resented having to pay taxes to the Anglican Church and had vague hopes of turning the trial into a protest against church-state ties. As would-be spectators streamed toward the courthouse, hawkers extolled the benefits of white lightning, patent medicines, livestock, young slaves, and whatever else they hoped to sell. As Patrick Henry approached the courthouse, he saw his uncle's carriage arrive and, fearing that his uncle's presence might sway jurors, he ran up to plead with him not to attend the trial.

"Why?" said the surprised clergymen.

"Because," young Patrick said disingenuously, "I am engaged in opposition to the clergy, and your appearance there might strike me with such awe as to prevent me from doing justice to my clients." Convinced that his nephew faced humiliation, the old parson climbed back into his carriage and rode home.[1]

Inside, the call to order brought presiding justice John Henry to the center of the long bench, followed by six other justices—all of them relatives of the Henry family by blood or marriage. Although twenty Anglican parsons had come to support the Reverend Maury, farmers made up the rest of the packed courtroom. After the clerk called the case, Justice Henry ordered the sheriff to summon a jury. Of the twelve called, at least four, including one of Patrick Henry's relatives, were Presbyterian dissenters. A fifth member of the jury was one of the parishioners whom Reverend Maury was suing. Maury objected, charging that the sheriff had gone "among the vulgar herd" and failed "to summon gentlemen." He complained that he knew one juror was "a party in the cause. . . . Yet this man's name was not erased. He was even called in court, and had he not excused himself, would probably have been admitted."[2]

Henry shot to his feet, demanding to know whether Maury was accusing the prospective jurors of dishonesty. Taken aback by Henry's aggressive challenge, Maury remained silent, and Henry turned to his father, proclaiming the jurors to be honest men and, therefore, "unexceptionable." Justice Henry agreed and the jurors took their oaths and their seats in the jury box to await the plaintiff's argument.

Maury's lawyer had a compelling case: The parish had paid him a mere £144 at a time when market prices of tobacco, according to the testimony of two tobacco dealers, would have yielded three times that amount had he received the usual 16,000 pounds of tobacco and sold it. With the Twopenny Act null and void and there being no excuse for underpayment,

Maury's lawyer demanded that the jury award his client the difference between £144 (about $8,800) and £432 (about $26,000) or £288 (about $17,500 today), plus legal fees and court costs.

The assembled parsons nodded their collective heads in agreement and turned to each other with self-satisfied smiles. Farmers among the spectators shuffled their feet uncomfortably and moaned softly over the huge losses they and their friends faced. As Maury's lawyer took his seat, Patrick Henry stepped onto center stage.

"No one had ever heard him speak, and curiosity was on tiptoe," according to William Wirt, a future U.S. attorney general. "He rose very awkwardly."[3]

In contrast to the dignified robes of the justices and men of the cloth, his coarse country clothes, though neat, gave him the appearance of a penitent rather than an attorney. Not a soul in the courtroom believed that his clients did not owe Parson Maury the difference between the amount they had paid him and the market value of 16,000 pounds of tobacco in 1758. Seconds passed—it seemed like minutes—as silence gripped the courtroom. Finally, Henry tilted his head upward, eyes fixed at the ceiling, lips pursed, and . . .

. . . still nothing. Not a word.

The spectators shifted uneasily in their seats, wondering with his father whether he was too young for the task ahead. Young Henry, however, had practiced long hours in the silence of the woods rehearsing for this moment—rehearsing rhetoric, trying out different acting techniques, reading plays aloud, memorizing lines with universal meanings that might apply in court. So he was ready when he stepped into court on December 1, 1763, and he opened his performance with a classic dramatic pause that gripped the courtroom with suspense.

When he finally spoke, he was nothing short of brilliant, modestly lowering his head at appropriate times, lifting his eyes to heaven in supplication at the right moment, roaring in rage, mewling in sorrow or pity, all but whispering one moment and thundering the next. In contrast to the pseudo-English inflections of most lawyers, he spoke the language of his jurors, with a mountain drawl. His days in the tavern across the road had taught him how to win their minds and hearts. Six feet tall, lean, cheek-bones protruding from his gaunt face, he marched back and forth, using every element of the stage. Instead of a defense attorney, he turned into a prosecutor, charging Maury and the Anglican clergy with un-Christian acts of extracting the last pennies from poverty-stricken farmers and forcing their wives and babies from their homes.

"We have heard a great deal about the benevolence and holy zeal of our reverend clergy, but how is this manifested?" he demanded to know.

> Do they manifest their zeal in the cause of religion and humanity by practicing the mild and benevolent precepts of the Gospel of Jesus? Do they feed the hungry and clothe the naked? Oh, no, gentlemen! Instead of feeding the hungry and clothing the naked, these rapacious harpies would, were their powers equal to their will, snatch from the hearth of their honest parishioner his last hoe-cake [cornbread], from the widow and her orphaned children their last milch cow! the last bed, nay, the last blanket from the lying-in woman![4]

The failed storekeeper and sometime tavern-keeper had found his voice and vocation.

"A wondrous change came over him," according to his grandson. "His attitude became erect and lofty, his face lighted up with genius, and his eyes seemed to flash fire; his gestures became graceful and impressive, his voice and his emphasis peculiarly charming. His appeals to the passions were overpowering. Those who heard him said he made their blood run cold and their hair to rise on end."[5]

Another witness said that spectators looked at each other "in disbelief" when he began his presentation. Then, "attracted by some strong gesture, struck by some majestic attitude, fascinated by the spell of his eye, the charm of his emphasis . . . they could look away no more. In less than twenty minutes, they might be seen in every part of the house . . . in death-like silence, their features fixed in amazement and awe, all their senses listening and riveted upon the speaker, as if to catch the least strain of some heavenly visitant."[6]

In the midst of his dramatic performance, Henry also presented constitutional arguments. He argued that the British government represented a compact between the king and his people, by which the former provided protection in exchange for obedience and support. Either party's refusal to fulfill its obligation, Henry declared, automatically released the other party from its obligations. Henry called the Twopenny Act necessary for the economic survival of the people. By annulling the act, the king had failed to fulfill his obligation to protect the people—indeed, "he had degenerated into a tyrant and forfeited all right to his subjects' obedience to his order of annulment."[7]

"Treason!" cried Maury's attorney.

"Treason!" cried clergymen in the audience.

"The gentleman has spoken treason!" Maury's lawyer shouted as he stood to address the court. "I am astonished that your worships can hear it without emotion or any mark of dissatisfaction."[8]

But Henry's oration had transfixed the justices as much as other spectators, and they remained silent as Henry ignored the interruption and continued—this time shifting his attack from the crown to the clergy. In refusing to abide by the Twopenny Act, the established church had abdicated one of its primary responsibilities to enforce obedience to the laws. "When clergy cease to answer these ends, the community have no further need of their ministry, and may justly strip them of their appointments," he declared. Instead of damages, he cried out, Mr. Maury deserved to be punished with signal severity.

With each phrase, Henry stripped away the veneer of reverence for the clergy that had suppressed the anger of country folk toward the church for generations. Citing "the natural rights" of Virginia freemen to keep the benefits of their labor, he so fired up farmer hatred of the Anglican Church that the clergymen who had come to support Reverend Maury "fled from the house in precipitation and terror." A long, satisfying silence followed, after which Patrick Henry intoned a soft-spoken warning to the jury that the court had already ruled for Reverend Maury in the clergyman's first trial—that he was indeed entitled to compensation, but "excepting they were disposed to rivet the chains of bondage on their own necks, he hoped they would not let slip the opportunity . . . of making such an example of him as might hereafter be a warning to himself and his brethren, not to have the temerity, for the future, to dispute the validity of such laws. . . ." Henry told the jury that the law required them to award Maury damages, but it had no obligation to award him more than a farthing.

Silence followed as the jury trooped out. After less than five minutes of deliberation, its members returned and awarded Reverend Maury one penny.

In the explosion of whoops, yells, and cheers that followed, Maury's lawyer shouted for a mistrial, but the justices dismissed the motion unanimously—setting off an even louder explosion of cheers as spectators hoisted Henry on their shoulders and carried him out of the courthouse in triumph.

Chapter 3

The Flame Is Spread

Patrick Henry was not unaware of his astonishing—almost frightening—gift to move men's minds, and, evidently guilt-stricken by the wounds he had inflicted on Reverend Maury, he sought out the injured priest to atone for his conduct in court.

"He apologized to me for what he had said," Maury recounted bitterly in a letter to an English friend, "alleging that his sole view in engaging in the cause, and in saying what he had was to render himself popular."

> You see, then . . . the ready road to popularity here is to trample under foot the interests of religion, the rights of the Church, and the prerogative of the Crown. If this be not pleading for the 'assumption of a power to bind the King's hands,' if it not be asserting 'such supremacy in provincial legislation' as is inconsistent with the dignity of the Church of England, and manifestly tends to draw the people of these plantations from their allegiance to the King, tell me, my dear sir, what is so, if you can . . . Patrick should have been guilty of a crime . . . he exceeded the most seditious and inflammatory harangues of the tribunes of old Rome.[1]

Some Anglican clergymen pressed the royal governor to prosecute Henry for treason, but the governor refused to risk his popularity with planters by involving himself in controversy that had no clear-cut legal resolution.

Except for Maury and the Anglican clergy, Patrick Henry's victory in the Parsons' Cause added to the joys of the 1763 Christmas season in Hanover County, which was still celebrating Britain's victory in the Seven Years' War. Earlier in the year, the Treaty of Paris had forced France to cede most of its territory on the North American mainland east of the Mississippi to Britain and opened the way for Virginians to settle western lands between the Appalachian Mountains and the Mississippi River, as far north as the Great Lakes. Many Virginians argued that Virginia went beyond the Mississippi to the Pacific Ocean (see Map 1, page 8).

Although some parsons continued their efforts to collect what they deemed was their due while the Twopenny Act was in effect, Henry's victory set a precedent that other Virginia courts refused to overturn. Henry's triumph propelled his name across the colonies and over the ocean to London. Hailed as the most eloquent lawyer in America, he became the champion of small farmers, adding 164 new clients and handling 555 cases in the year following the Parsons' Cause. Each court appearance saw him hone his rhetorical weapons and slice his opponents' arguments with increasingly deadly precision. He used every rhetorical device he could find or invent. On clear days, he embraced the sunshine and lifted jurors' hearts; on grey days he pointed to the clouds and rain to provoke their tears; and on the darkest days, he saw omens of destruction in the heavens that left jurors cowering in fear as he cited each thunderclap or lightning bolt as nothing less than "the wrath of God."

"Whenever he rose to speak," said the losing attorney in the Parsons' Cause, "although it might be on so trifling a subject as a summons and petition for twenty shillings, I was obliged to lay down my pen and could not write another word until the speech was finished."[2]

After the 1764 elections, Henry's friend and neighbor Nathaniel West Dandridge contested his defeat in a close contest for the House of Burgesses and retained Henry as counsel before the Committee on Privileges and Elections at the colonial assembly, in the capitol at Williamsburg. As Henry entered the stately House of Burgesses and peered into the assem-

The Capitol in Williamsburg, where Patrick Henry sat as a member of the House of Burgesses under British rule and the House of Delegates after Virginia declared independence from Britain. (From a nineteenth-century drawing)

bly hall where committee members awaited, he fixed his eyes on one of the seats and determined to make it his own.

"The proud airs of aristocracy, added to the dignity of that truly August body, were enough to have deterred any man possessing less firmness and independence of spirit than Mr. Henry," Henry's friend Judge John Tyler recalled.

> He was ushered with great state and ceremony into the room of the committee . . . dressed in very coarse apparel . . . and scarcely treated with decent respect . . . but the general contempt was soon changed into general admiration, for Mr. Henry distinguished himself by a copious and brilliant display on the great subject of the rights of suffrage, superior to anything that had been heard before within those walls. Such a burst of eloquence from a man so very plain and ordinary in appearance struck the

committee with amazement, so that a deep and perfect silence took place during the speech, and not a sound, but from his lips, was to be heard.[3]

Henry lost his plea for Dandridge, but his plain, farmer's work clothes, his occasional—and carefully measured—country twang, his long dramatic pauses, his self-deprecation in the face of "learned" judges or opponents, and his occasional appeals to heaven became his standard rhetorical instruments, designed simultaneously to lower juror expectations and arouse their sympathies before startling them with a thunderous—and brilliant—exposition of irrefutable truths. He left courtroom spectators stunned, breathless, helpless—in effect, captives.

In the wake of the Parsons' Cause, vestrymen from across the colony trooped to the hill country to plead with Henry to defend them against clergymen who refused to accept the Parsons' Cause verdict. Henry defeated the claims of every parson he faced, including those of his own uncle, Reverend Patrick Henry. In the end, the clergymen succeeded only in stirring up dissent against the church—and the crown, for sustaining the church with a universal tax on every landowner, regardless of religious convictions.

In 1764, Sarah Henry's father sold the Hanover Tavern, and Patrick Henry sold their farm for £350, to which he added £250 from legal fees to purchase 1,700 acres just north of Hanover town, but close enough for him to walk to court, his musket slung over his shoulder to pick off small game for Sarah's table. A one-and-a-half-story wooden structure, his house had three large rooms on the main floor and two upstairs, with the kitchen in a separate outbuilding to prevent fires from burning the house. Other outbuildings included a pantry, a smokehouse, a woodshed, and a spare room for the boys to use if guests needed their quarters in the main house. "His furniture was all of the plainest sort," his long-time friend and brother-in-law Samuel Meredith remarked. "They consisted of necessities only; nothing for show or ornament."[4]

Popular resentment against the Anglican clergy generated by the Parsons' Cause continued to increase in the winter and spring of 1765, when news arrived that Britain's Parliament had passed the Stamp Act, the first direct tax Parliament had ever imposed on American colonists. For generations, Parliament had only collected indirect "hidden" taxes such as import duties, and allowed each colony's elected legislature to impose direct taxes such as sales taxes and property taxes to pay costs of colonial administration.

Although England had won the Seven Years' War, her victory left the government nearly bankrupt, with a national debt of £130 million (nearly $8 billion today) and £300,000 in annual costs of military garrisons to protect American colonists against Indian attacks. To pay for the garrisons, Parliament raised taxes at home first, but the increases plunged 40,000 Englishmen into debtor's prisons and provoked widespread antitax riots. Threatened with a national uprising, Parliament rescinded some tax increases at home and compensated by raising duties on America's imports and exports—and extending the reach of the British Stamp Tax to the colonies. Parliament—and, indeed, most Englishmen—believed Americans should pay for their own military protection, and the stamp tax seemed the most innocuous way to do so. In effect for decades in England, the stamp tax required the purchase and affixment of one or more revenue stamps—often worth less than a penny—on all legal documents (wills, deeds, marriage certificates, bills of lading, purchase orders, etc.), newspapers and periodicals, liquor containers, decks of playing cards, and a host of other industrial and consumer goods. All but negligible when added to the cost of any individual item, it nevertheless amounted to a considerable—and reliable—revenue source for the government when collections from the stamps on tens of thousands of documents and products poured into the treasury. British Chancellor of the Exchequer Lord Grenville estimated that stamp tax collections in America would reap about £60,000 a year, or about 20 percent of troop costs there.

Although costs of the stamp tax to the average American was trivial, Parliament chose just the wrong moment to impose it. Increased duties were already strangling the American economy in the spring of 1765. Importers were collapsing under the weight of debts to English suppliers; shopkeepers and craftsmen closed their doors; even the largest merchants struggled to stay in business, leaving farmers without their usual outlets for crops and at the mercy of speculators. Patrick Henry loaned his father-in-law, John Shelton, several hundred pounds to help Shelton keep his farm and stave off personal bankruptcy.

Further inflaming colonist anger were frantic warnings from Boston's ambitious political malcontents—the emotionally unbalanced lawyer James Otis and the failed merchant Samuel Adams. In a pamphlet entitled *The Rights of the British Colonies Asserted and Proved,* Otis raised the first specious cry against parliamentary imposition of direct taxation without representation, conveniently overlooking the absence of parliamentary representation for almost all English taxpayers in England as well as in America. Indeed, only one million of Britain's nine million adult males were permitted to vote.

"Copyholders, leaseholders, and all men possessed of personal property choose no representatives," explained a member of parliament in defense of colonial taxation. "Manchester, Birmingham, and many more of our richest and most flourishing trading towns send no members to Parliament."[5]

Helping Otis generate his evocative propaganda was Harvard-educated Samuel Adams, the son of a politically powerful Boston brewer. After his parents died, young Adams inherited the family brewery and Boston mansion, but allowed both to deteriorate, and he sank deeply in debt. His father's political friends saved him from bankruptcy by appointing him Boston tax collector, but within a short time he owed the town £8,000 for taxes that he had either embezzled or failed to collect. Mired in poverty after fifteen years of failure, he festered with hatred for royal rule and those who profited from it, and he blamed them for all the ills of the world, including his own.

Teaming with Otis, Adams all but smothered Boston's editors with propaganda leaflets that the proroyalist *Boston Evening Post* labeled "mad rant and porterly reviling." Indeed, few but the world's most disgruntled citizens would have paid any attention to it except in North America, where settlers isolated in the hamlets and woods of New England had lived free of almost all government authority for more than 150 years. They had cleared the land, felled great forests, built homes and churches, planted their fields, hunted, fished, and fought off Indian marauders on their own, cooperating with each other, collectively governing themselves, electing their militia commanders and church pastors and turning to assemblies of elders to mediate occasional disputes. Self-reliant—often courageously so—they had thought and acted independently for four or more generations, seldom hearing, let alone responding to, utterances from the church, throne, or Parliament in far-off London. Like Patrick Henry, they had lived in freedom, without government intrusion in their lives and saw little need for it.

Nor had London objected. With a wealth of lumber, furs, pelts, and other resources flowing across the Atlantic to enrich British merchants, the British government had left the American colonists free to govern themselves and trade with the world. In 1651, however, Parliament began to interfere in colonial affairs after Dutch cargo ships began capturing more and more of the trade between America and Europe, threatening the health of Britain's merchant fleet. Parliament passed a series of "Navigation Acts," which, one by one, over the next fifty years, banned all American trade with any country but England and forced all ocean-going trade onto British or American bottoms.

Although galled by parliamentary intrusions in their affairs, most New England lumbermen and shipbuilders profited handsomely from the Navigation Acts and the massive expansion of the British and American fleets they engendered. In any case, smuggling goods onto unguarded landing points avoided duties altogether. The unexpected economic collapse that followed the Seven Years' War, however, left New Englanders easy prey for Boston's rabble-rousers and the frenzied warnings that the stamp tax would bankrupt them.

With their economy tied to tobacco and agriculture rather than shipbuilding, Virginians and most other southerners were less agitated. Even Otis conceded that "nine hundred and ninety-nine in a thousand of the colonists will never once entertain a thought but of submission to our sovereign and to the authority of parliament. . . ."[6] The Stamp Act, therefore, was not the first item on the agenda as Virginia's House of Burgesses assembled at the end of May 1765, when Patrick Henry arrived as a newly elected burgess, nine days short of his twenty-ninth birthday.

Williamsburg boiled with festive activity whenever the burgesses arrived: The population tripled; ornate coaches—some pulled by four horses, even six—rolled along the beautiful tree-shaded boulevard through the center of town; a colorful assortment of horsemen trotted about—farmers, hunters in buckskin, elegantly dressed gentlemen, English officers in bright red uniforms, swords flashing in the sun, their eyes trained on ladies in satins and lace, gliding in and out of the fashionable shops.

The House of Burgesses met twice a year, in May and October, and the arrival of burgesses and their wives opened a season of pomp and ceremony, with dances at the elegant Apollo Room of the Raleigh Tavern, concerts and plays at the town's two theaters, horse races and foxhunts at nearby plantations. Wealthy merchants and burgesses, almost all of them planters, hosted nightly dinners at their elegant town houses, while the Governor's Palace—the site of grand banquets throughout the legislative session—exploded in brilliance on the night of the Governor's Ball, to mark the official celebration of the British monarch's birthday.

Henry arrived in his drab, farmer's work clothes, but went unnoticed until he tethered his horse at the House of Burgesses and tried to walk past sentries. Ordered to stop, he extracted his official papers and showed his election certificate to the sergeant at arms, who rather warily let him pass. For the second time in his life, Henry strode into the hall, this time to assume a seat of power with the elite assemblage of 116 members who ruled Virginia—the largest, wealthiest, and most populated English colony in the New World, with 800,000 people, or nearly 27 percent of the 3 million people in the thirteen colonies. In contrast, Massachusetts, the second largest colony had 400,000 people, or just over 13 percent of the colonial population. (Eighty-one percent of Americans were white, and 19 percent were black, of whom 96 percent of blacks were slaves.)

Virginia's stately looking burgesses—bewigged and dressed in formal morning clothes—drew reverent stares as they marched into the House, legends all: four members of the Lee family, including Richard Henry Lee, acclaimed as the "Cicero of America," and his brother Francis Lightfoot Lee; law professor George Wythe; former attorney general John Randolph and his son Peyton, who succeeded him to that post; John Blair, the Scottish-born chancellor of the College of William and Mary; George Washington, the soft-spoken, heroic warrior; and Colony Treasurer John Robinson, who had been Speaker of the House for twenty-five years.

Together, they *were* Virginia.

Nearly three-fourths owned properties of more than 10,000 acres. Washington owned more than 20,000—with 300 slaves—and Speaker Robinson, 30,000 acres and 400 slaves. The median holding of burgesses was 1,800 acres with 40 slaves. In comparison, Henry owned 1,700 acres, but no slaves. Some 85 percent of burgesses had inherited their properties and what they deemed their right to rule the colony.[7] Of the 116 members, forty had attended the College of William and Mary and nearly one hundred had served as justices in their home counties before entering the House. Almost all had won election to the House without opposition. During the fifty previous years, four families—the Randolphs, Carters, Beverlys, and Lees—had dominated House leadership, providing thirty-four of the speakers. The only serious political division in the House reflected the deep split in Virginia society between Tidewater aristocrats from the large tobacco plantations in the East and the isolated upland farmers and backwoodsmen from the western Piedmont hills. Thirty-five of Virginia's fifty-six counties, however, were in the Tidewater region, and only twenty-one were upland. With each county electing two burgesses, the well-organized, closely connected aristocrats gained overwhelming control of the House of Burgesses. Adding to their majority were four additional burgesses, two representing Williamsburg and two representing Richmond.

With his half-brother John Syme Jr. already sitting in the House as a burgess from Hanover County, Henry found a warm welcome among the disorganized, younger, upland Burgesses. "They wanted a leader," explained former Attorney General John Randolph's son Edmund, who was a young burgess himself when Henry entered the House.

> From birth he derived neither splendor nor opulence. . . . The mildness of his temper . . . rendered him amiable. . . . He was never profound . . . [but] had no reason to shrink from a struggle with any man. Not always grammatical and sometimes coarse in his language, he taught his hearers how to forget his inaccuracies by his action, his varying countenance and voice. . . . He was naturally hailed as the democratic chief."[8]

After only four days in his seat, Henry openly challenged House elders by asking for recognition—an unheard-of impudence for a first-term burgess, especially a coarsely dressed uplander with no firsthand knowledge of the sensitive issue at hand. The central figure in the discussion was John Robinson, the good-hearted Speaker of the House and colony treasurer since 1735. Robinson was Virginia's most influential politician and one of its wealthiest planters, whom colleagues in the House had, over the years, approached for personal loans—often to forestall financial ruin after a poor tobacco crop. As owners of Virginia's largest plantations, linked by generations of intermarriage, their survival was essential to the colony's economic survival. As noted, they—and he—*were* Virginia.

With the colony's funds at his disposal, Robinson started making loans from the treasury, fully prepared to cover any losses with funds from his own, seemingly infinite fortune—until the Seven Years' War reduced it to a dangerously low, finite amount. As he took the speaker's chair, he was "sensible that his deficit to the public was become so enormous that a discovery must soon take place," and he and his colleagues in the House—all of them his debtors—proposed creation of a public loan office, with £240,000 that the colony would borrow from Britain, in part to cover the losses the colonial treasury had suffered from Robinson's malfeasance.

"It had been urged, that from certain unhappy circumstances of the colony, men of substantial property had contracted debts, which, if exacted suddenly, must ruin them and their families, but with a little indulgence of time, might be paid with ease," Thomas Jefferson recalled. Still a student at the College of William and Mary, Jefferson often stood near the doorway listening to House debates.[9]

"What, sir?" roared the outraged Patrick Henry. "Is it proposed then to reclaim the spendthrift from his dissipation and extravagance by filling his pockets with money?"[10]

Infuriated by the young uplander's insult to the most revered of their number, the burgesses ignored Henry's objections without a response and created the loan office, from which Robinson was able to salvage his wealth. But Henry's public attack shattered the Speaker's reputation, and Robinson died in disgrace a year later. After Henry's initial address to the House, older conservatives—all Robinson allies—stared at the ill-mannered young up-lander with a mixture of loathing and dread, but "what he lost on one side of the House he gained on the other," Edmund Randolph explained. "Members who, like himself, represented the yeomanry of the colony were filled with admiration and delight. They rallied around the man who was one of themselves, and who showed himself able to cope with the ablest of the old leaders."[11]

Randolph called Henry "the first who broke the influence of that aris-tocracy" and ascribed his success to his "abounding . . . good humor." Henry's "peculiar and even quaint" language, which he expressed with "a certain homespun pronunciation," won "the hearts" of Virginia's popular majority. "He identified with the people, [and] they clothed him with the confidence of a favorite son."[12]

Five days after Henry's impertinent outburst against the venerable Speaker of the House, the Burgesses began the Stamp Act debate. Older members, such as Edmund Pendleton of Caroline County, had close fam-ily and business ties to England and hoped for quick approval of the new law without debate, followed by a motion to adjourn for the summer. In-deed, some members had already left Williamsburg. Most colonies to the north had already approved the Stamp Act quite routinely, with little de-bate, and Virginia expected to follow suit. As older burgesses gasped with outrage, Patrick Henry stood and refused to allow the House "to end its session in feeble inaction."

"I had been for the first time elected a burgess a few days before," he recalled later. "I was young, inexperienced, unacquainted with the forms of the House and the members that composed it. . . . All the colonies, either through fear, or want of opportunity to form an opposition . . . had remained silent. Finding men of weight averse to opposition, and the commencement of the tax at hand, and that no person was likely to step forth, I determined to venture, and alone, unadvised and unassisted, on a blank leaf of an old law book wrote . . . the first opposition to the Stamp Act and the scheme of taxing America by the British Parliament."[13]

On May 29, 1765, his twenty-ninth birthday, Henry startled the House by asking for recognition and, as older burgesses demanded that he sit, he proposed five resolutions that they shouted down as preposterous. The first three were harmless enough, reiterating the principle that colonists were entitled to "all the privileges, franchises, and immunities . . . possessed by the people of Great Britain." The fourth resolution declared speciously that "taxation of the people by themselves, or by persons chosen by themselves to represent them . . . is the distinguishing characteristic of British freedom. . . ." In fact, few British subjects had any say over taxes, although Virginia, as Henry stated correctly in his fourth resolution, had "uninterruptedly enjoyed the right of being . . . governed by their own Assembly in the article of their [direct] taxes. . . ."[14]

The last Henry resolution was the most preposterous, and provocative, of all, and he was too well versed in British law by then not to have realized it. Inspired, perhaps, by the overwhelming popular support he had received in the Parsons' Cause, he evidently saw opposition to taxes as a way to ensure and even broaden that support. In his fifth resolution, he declared that "the General Assembly of this colony have the only and sole exclusive right and power to lay taxes . . . upon the inhabitants of this colony, and that every attempt to vest such power in any person or persons . . . other than the General Assembly . . . has a manifest tendency to destroy British and American freedom."[15]

Their faces reddening with rage as Henry read his resolutions, House elders erupted in fury, calling out to him to be silent and sit down. They were not used to airing their disputes in public. They normally settled "difficulties" quietly, behind closed doors in a private room at Raleigh Tavern. They saw Henry as a threat not only to their own leadership but to their profitable ties to the mother country. As Henry realized, his resolutions not only violated House protocol, they represented the first colonial opposition to British law.

The most heated of the debates revolved around the fifth resolution, with Henry raging against the tyranny of the Stamp Act and warning, "Caesar had his Brutus, Charles the First his Cromwell, and George the Third. . . ."

"Treason, sir!" the aging Speaker interrupted.

"Treason!" shouted the older burgesses one after another, some standing to shake their fists at the insolent renegade. "Treason! Treason!"

An idealized painting of Patrick Henry delivering his oration denouncing the Stamp Act in 1765, with a warning to King George III that "Caesar had his Brutus, Charles the First his Cromwell . . . ." (FROM A NINETEENTH-CENTURY PHOTOGRAPH)

Henry arched his back and stood as tall as his height permitted until the shouting faded.

" . . . and George the Third," he boomed in defiance, "may profit by their example! If *this* be treason, make the most of it!"[16]

The House erupted in a cacophony of angry shouts and jubilant cheers. "Violent debates ensued," Henry recalled. "Many threats were uttered, and much abuse cast on me. After a long and warm contest, the resolutions passed by a very small majority, perhaps of one or two only."[17] With many older members out of the Assembly making preparations to adjourn for summer, populists and young uplanders commanded a bare majority of the forty-one members present, and they forced through the vote approving Henry's resolutions—with George Washington and, most surprisingly, Richard Henry Lee among them. Both Washington and Lee were Tidewater planters with huge properties of more than 20,000 acres each. Although Washington had married into the Tidewater aristocracy, Lee was born to a family of great wealth for many generations and, like his peers, went to England for his higher education. He was so integrated in Virginia's British establishment that he had applied for the post as distributor of stamps and collector of stamp revenues for the British government. After hearing Henry's condemnation of the Stamp Act, however, he realized, as did Washington, that the act would undermine the rights of all Virginians, the wealthy planters as well as Henry's uplanders. Lee and Washington immediately abandoned the pro-British bloc of burgesses and became two of Patrick Henry's staunchest political allies, with Lee resigning his ties to stamp distribution. Thomas Jefferson explained why:

> I attended the debate at the door of the lobby of the House of Burgesses, and heard the splendid display of Mr. Henry's talents as a popular orator. They were great indeed; such as I have never heard from any other man. . . . By these resolutions and his manner of supporting them, Mr. Henry took the leadership out of the hands of those who had theretofore guided the proceedings of the House. . . .[18]

Henry had two additional resolutions that called for outright disobedience of the Stamp Act, but he decided he had gone far enough with his first five resolutions and stopped short of espousing revolution—for the moment.

"Mr. Henry plucked the veil from the shrine of parliamentary omnipotence," Edmund Randolph wrote. "It was judicious in Mr. Henry to suspend his resolutions . . . until a day or two before the close of the session. At this stage of business those who would be most averse . . . had retired. Those who were left behind . . . clung to Mr. Henry."[19]

Outraged by what he considered nothing less than a coup d'état, Speaker Robinson acted swiftly to reassert his authority and that of senior members by recalling absent burgesses to the House for the next morning's session. When the House reconvened, Robinson's aristocrats, led by Edmund Pendleton, took control and moved to erase the resolutions from the public record. All the burgesses strained their necks looking for Henry to protest, but he was nowhere to be seen. In fact, after stirring the political pot to a boil the previous afternoon, he had disappeared into the crowd outside the House, slipped away to the stable to find his horse and trotted off on the road to Hanover County, indistinguishable in the stream of farmers riding home from market.

"Mr. Henry," an Anglican minister reported to the Bishop of London, "is gone quietly into the upper parts of the country to recommend himself to his constituents by spreading treason and enforcing firm resolutions against the authority of the British Parliament."[20]

Henry's absence startled the entire House of Burgesses. Even more startling were the votes of Lee and Washington and younger Tidewater planters, who rebelled against their elders by joining Henry's uplanders in defeating Pendleton's omnibus motion to erase all of Henry's resolves from the record. Although senior burgesses managed to remove the most virulent resolutions, their efforts came too late. Before leaving Williamsburg the previous day, Henry had given the editor of the *Virginia Gazette* all seven resolutions to copy, and, under a news-sharing agreement among newspaper printers in most of the colonies, he had already sent them on their way to newspapers across America. The entire continent soon heard the lion's roar.

"The alarm spread . . . with astonishing quickness," Henry chuckled, "and the ministerial party were overwhelmed. The great point of resistance to British taxation was universally established in the colonies."[21] The royal governor responded to Henry's resolves by abruptly dissolving the House of Burgesses on June 1, without the usual ceremony or closing speech. He would not reconvene the House for a year.

A week later, Henry's resolves appeared in the Annapolis, Maryland, newspaper; by mid-June they were in the Philadelphia, New York, and Boston papers, and by early August, in the Scottish and British press. Newspaper publishers in Britain were at one with American publishers in despising the Stamp Act, which required them to put a stamp on every copy they sold. With each publication of Henry's resolves, exaggerations, misinterpretations, and copying errors transformed them into nothing less than a call to revolution. His sixth resolution, according to the *Maryland Gazette*, declared that Virginians were "not bound to yield obedience to any Law or Ordinance whatsoever, designed to impose Taxation upon them, other than the Laws or Ordinances of the General Assembly . . . " and his seventh resolution called anyone who supported Parliament's efforts to tax Virginians "AN ENEMY TO THIS HIS MAJESTY'S COLONY."[22]

The *Boston Gazette* also printed all seven of what they called Henry's original resolutions, but claimed, in addition, that Virginia had adopted them all intact—a lie planted by Samuel Adams.

With or without lies, publication of Henry's resolutions fired up colonist antipathy toward British government intrusion in their affairs and Parliament's efforts to tax them, directly or indirectly. Stamp Act opponents rallied in every city, forming secret societies called the Sons of Liberty.

"The flame is spread through all the continent," Virginia's royal governor Francis Fauquier warned his foreign minister in London, "and one colony supports another in their disobedience to superior powers."[23] Governor Sir Francis Bernard of Massachusetts agreed, warning the ministry that Henry's resolutions had sounded "an alarm bell to the disaffected."[24]

After reading Henry's resolutions in the *Boston Gazette*, the Massachusetts Assembly called on all colonies to send delegates to an intercolonial congress to be held in New York City in October, one month before the Stamp Act was to take effect.

Having sparked the fires of rebellion across the colonies, however, Henry remained curiously absent from the turmoil he had created, having vanished into the Piedmont hills to attend to the mundane tasks of raising and supporting his family. Unlike many of his contemporaries, Henry derived far less pleasure from the pomp, power, and formality of the capital than he did from the sense of freedom he felt in his fields at home and the joys he derived from his children. After planting his grain and tobacco, he set to work expanding his law practice—and his family. He was already father of three—a daughter and two younger sons—and his wife was pregnant again. To accommodate his growing family, he began building a new, larger, and more comfortable home on the 1,700-acre parcel of land he had bought from his father in Louisa County, just west of Hanover County.

On a hill above the South Anna River on Roundabout Creek, it overlooked a broad valley checkered with grain and tobacco fields, interspersed with uncleared stretches of forests thick with game. Although a few wealthier planters had built ostentatious pseudo-English structures such as nearby "Roundabout Castle," Henry would have none of it. His was to be traditional hill-country rustic: a one-and-a-half-story structure built of rough, hand-hewn lumber, with three large rooms downstairs and two upstairs, and the usual outbuildings surrounding the house. Hewing to hill-country tradition, Henry paid his carpenter and mason a mixture of cash, corn, livestock feed, and rum that he had received as fees from his own clients—including a twenty-five-gallon barrel of rum from one of the vestrymen in the Parsons' Cause.

In contrast to Tidewater burgesses such as George Washington, hill-country burgesses seldom brought their wives to Williamsburg. Their homes lay several days distance over rough roads and often narrow trails that made travel by horse difficult and travel by wagon a bone-shattering experience that few women could or would tolerate. With only babies and slaves as daily companions, however, Sarah Henry grew noticeably despondent, often teetering on the edge of madness. Even Henry's exuberant fiddling failed to cheer her. More and more, her oldest child, ten-year-old Martha, intervened to look after the younger children.[25]

At the beginning of August, the British government published the names of the colonial distributors who would sell tax stamps. With Henry's resolves still echoing across the colonies, Bostonians—particularly hard hit by the economic downturn—snapped as one. Debts had piled high; there was no work; shops had closed. With nothing left for rent or food, some tramped off into the wilderness, hoping to stumble on some unfortunate beast whose flesh and hide might provide sustenance and clothing.

On the morning of August 14, a straw effigy of Boston's designated stamp collector, the wealthy Tory merchant Andrew Oliver, dangled from the limb of an oak tree on High Street. Immediately dubbed the Liberty Tree, it drew an ever-thickening crowd, which metamorphosed into an angry mob. At day's end, a rougher crowd of waterfront workers and laborers set to drinking courtesy of Sam Adams and raged out of control, pulling down the effigy and carrying it to the governor's office, chanting, "Liberty, Property, and No Stamps." Growing in number, they moved toward a half-finished brick building that Oliver owned near the waterfront, which they believed would house the tax offices. The mob clawed it down, then surged off on the road to Oliver's beautiful estate and began stoning the windows. Unsatisfied, they beheaded and burned the straw effigy, cried for a hangman's rope, and broke down the mansion's doors. When they realized that Oliver and his family had fled, they set fire to the magnificent furniture, art, and other contents of the house. The governor ordered the militia summoned, but the drummers who normally sounded the alarm were part of the mob, as were many of the militiamen.

A few days later, a second mob gathered around a bonfire, drank themselves into a frenzy, and marched to the home of a marshal of the vice-admiralty court to burn it down. Wiser than most targeted victims, he saved his home—and life—by guiding mob leaders to a tavern and buying them a barrel of punch. Another mob, however, was on its way to the home of Royal Governor Thomas Hutchinson, a prominent Boston merchant who was a direct descendant of Anne Hutchinson, the early-seventeenth-century religious leader. One of the architectural jewels of North America, Hutchinson's Inigo Jones–style residence bore Ionic pilasters on its façade and a delicate cupola atop its roof. The mob broke down its massive doors and, room by room, set fires in each, and destroyed everything, including Hutchinson's legendary collection of manuscripts—many of them significant public papers documenting the history of Massachusetts. It took the mob three hours to dislodge the cupola from the roof and tumble it onto the huge fire below.

The violence in Boston set off an epidemic of violence across the colonies, spreading first to Newport, then to New York, Philadelphia, and Charleston. A mob in Newport, Rhode Island, built a gallows for the designated stamp collector, who fled to a British warship in the harbor and promised to resign. As rioting spread, stamp officers resigned in New Hampshire, Connecticut, New York, New Jersey, Pennsylvania, Maryland, Virginia, North and South Carolina, Georgia, and even offshore in the Bahamas. In New York City, a mob of about 2,000 protestors marched through the city, broke open the governor's coach house, and seized his ornate gilded coach and three other vehicles. After seating effigies of the governor and royal officials, they paraded the carriages through town, hung the effigies on a makeshift galley, and burned all the vehicles.

Delegates from eight colonies responded to the Massachusetts call for an intercolonial congress in New York. New Hampshire, North Carolina, Georgia, and, most noticeably, Virginia—the most important colony— failed to respond or send delegates. In the case of Virginia, the governor had dismissed the House of Burgesses before word of the congress arrived. Speaker Robinson eventually received the invitation, but was far too loyal to the crown to do anything but discard it.

Although physically absent from the Stamp Act Congress, Henry was nonetheless there, as delegates continually cited his seven resolutions. After eleven days of deliberations, the congress approved a "Declaration of Rights and Grievances of the Colonists in America," with fourteen resolutions that condemned the Stamp Act for depriving colonists of the right of taxation by consent, which it called "essential to freedom." With moderates outnumbering radicals, however, the Congress stopped short of embracing Henry's positions and asserted, instead, that colonists "glory in being the subjects of the best of kings. . . . That we esteem our connection with . . . Great Britain as one of the great blessings. . . ." It concluded with an obsequious assertion that "subordination to the parliament is universally acknowledged."[26] Even the whimper that ended the declaration could not coax a single delegate to risk treason by penning his name on the document. The only signature that appeared was that of the paid clerk.

Boston's Otis was furious as he stomped out of the meeting to begin the ride home. Once there, he strode into the colonial assembly in

Boston and shouted a challenge to Lord Grenville—by then prime minister—to duel on the floor of the House of Commons in London, to determine whether the colonies were to be free or enslaved by British tyranny. Royal Governor Hutchinson responded by calling Otis "more fit for a madhouse than the House of Representatives."[27]

After the Stamp Act Congress, Henry's words permeated the debates in every legislature, slipping off every tongue as easily as scriptural passages and provoking adoption of similar resolutions in eight colonies. British authorities recognized they would now need an army to enforce the Stamp Act. "Mr. Henry," Jefferson declared, "gave the first impulse to the ball of the revolution."[28] Without knowing it, Patrick Henry's outrage at government taxation had provoked a war for independence that would free his countrymen from British rule.

Chapter 4

We Are Slaves!

As the effective date approached for the Stamp Act to go into effect, Patrick Henry's new friend and political ally, planter Richard Henry Lee, of Westmoreland County, put his name and fortune at risk by calling on Virginians to boycott all things British until Parliament repealed the Act. In what was essentially an act of treason, more than one hundred Virginia planters signed Lee's Westmoreland Protests and inspired similarly prominent men in other colonies to follow suit. Some 200 merchants in New York City, 250 in Boston, and 400 in Philadelphia pledged to stop importing all but a select list of goods from England until Parliament repealed the Stamp Act. Boston's leading merchant banker John Hancock warned his London agent that "the people of this country will never suffer themselves to be made slaves of by a submission to the damned act."[1]

By the time the Stamp Act became law, every stamp officer in the colonies had resigned, and, with no distributors to sell stamps, the act could not take effect. Americans nonetheless greeted November 1 as a day of mourning, with church bells tolling throughout the day, from St. John's in Richmond, Virginia, to Boston's North Church. The Sons of Liberty gathered about Liberty Trees in towns and cities across the colonies to hang effigies of Grenville, their royal governors, and any other government official they could think of to blame for their economic woes.

*Richard Henry Lee, the Virginia planter whose
resolution in the Continental Congress—that
Britain's colonies "are, and of right ought to be,
free and independent States"—provoked the
Declaration of Independence on July 4, 1776.*
(LIBRARY OF CONGRESS)

The boycott against English imports had terrible economic consequences for English merchants. Colonial merchants owed them about £4
million, and the flow of orders from America had all but dried up. British
exports dropped 14 percent, and goods piled up inside and outside British
warehouses. Merchants in London, Bristol, Liverpool, Manchester, Leeds,
Glasgow, and every other trading town in Great Britain inundated Parliament with petitions demanding repeal of the Stamp Act.

George Washington observed that,

> whatsoever contributes to lessen our importations must be hurtful to
> their manufacturers. And the eyes of our people . . . will perceive that
> many luxuries which we lavish our substance to Great Britain for, can

well be dispensed with whilst the necessities of life are (mostly) to be had within ourselves. . . . As to the Stamp Act . . . I fancy the merchants of Great Britain will not be among the last to wish for a repeal of it.[2]

Washington proved a good prophet. By mid-January 1766, English merchants warned Parliament that they faced bankruptcy unless normal trade with North America resumed immediately. Letters from their trading partners in America promised nothing but armed rebellion if Britain sent troops to enforce the Stamp Act. If Parliament wanted to tax the colonies, they counseled, it should continue the tradition of using indirect, hidden taxes such as import duties. By the end of February, pressure for repeal grew overwhelming and, only four and a half months after the Stamp Act had taken effect, Parliament yielded, without a single stamp having been affixed to a colonial document. In addition, it lowered duties on imported molasses from the French West Indies that New Englanders used to make rum, and it eliminated duties on sugar from the British West Indies, thus reducing mainland prices for two key commodities.

Repeal of the Stamp Act was a humiliating defeat for Grenville and his party in Parliament—particularly because it came at the hands of a constituency without a single vote in either the House of Commons or the House of Lords. In the end, the British government had collected no new taxes and left its own treasury and many British merchants far poorer than they would have been had it never passed the act. A far more ominous consequence of the act, however, was the appearance of the first organized opposition to royal rule in the colonies—provoked by Patrick Henry and joined by others chafing under the London government's arbitrary regulations and restrictions.

In mid-May, about a month after the actual vote in Parliament, news of America's success arrived in Boston, New York, Philadelphia, and other ports. Across the colonies, Americans set aside a day they named "Repeal Day," to celebrate their triumph over the government of the world's most powerful nation. Merchants broke open barrels of rum, wine, beer, and other beverages for employees, clients, and passersby to toast his Majesty's health, believing false rumors that the young King George III himself had intervened on behalf of the Americans. In Virginia, jubilant city fathers illuminated Norfolk and Williamsburg and sponsored balls that lasted until dawn. The royal governor would not recall the House of Burgesses until November 1766, but when it reconvened it voted to erect a statue of King George III and an obelisk in recognition of Henry and other patriots who had fought for repeal. (Neither was ever built.) Even Londoners rejoiced over repeal of the Stamp Act. The city illuminated its streets, and its merchants—ecstatic over prospects of renewed trade with America—rolled out kegs of wine to serve to dancing celebrants in the lanes outside their doors.

As Americans and Englishmen feted the prospects of economic recovery, bitterness gripped the hearts of the humiliated parliamentary tyrants who had provoked the crisis. Refusing to accept defeat or seek reconciliation, they lit the fuse for the next colonial explosion by quietly passing a Declaratory Act on the very day they repealed the Stamp Act. The act asserted that "the Parliament of Great Britain had, hath and of right ought to have, full power and authority to make laws and statutes of sufficient force and validity to bind the colonies and people of America Subjects of the Crown of Great Britain in all cases whatever."[3]

When the House of Burgesses reconvened at the end of 1766, Patrick Henry and his young rebels held a clear majority of votes. Speaker Robinson had died and many of his closest allies had either followed him to the grave or retired in disgust at Henry and other blasphemers intent on undermining the standards of British decency and respect expected from loyal subjects of the crown.

With their Stamp Act victory, Henry and the Sons of Liberty in other colonies stowed their torches and banners, took the helms of their little ships of state and set sail over the uncertain seas to utopia. When Henry reentered the House of Burgesses, he walked with authority. Elected a vestryman in his home county, he was a leader of the established church as well as political leader of the western part of the largest American colony. Indeed, his own family—his half-brother, John Syme Jr., his friend and future brother-in-law, Samuel Meredith, and relatives from five western counties—made up a powerful backcountry voting bloc that Henry used effectively to influence House of Burgesses legislation. Like other burgesses,

Henry took the traditional oath of office at the beginning of each new session and swore allegiance to King George III, but he followed his oath with proposals for social, economic, and political reforms to dilute royal powers. He also called for separation of church and state, an end to slave importation, expansion of Virginia's domestic manufacturing to ease dependence on British imports, and new rules to prevent political corruption. Named to several key committees, he proposed—and the burgesses approved— prohibiting the Speaker of the House from serving simultaneously as colonial treasurer—as Speaker Robinson had done. "Away with the schemes of paper money and loan offices, calculated to feed extravagance and revive expiring luxury," Henry barked at the House.

Although Henry sought to ban importation of slaves, the Assembly agreed only to slow the influx of slaves with a tax that would make importation more costly but not prohibitive. Virginia had actually voted to ban slavery early in the century, but the government of "Good Queen Anne" overruled the act because of the royal treasury's dependence on revenues from British slave traders. At the time, only 25,000 slaves had arrived in Virginia, and an outright ban might have permitted most, if not all, to sail home to Africa, thus aborting the growth of slavery in America. In the next half century, however, Virginia's many appeals to end slave importations brought nothing but rejections from the three Georges who mounted the British throne in succession. By 1770, more Africans had crossed the Atlantic— albeit involuntarily—than Europeans, and Virginia's slave population grew almost eightfold, to nearly 190,000, the equivalent of 20 percent of the white population. The slavery issue had grown insoluble. "To re-export them is now impracticable," Henry lamented, "and sorry I am for it."[4]

Ironically, the increase in the number of slaves proved more of a burden than a benefit to most Virginia planters. Unable to speak English when they arrived and usually unskilled, slaves had fewer incentives to work than piece workers in the North, and, as they aged and fathered children, they added enormous numbers of nonproductive infants and infirm elderly to the population that planters had to support. "How comes it," Henry railed at the House of Burgesses, "that the lands in Pennsylvania are five times the value of ours? Pennsylvania is the country of the most extensive privileges with few slaves. . . . Europeans instead of Africans till the lands and manufacture. Is there a man so degenerate as to wish to see his country the gloomy retreat of slaves?"

"No!" he answered his own question.

"While we may, let us people our lands with men who secure our internal peace, and make us respectable abroad."

Like Henry, most tobacco planters favored ending slavery, but none had a practical way to do so. "There is not a man living," George Washington declared, "who wishes more sincerely than I do to see a plan adopted for the abolition of slavery in this country. . . . an evil exists which requires a remedy. . . ."[5]

For Washington, like Henry and other well-meaning planters, straightforward abolition appeared as cruel as perpetuation of their bondage. To set loose nearly 190,000 largely unskilled, illiterate, or semiliterate people—one-third of them children and an equal number of crippled or overaged men and women—was unthinkable. Where would they go? What would they do? How would they eat? The urbanized North had relatively few slaves and offered an array of apprenticeships in craft shops and manufactories to impart a range of skills; the South was a land of vast plantations, one after another, abutting each other, and worked by mostly unskilled, largely illiterate labor. With few towns or cities, few opportunities existed for work off the fields that paid freedmen enough to support themselves, let alone their families. The only opportunities for runaway slaves were in outlaw bands, pillaging isolated farms in the wilderness.

"I believe a time will come when an opportunity will be offered to abolish this lamentable evil," Patrick Henry wrote to his friend, Quaker leader Robert Pleasants. "If not, let us transmit to our descendants, together with our slaves, a pity for their unhappy lot, and an abhorrence of slavery. If we cannot [produce] this wished-for reformation . . . let us treat the unhappy victims with lenity. It is the furthest advance we can make toward justice."[6]

The conflict of his moral opposition to slavery and his ownership of slaves tore at Patrick Henry's heart and mind throughout his life. Although he acquired only slaves attached to farmlands he purchased, he rued his ownership of other human beings and could not reconcile it with his moral and religious beliefs. "Would anyone believe I am the master of slaves of my own purchase!" Henry all but sobbed to his Quaker friend Pleasants. "I will not, I cannot justify it."

"Is it not amazing," he went on, "in a country above all others fond of liberty, that in such an age and such a country we find men professing a religion the most humane, mild, meek and generous, adopting a principle as repugnant to humanity as it is inconsistent with the Bible and destructive to liberty."[7] Henry said he hoped that "the disadvantage from the great number of slaves may perhaps wear off when the present stock and their descendants are scattered through the immense deserts in the West."[8]

Beyond the confines of the House of Burgesses, Henry took advantage of his triumph in the Stamp Act controversy to expand his law practice, building his client base to more than 550 in 1767. His renown—and popularity—were such that he could afford to champion such unpopular causes as separation of church and state. Indeed, he succeeded in winning an exemption for Quakers from military service. Still bitter over Anglican Church treatment of his mother and other dissenters as treasonous heretics, Henry championed the rights of Baptists and other sects to practice their faiths. When he learned that Baptist minister John Weatherford had languished in Chesterfield County jail south of Richmond for five months, he rushed to court and won a judge's order of release. The jailer, however, refused to set Weatherford free until he paid the costs of his imprisonment. All but destitute, the minister faced perpetual imprisonment until an anonymous donor met the jailer's demands. It was Patrick Henry.

"From that time until the day of their complete emancipation, the Baptists found in Patrick Henry an unwavering friend," according to his grandson.[9] As the colony's leading advocate of church-state separation and defender of dissenters, Henry traveled the colony to defend them against oppression for "worshiping God according to the dictates of their own consciences."[10] Some Baptist ministers opted for martyrdom, however, refusing Henry's offers to pay the often small, albeit unjust, fines for preaching without a license and choosing to remain in jail rather than posting bond. Their tactic combined with the soaring oratory of leading Baptist preachers to capture the minds, hearts, and souls of thousands across the South. Unlike the Anglican Church, which shunned the poor and disenfranchised, the Baptists welcomed all—and the effects were evident immediately. From the founding of Virginia's first Baptist church near the James River in 1767, the number of Baptist churches mushroomed to fifty by 1774, with the burgeoning numbers of worshipers cleaving to the Anglican Patrick Henry as their most committed political supporter.

Living as he did near the edge of the vast western wilderness, Henry befriended and accumulated supporters among the disenfranchised. His new home at Roundabout stood in the middle of Louisa County, a way station for men in buckskin—some with families—caught in the mania to claim and settle western lands. Many disappeared into nearby forests only to return from the forbidding wilderness weeks later, shattered by a devastating encounter with nests of snakes, bears, brigands, Indians. Many had no conception of the dangers they faced when they left or the unspeakable violence that awaited in the anarchic world of the frontier.

The Louisa County Courthouse stood nine miles north of Roundabout. Henry covered the distance on horseback, dressed in coarse clothes, leather breeches, and leggings, a musket at the ready to fell deer, rabbits, and game birds for his and Sarah's table. He often strode into court adorned with burrs and splashes of blood from eviscerated game—as did many of his clients and, often, the judge. This was deep country, and Patrick Henry—eloquent though he was before the bench—blended perfectly with Louisa County's hill folk, even striking up his fiddle in the nearby tavern after overwhelming a prosecuting attorney with an impossibly artful oration.

In court, he seemed otherworldly—even Godlike—his rude dress transformed into saintly robes, his voice soaring, defending rich and poor alike—planters, craftsmen, Anglicans, and dissenters—against the crown, church, colonial or local government, and the law itself—fierce in his constant struggle against government intrusion in the lives of free men. Whatever the verdict—and it usually was in his favor—he bought everyone, clients, jurymen, judges, and prosecuting attorneys, drinks in the tavern across the road and serenaded them on his fiddle. And win or lose, they adored him, stood in awe of him, and pledged their loyalty to him. He brought joy into everyone's life—and a promise of protection against injustice. As he pursued fame and fortune, however, his wife Sarah languished at home, tending her—and his—flock of children, all but unseen by the outside world, alone, socially isolated, and sinking into depression.

In 1769, Henry obtained a license to practice before the General Court, the highest court in the colony, where the breadth of each case allowed him to raise his fees and reduce the number of petty disputes he handled in county courthouses. His smaller caseload, however, did not reduce his time in court—away from home. As much as he disliked separating himself from his family, he had little choice but to increase his income to meet their ever-increasing needs. He and Sarah had added two more girls to the family, making him father of six.

The General Court met for about two weeks each in April and October for civil cases and two weeks each in June and December for criminal cases. The House of Burgesses also convened twice a year, in May and November, which meant that Henry now spent four to six months a year in Williamsburg.

"His countenance was grave, penetrating, and marked with the strong lineaments of deep reflection," according to one of his fellow burgesses. "His visage was long, thin . . . his profile was of the Roman cast . . . his eyebrows dark, long, and full; his eyes a dark gray, not large, penetrating, deep-set in his head."[11]

He astounded lawyers in the General Court as much as he had the lawyers in the most insignificant county court, now adding a broad-based legal knowledge to the histrionics he brought to rural courtrooms. Henry had accumulated a substantial law library, but disguised his broad knowledge of the law behind a scrim of self-deprecatory remarks and a mountain twang that lured opposing lawyers and judges into underestimating his skills and knowledge. After Henry successfully defended a Spanish ship captain against government efforts to seize his vessel and cargo, Judge William Nelson said he had never heard "a more eloquent or argumentative speech" in his life. He said he was "astonished how Mr. Henry should have acquired such a knowledge of maritime law, to which he had never before turned his attention."[12]

Patrick Henry, probably as a delegate to the House of Burgesses and the Continental Congress in 1775. Painted by Alonzo Chapelle. (Red Hill Museum Collection, Patrick Henry Memorial Foundation, Brookneal, VA.)

He began most cases the same way: lips pursed, head bowed in thought, allowing the suspense of his silence to grow all but unbearable. Only then did he lift his face and peer at the judges with a sad, humble look:

"I stand here, may it please your honors, to support, according to my power, that side of a question. . . ." The questions he supported could vary from a dissenter's right to avoid the whip for not attending Anglican services, to the right of a starving migrant to steal a chicken.

"I beg leave to beseech the patience of this honorable court, because the subject is very great and important, and because I have not only the greatness of the subject to consider, but those numerous observations which have come from the opposing counsel to answer. . . ."

As spectators sat at attention to watch the master swordsman at work, Henry would launch a series of devastating thrusts:

> I know, sir, how well it becomes a liberal man and a Christian to forget and forgive.
>
> Our mild and holy system of religion inculcates an admirable maxim of forbearance.
>
> In considering this subject, it will be necessary to define what a debt is.

These and other arguments, of course, had nothing to do with the central question of the case, but his presentation left judges, juries, and spectators transfixed, often in tears, and usually prepared to decide in Henry's favor when he finally dispensed with rhetoric and presented his legal argument in short, pithy, logical declarations that resisted refutation. He was not only a great orator, he was a great lawyer—so great, in fact, that Robert Carter Nicholas, the renowned attorney who had examined Henry when he applied for a law license, turned over his General Court practice to Henry when Nicholas became colony treasurer.

Henry's first cousin, Judge Edmund Winston, asserted that Henry "did not lose in comparison with any man . . . in reasoning on general principles . . . and I never heard that he betrayed a want of legal knowledge. It will naturally be asked, 'How was this possible?' To which I can only answer that without much labor he acquired that information which in the case of other men is the result of painful research. I have been told in Mr. Henry's family that he employed a considerable part of his life in reading."[13]

If Henry proved indomitable before the General Court, he was even more overpowering in jury trials. "His power over juries was something wonderful," his grandson recounted, "and as a criminal lawyer he had no equal. He understood the human character so perfectly; knew so well all its strength and all its weakness . . . that he never failed to take them, either by stratagem or storm. Hence he was, beyond doubt, the ablest defender of criminals in Virginia, and will probably never be equaled again."[14]

More than most lawyers, Henry knew his jurors well. Indeed, he was one with them, having lived with them as a boy, fishing, hunting, and roaming the Piedmont hills together. Most resented oppressive laws and government restrictions that limited their "natural rights" to hunt, fish, farm, and, indeed, live as they saw fit. They cared less about legal technicalities and entitlements of the powerful than they did about justice for the weak and powerless. Henry disarmed the powerful and empowered the weak and defenseless.

With his booming practice came wealth, which he used to expand his land holdings—often speculating with colleagues from the House of Burgesses. Only land, not money, represented wealth in Patrick Henry's America. Any bank could—and, indeed, did—print paper money, but land was "real" estate, producing income from crops, timber, the pelts and flesh of wildlife, and, sometimes, ore. After the Stamp Act controversy, the royal governor sought to restore good relations with burgesses by offering them extensive land grants in the West for token investments. A wave of settlers had washed across the West after the French and Indian War, and George Washington, Richard Henry Lee, George Mason, Edmund Pendleton, and other burgesses poured their money into the governor's land offerings, some of which stretched west to the Mississippi River and north to the Great Lakes over present-day Kentucky, Ohio, Indiana, and Illinois. Henry's maternal cousins, the Winstons, snapped up 50,000 acres, and Henry bought 5,000 acres along the upper James River, along with some lands on the Mississippi River. He joined a group of burgesses in purchasing 50,000 acres along the Ohio River that they divided into hundred-acre parcels for resale to 500 families. His interest in the West intensified after his sister Anne married Colonel William Christian, the son of a prominent merchant in Staunton, the county seat of Augusta County in the Shenandoah Mountains. As other relatives moved west, Henry rode out to visit many of them and usually returned with saddlebags full of commissions to represent them in the House of Burgesses and General Court. He quickly became spokesman in the House of Burgesses for much of the West.

In May 1767, Henry turned thirty-one and Britain's Parliament again intruded into the lives of Americans. Tax riots had forced Parliament to placate English farmers by reducing property taxes 25 percent, and Chancellor of the Exchequer Charles Townshend believed he could do what his predecessor George Grenville had failed to do: make colonists pay the costs of British government operations in America, including costly efforts to stop the smuggling trade. He gave no thought to taxing the profligate British nobility or reducing the king's £800,000-a-year allowance (about $50 million today). Townshend's opponents argued against sowing more seeds of discontent in America, but those seeking to avenge the humiliation of the Stamp Act repeal insisted that the colonies had usurped powers of the king by granting amnesty to Stamp Act rioters.

At the end of June, Parliament passed the first of four Townshend Acts, which imposed duties on American imports of glass, lead, paint, paper, and tea, worth about £40,000 a year for "defraying the charge of the administration of justice and the support of the civil government." A second act transferred responsibility for paying colonial governors and judges from colonial assemblies to the British government. And another Townshend Act called for transport of defendants in the colonies to offshore admiralty courts for trials without juries.

Infuriated by the new laws, merchants in Boston and other port cities called for a selective boycott of British goods. "It is surprising to me," wrote Boston merchant John Hancock in an angry letter to his London supplier, "that so many attempts are made on your side to cramp our trade, new duties every day increasing. In short we are in a fair way of being ruined. We have nothing to do but unite and come under a solemn agreement to stop importing any goods from England."[15]

Virginia's George Washington agreed. "I think the Parliament of Great Britain," he complained to a British merchant, "hath no more right to put their hands in my pocket, without my consent, than I have to put my hands into yours for money. . . ."[16]

To sustain their boycott, Boston merchants, led by John Hancock, took a step towards commercial independence by setting up manufactures to produce goods that British laws had previously forced them to buy from England—clothing, jewelry, cordage, and similar easy-to-make staples. A month later, the *Pennsylvania Chronicle* and *Virginia Gazette* published the first of twelve stirring essays by John Dickinson, a London-educated lawyer and member of the Pennsylvania Assembly who had drafted the final declaration of the Stamp Act Congress. Printed in twenty of the twenty-six newspapers in the thirteen colonies, *Letters from a Farmer in Pennsylvania* provoked protests against further parliamentary legislation affecting the colonies. The *Letters* called British taxes unconstitutional and charged Parliament with bleeding the colonial economy. "If Britain can order us to come to her for necessities . . . and can order us to pay what taxes she pleases before . . . we land them here, we are . . . slaves," Dickinson argued. He then attacked the second of the Townshend Acts that stripped colonial assemblies of financial control over judges and governors:

> Is it possible to form an idea of slavery more *complete*, more *miserable*, more *disgraceful*, than that of a people where *justice is administered, government exercised* . . . AT THE EXPENSE OF THE PEOPLE, and yet WITHOUT THE LEAST DEPENDENCE AMONG THEM. . . . If we can find no relief from this infamous situation . . . we may bow down our necks, and with all the stupid serenity of servitude, to any drudgery which our lords and masters shall please to command.[17]

After the appearance of Dickinson's *Letters,* Rhode Island and New York joined the Massachusetts boycott, and the Massachusetts Assembly petitioned the king to repeal the Townshend Acts "as violations of their sacred rights as Englishmen of being taxed only by representatives of their own free election." Virginia, New Jersey, and Connecticut issued their own petitions, with Virginia also sending a circular letter urging other colonies to support the Massachusetts boycott. In their petition to the king, Virginia burgesses used Henry's arguments in the Stamp Act resolutions, calling the Townshend taxes "internal to all intents and purposes" and therefore unconstitutional.[18] By the end of 1767, Maryland, Pennsylvania, Delaware, New Hampshire, South Carolina, North Carolina, and New York had each petitioned the king to repeal the Townshend Acts. Far from considering repeal, however, King George ordered stricter enforcement of the acts in rebellious colonies.

At sunset on May 9, 1768, John Hancock's small sloop *Liberty* sailed into Boston harbor after crossing the Atlantic from Madeira with what appeared to be a shipload of wine. Darkness forced customs inspectors to postpone their inspection until morning, but when they went to board at dawn the next day, they found the ship bobbing high in the water, its hold more than three-quarters empty and the remaining cargo not subject to duties. A month later, a fifty-gun British man-of-war, the *Romney*, sailed into Boston harbor, its captain thundering to all within earshot, "The town is a blackguard town and ruled by mobs . . . and, by the eternal God, I will make their hearts ache before I leave."

As British press gangs swarmed ashore to terrorize the waterfront, a detachment of marines boarded the *Liberty* and tied her fast to the *Romney*. A mob of about five hundred gathered on the wharf and pelted the marines with paving stones ripped from the streets, but the *Romney* towed the *Liberty* out of range. The mob refocused its attack on customs officials, beating them as they ran to their houses. They caught one and dragged him through the streets, pelting him with rocks and filth, then turned and smashed the windows of his house. Another group at the harbor burned the customs officer's boat. As the royal governor prepared to flee, he sent an urgent message to General Thomas Gage who ordered ten regiments to march on Boston "to rescue the Government out of the hands of a trained mob."[19]

In contrast to its response in Boston, the British government sought to calm and, indeed, ingratiate itself with the people of Virginia, America's largest and richest colony. As its new royal governor, it sent Norborne Berkeley, Baron de Botetourt, a personal friend of the king and self-professed "friend to decency and moderation."[20] Although personally bankrupt because of his gambling addiction, he arrived aboard a seventy-four-gun Royal Navy ship of the line, with a maximum amount of pomp, ceremony, and cannon blasts intended to flatter Virginians by showing how high they ranked in Britain's estimation. On board was a coach of state and six magnificent white Percheron drays to carry the new governor from pierside to Williamsburg and transport him about the capital. When the House of Burgesses gathered for their first session on May 8, Botetourt emerged from the palace in a gold-threaded ceremonial robe, climbed into his coach, and rode slowly down the town's main boulevard, Duke of Gloucester Street, toward the House of Burgesses, waving his hand patronizingly and nodding serenely to his new constituents. Later in the day, he entertained more than four dozen government officials and burgesses, including Patrick Henry, at a lavish dinner at the ornate Governor's Palace. As a chamber orchestra entertained his guests, he engaged in jovial conversations, proclaiming himself one with Virginia's colonials.

Apart from Botetourt's appearance, the opening session of the House of Burgesses that year was notable for the first appearance of a burgess from Albemarle County in the Piedmont—a tall, freckle-faced redhead named Thomas Jefferson. No stranger in Williamsburg, Jefferson had studied three years at the College of William and Mary and studied law under burgess George Wythe. Once admitted to the House, he immediately drifted to the side of Patrick Henry and the other young radicals.

"The exact conformity of our political opinions," Jefferson recalled, "strengthened our friendship, and, indeed, the old leaders of the House being substantially firm, we had not after this any differences of opinion . . . on matters of principles, though sometimes on matters of form."[21] Jefferson called Henry "far above all in maintaining the spirit of the Revolution. His influence was most extensive with the members from the upper counties, and his boldness and their votes overawed and controlled the more timid aristocratic gentlemen of the lower part of the state." As puzzled as most of his contemporaries by the magic of Patrick Henry's eloquence, Jefferson questioned whether "it should be called eloquence." Calling it "peculiar," Jefferson described Henry's oratory as "impressive and sublime, beyond what can be imagined . . . while he was speaking, it always seemed directly to the point. When he had spoken . . . it produced a great effect, and I myself had been highly delighted and moved, but I have asked myself when he ceased, what the devil has he said?"[22]

A week after it had convened, the House of Burgesses adopted four resolutions written by Henry, Lee, Blair, Nicholas, George Mason, and Benjamin Harrison, with Henry presenting them in an eloquent address that reiterated colonist rights to tax themselves and petition the king for redress of grievances. They condemned as unconstitutional the creation of admiralty courts to try colonials beyond the borders of their own colonies, without juries and without the right to call witnesses. To the astonishment

The Raleigh Tavern was Williamsburg's most elegant restaurant. Its beautiful Apollo Ballroom was the site of major civic events and magnificent dances. Patrick Henry and the other burgesses repaired to the Apollo Room after the royal governor Norborne Berkeley, Baron de Botetourt, dismissed the House of Burgesses in 1774 after the House protested the repressive British Townshend Acts. (FROM A NINETEENTH-CENTURY PRINT)

of the burgesses, the jolly royal governor, who had befriended and entertained them in the palace a week earlier, summarily dissolved the House. "I have heard of your resolves," he declared in somber tones, "and augur ill of their effect."[23] With that, he ordered sentries to clear the chamber and, with guns at the ready, they escorted Henry and the other burgesses into the streets and shut down representative government in Virginia.

Infuriated by the governor's evident hypocrisy, Henry and the others marched out and reconvened in the Apollo Room at Raleigh Tavern. After reconfirming their resolutions, they voted unanimously to enlarge the partial boycott into a total ban on British imports and to send this warning to Parliament: "An attack, made on one of our sister colonies . . . is an attack on all British America. . . ."[24] In a final decision—again, unanimous—they ordered a round of drinks . . . and another . . . until they had toasted and emptied their glasses thirteen times.

"To some," Richard Henry Lee explained to British secretary of state Earl of Shelburne, "the proceedings may appear the overflowings of a seditious and disloyal madness, but your lordship's just and generous attachment to the proper rights and liberties of mankind will discover in them nothing more than a necessary assertion of social privileges founded in reason . . . and rendered sacred by a possession of near two hundred years."[25]

Chapter 5

To Recover Our Just Rights

As they had after Henry's Stamp Act resolutions, North Carolina, Maryland, New York, Massachusetts, and Rhode Island joined Virginia in boycotting British imports. Britain felt the effects immediately, and British merchants joined reform-minded political leaders in demanding that Parliament repeal the Townshend Acts. Too many members of Parliament, however, represented single-family "pocket boroughs" and underpopulated "rotten boroughs," leaving them with no inclination or motives to respond to popular demands—in either the colonies or England. While the king "plumes himself upon the security of his crown," warned an anonymous critic in the *Virginia Gazette*, "he should remember that, as it was acquired by one revolution, it may be lost in another."[1]

The disruptions in trade with Britain affected every American, including Patrick Henry. Like most farmers, he cleared new fields to grow hemp and flax for making cloth and clothes for himself and his family. Henry installed spinning wheels and a loom and began wearing Virginia cloth made on his own plantation. By the end of 1769, the effects of colony-wide home manufacturing helped cut imports from Britain nearly 40 percent, from about £2.2 million to just over £1.3 million.

Early in 1770, an ugly confrontation between British soldiers and the Sons of Liberty in New York City left both sides with cuts and bruises, but no fatalities. Boston was the scene of uglier incidents though—many, the result of Boston's unruly street children pelting Redcoats and suspected Redcoat sympathizers with snowballs. When a small mob broke down the door of a Tory shopkeeper, a friend came to his help and fired his musket at the mob, wounding a nineteen-year-old and killing an eleven-year-old. "Young as he was," the *Boston Gazette* proclaimed, "he died in his country's cause."[2]

Rabble-rouser Samuel Adams turned the boy's funeral into the largest ever held in America—an enormous mass mourning of a martyr that stretched more than a half mile, with more than four hundred, carefully groomed, angelic children leading the coffin and 2,000 mourners walking behind, followed by thirty chariots and chaises.

"Mine eyes have never beheld such a funeral," John Adams all but sobbed. "This shows there are more lives to spend if wanted in the service of their country. It shows too that the faction is not yet expiring—that the ardor of people is not to be quelled by the slaughter of one child and wounding of another."[3]

Relations between Boston colonists and British troops deteriorated badly. The air filled with a constant staccato of catcalls and cries of "Lobster, Lobster!" at passing British Redcoats. Fights erupted between "lobsters" and waterfront thugs, the latter often goaded (and surreptitiously remunerated) by Samuel Adams. On the evening of March 5, belligerent bands of laborers and soldiers roamed the streets, only narrowly avoiding conflict until nine o'clock that evening, when a young barber's apprentice provoked a sentry at the customs house. The sentry knocked the boy down and sent him off screaming for help. A crowd of boys gathered and pelted the sentry with snowballs, shouting, "Kill him, kill him." A crowd of men joined in. Suddenly the town's church bells began to peal; townsmen rushed from their homes thinking a fire had broken out; mobs surged through the streets. Hearing of the sentry's predicament, Captain Thomas Preston, the officer of the day, led a squad of six privates and a corporal to the scene, their muskets unloaded but bayonets fixed, with orders to escort the sentry into the customs house, away from the mob's missiles and taunts. By the time they reached the sentry's post, small gangs had swept in from all directions. A mob of waterfront thugs made it impossible for Preston to march away. Volleys of ice, oyster shells, and stones rained on the troops, with one of the rocks finding its mark. A soldier fell, staggered to his feet, loaded his rifle, and fired into the crowd. A second soldier loaded his weapon and fired a hole into the skull of one of the attackers. Before his body hit the ground a volley of shots left two others dead and eight wounded. Two of the injured later died of their wounds.

"Endeavors had been systematically pursued for months by certain busy characters to excite quarrels, encounters and combats," wrote John Adams. "I suspected this was the explosion which had been intentionally wrought up by designing men who knew what they were aiming at better than the instruments employed."[4]

Samuel Adams elevated the thugs to near sainthood by staging a grandiose procession with more than 10,000 mourners to carry them to their graves. He encouraged James Bowdoin, a friend from Harvard days, to write (anonymously) an inflammatory pamphlet entitled *A Short Narrative of the Horrid Massacre of Boston*. Although born to mercantile wealth, Bowdoin was a radical who seldom let facts stand in the way of his conclusions. His pamphlet, which called the shootings part of an army conspiracy to silence critics of British rule, was sent to newspapers across the colonies and Britain. Boston silversmith Paul Revere made a grossly inaccurate engraving that showed soldiers, muskets drawn, slaughtering helpless, unarmed townsmen.

As Boston and the rest of the nation waited for the Boston Massacre to expand into a wider conflict, American-born Governor Thomas Hutchinson acted swiftly, promising, "The law shall have its course." He ordered Preston and the eight soldiers under his command arrested for murder.[5]

After their arrest, news arrived that a new prime minister, Lord Frederick North, had yielded to merchant pressure and pledged not to levy any new direct taxes on the colonies. At his behest, Parliament repealed all the Townshend Act taxes but the one on tea. The concessions brought an immediate end to American boycotts and a return to normal trade relations for most of the colonies. Renewed prosperity created jobs and weakened popular support for revolution in Boston and other cities. Boston also lost its appetite for vengeance after two Patriot lawyers, John Adams and Josiah

Paul Revere's engraving of the Boston Massacre appeared in newspapers across America and inflamed colonist passions against British rule. (Bostonian Society)

Quincy, agreed to represent the British soldiers at the massacre and presented thirty-six witnesses to testify that civilians had plotted the attack. In addition, they presented the deathbed confession of one of the thugs that the soldiers had not fired until attacked. At the end of Captain Preston's six-day trial, the jury acquitted him, and, in a second trial of the eight soldiers, the jury acquitted six of them and found two guilty of manslaughter with mitigating circumstances. They were punished in the courtroom by being branded on their thumbs and released.

Despite Samuel Adams's polemics and Paul Revere's provocative engraving, the wave of prosperity that followed the repeal of most import duties all but ended tensions between the colonies and their mother country. Indeed, under prodding from leading merchants, colonial assemblies across British America agreed to hold an intercolonial assembly in New York in midsummer to discuss ways to improve major colonial waterways. The House of Burgesses selected Patrick Henry and lawyer Richard Bland as Virginia's delegates. For Henry, it was his first journey out of the colony into populated urban areas—Annapolis, Philadelphia, and New York. The trip took him through lush Pennsylvania and New Jersey farmlands, where he saw how workers paid by the piece had turned the soil into the most productive fields on earth. For the first time, he saw the reality of English clergyman Jonathan Boucher's pronouncement from the pulpit of Henry's own Hanover County church: "The free labor of a free man who is regularly hired and paid for the work he does and only for what he does, is in the end cheaper than the eye-service of the slave."[6]

Henry and his party arrived in New York City on July 10—only to learn that New York's gruff royal governor John Murray, Earl of Dunmore, had cancelled the conference for fear that delegates might plot against British rule. Henry and the others had little choice but to return home.

With Henry's increased wealth came a commensurate increase in his family, which now included three boys and three girls, besides his wife, himself, their servants, and slaves. He needed nothing less than a genuine mansion. Throughout his childhood years, Henry had eyed with reverence the estate called Scotchtown. Its previous owner had been John Robinson, the late Speaker of the House of Burgesses, whose malfeasance Henry had exposed. Not far from his Hanover County boyhood home, where his father still lived, Scotchtown was, for the Piedmont at least, a palatial mansion, shaded by stately oaks and elms and landscaped with trimmed boxwood. Approached by a grand staircase of polished stone, Scotchtown measured ninety-four feet long and thirty-six feet deep and boasted sixteen

Patrick Henry's home at Scotchtown, after its abandonment by its last residents at the beginning of the twentieth century. (FROM A 1906 PHOTOGRAPH.)

rooms. Unlike the utilitarian central hall of Virginia's traditional farm-houses, the large central hall at Scotchtown was a reception area that opened into eight other spacious rooms: one of them a grand dining room, another an equally splendid living room. Other rooms—some with walls paneled with solid mahogany—included a study, music room, card and game room, a small sitting room, and a private dining room for breakfast and informal meals. Eight bedrooms spread across the second floor, while an unfinished attic lay under the roof on the third floor. A hidden staircase built into the rear wall provided an escape in case of assault by Indians or brigands. Two huge chimneys climbed the outer walls at either end of the mansion, while the large kitchen and pantry stood in a nearby outbuilding.

Twenty miles north of Richmond, Scotchtown was near the main road to Williamsburg and within easy riding distance to both Hanover Court-house and his father's home at Mount Brilliant. Purchased for a mere £600, Scotchtown boasted 960 acres, where his two boys "were permitted to run quite at large . . . as wild as young colts," according to Henry's brother-in-law Samuel Meredith.

In the management of children, Mr. Henry seemed to think the most important thing . . . is to give them good constitutions. They were six or seven years old before they were permitted to wear shoes, and thirteen or fourteen before they were confined to books or received any kind of literary instruction. . . . He seemed to think that nature ought to be permitted to give and show its own impulse. . . . His children were on the most familiar footing with him, and he treated them as companions and friends.[7]

Another of Henry's brothers-in-law said Henry's sons at fourteen ran "bareheaded, barefooted, hallooing and whooping about the plantation in every direction, and as rough as nature left them."[8] Henry derived unbounded joy from watching his son's antics, describing them as living in pure liberty.

In addition to luxurious living, Scotchtown added to Henry's annual earnings, as thirty slaves produced profitable crops of tobacco and wheat from the 600 acres under cultivation. Elated by the spaciousness of his new home, Patrick Henry hoped the rich new surroundings would lift his wife's spirits, but she spurned his advances, and they slept in separate rooms for the first time. The marriage of their oldest daughter, sixteen-year-old Martha, to John Fontaine lifted his but not her spirits. She had grown so dependent on Martha to care for the younger children that she was unable to cope with even their simplest needs.

The son of a prominent Hanover County tobacco planter, Fontaine was the youngest in a long line of wealthy Huguenots whose noble ancestors—the de la Fontaines—fled persecution in France and embraced Quakerism when they arrived in America. Flocks of Fontaines and Henrys filled Scotchtown for the wedding. The ceremony took only a few minutes, but newlyweds in colonial times often eschewed honeymoons in favor of at-home celebrations with friends and relatives over several days and often as long as a week. Many of the invited had traveled great distances—sometimes for days—by horse or wagon over dusty, bumpy roads. They were not about to turn around and drive home the same day.

When celebrants and newlyweds had finally left, however, Sarah Henry felt a deep sense of loss and sank into depression. She seemed dazed, distant from her five children; she looked into her husband's face, saw him speak and heard nothing. According to the Henry family physician, Sarah Henry had "lost her reason and could only be restrained from self-destruction by a strait-dress."[9]

Although a penitentiary for the insane had opened in Williamsburg, eighteenth-century institutions often treated mental illness as the devil's work and offered little but ghastly exorcisms, with bloodletting, dunking, and restraints that left patients maimed or dead. Unwilling to submit his wife to such horrors, Henry confined her to a large sunny room in the half basement at Scotchtown. "Here she was in her own home with loyal and faithful servants giving her ever tender loving care," according to a family descendant. Although Henry often brought her food, and her children made persistent efforts to engage her in conversation and games, she developed "a strange antipathy" towards them all, rejecting her children and distressing Henry so much that he described himself as "a distraught old man."[10] Henry's oldest daughter, Martha, and her husband, John Fontaine, came to stay at Scotchtown, with Martha becoming mistress of the household, nursing her mother and becoming a second mother to her younger brothers and sisters. Her husband, meanwhile, managed the plantation and freed Patrick Henry to tend to his law practice and pursue his public service career.

To add to Henry's personal tragedy, a natural disaster befell much of Virginia in the spring of 1771, when ten days of heavy rains drenched the Piedmont hills and sent a forty-foot-high wall of water over the banks of Virginia's low-lying rivers. The flood waters carried away houses, outbuildings, and, farther downstream, tobacco warehouses bulging with the previous year's harvest—and the fortunes of hundreds of planters, large and small. Upriver planters on small hillside properties in the Piedmont suffered the worst losses. Unlike large plantations with ample room for their own storage sheds, small farms seeded every square inch of soil and depended on commercial warehousers at dockside to store crops until a cargo vessel came to transport them to market. Not only did the floods wash away warehouses, the torrential rains that produced the floods washed away the precious topsoil that nourished hillside crops. James River planters alone lost 2.3 million pounds of warehoused tobacco.

When the waters receded, many farmers were penniless, searching for missing children and other family members and family retainers. Hundreds died; thousands of livestock vanished; tens of thousands of acres of spring plantings and top soil flowed away into the maelstrom, leaving direct losses estimated at £2 million (more than $150 million) today. Thousands of slaves had disappeared. Although the roaring floodwaters swallowed some, many took advantage of the chaos to flee into the wilderness—some to die, some to prey on passersby, some to settle in or near Indian encampments. A few who were unable to cope retraced their steps to their masters' plantations. Rather than face starvation—or possible abduction by bounty hunters and shipment to the horrors of the West Indies—they chose to face their master's whip.

When Henry rode into Hanover town over the washed-out trails, farmers—many with their wives and children huddled about them—gathered near the courthouse and tavern, trying to comfort each other. After listening to their tales of trouble, he pledged to ride to Williamsburg for help and urged those with homes still intact to shelter the homeless. Before leaving, he made the difficult decision to separate his five children from their mother after his oldest daughter, Martha, and her Quaker husband, John Fontaine, agreed to care for them.

Patrick Henry rode at a gallop at times, reaching the capitol in a cloud of dust that left him looking more like a crazed chimney sweep than a distinguished burgess. Once in the House, his colleagues yielded the floor to hear his appeal for help to rescue Virginia's hill folk from the ravages of the Great Flood of 1771. The Pamunkey River, the James River, and countless streams were clogged with debris. The colony's entire navigation system—its trading lifelines to Chesapeake Bay, the Atlantic Ocean, and Britain—was in peril. Courageous hill folk were toiling night and day to clear the debris, he pleaded, but they needed tools, food, clothes, and compensation for their labors. All Virginians would suffer if they failed; all Virginians had an obligation to ensure their success.

It was vintage Henry oratory, this time fighting for his up-country hill folk—the farmers, hunters, frontiersmen, the disenfranchised and homeless who trusted him. He expected the Tidewater majority to reject his pleas—and they did—until news arrived that Piedmont uplanders in neighboring

North Carolina had rebelled against their colony's assembly. North Carolina's Royal Governor William Tryon had to lead a force of 1,200 troops into the Piedmont to subdue the rebels, who called themselves "Regulators." Largely unarmed, they had little choice but to surrender. The governor ordered one Regulator leader executed on the spot. Of the dozens tried for treason, twelve were found guilty and six executed. The governor gave the other six—along with some 6,500 other Piedmont Regulators—a choice of a similar fate or swearing allegiance to the Crown and the British government.

Fearing the North Carolina Piedmonter rebellion would spread into their colony, Virginia burgesses reluctantly supported Patrick Henry's appeal for the Pamunkey River cleanup and improvements to help up-country farmers transport harvests to market more efficiently. Henry's legislation would prove one of the last constructive acts of the House of Burgesses as an arm of colonial rule.

Late in 1771, Lord Botetourt died, and the British government shifted the hateful New York Governor Lord Dunmore to Williamsburg to replace him. Dunmore was Virginia's first royal governor to be paid by the king's treasurer instead of the colonial legislature, thus becoming the first governor to rule the colony financially independent of those he governed. With the royal blood of Stuarts flowing in his veins, he scoffed at self-government, dismissed the House of Burgesses, and slammed shut the door of the Governor's Palace, refusing to make himself available to discuss public needs.

When the House of Burgesses reconvened in February 1772, many delegates came to the capital hoping once again to end Virginia's costly slave trade. Virginians owned 40 percent of all the slaves in America, and, with record numbers of slave traders streaming up the James River, burgesses feared blacks would soon outnumber whites and stage an uprising that would end in widespread massacres.

"The colony was filling up rapidly with a barbarous population taken from the wilds of Africa," Henry's grandson explained. "As slaves," he added, "they retarded the prosperity of the country, and to give them the rights of citizenship seemed certain destruction to every interest held dear by the English."[11]

Time after time, the House had petitioned the king to end the slave trade, but the king himself shared the profits of the trade and refused even to respond. The winter of 1772, however, made ending the slave trade more urgent. The floods had destroyed hundreds of farms and left thousands of slaves roaming the countryside hungry, desperate, ready to assault or even kill for food. Some had organized gangs to attack and kill plantation owners and their families and seize control of properties. With thousands more angry, half-starved, black captives arriving from Africa each day, a full-scale rebellion seemed likely.

Playing on their fears, Henry rallied burgesses to petition the king to help avert "a calamity of a most alarming nature. The importation of slaves into the colonies from the coast of Africa hath long been considered as a trade of great inhumanity, and, under its present encouragement, we have too much reason to fear it will endanger the very existence of your Majesty's American dominions."[12]

The ill-tempered royal governor, however, dismissed the Assembly on the assumption—a correct one, as it turned out—that George III profited too much from the slave trade to consider the petition and that asking him to do so represented an impertinence. The governor would not recall the Assembly for another year.

In the spring of 1772, the embers of antipathy towards the motherland burst aflame again in New England after the British customs schooner *Gaspée* ran aground near Providence and a mob rowed out in boats to burn it. What many Americans might have dismissed as an act of vandalism turned into a cause célèbre when British officials announced they would send the culprits to England for trial. Although the British never caught the attackers, colonists saw the threat of trying American colonists in England as an infringement on their rights as British subjects to trial by a jury of peers in their own vicinage [district].

Samuel Adams used the *Gaspée* incident to call for revolution. "Let every town assemble," he wrote in the *Boston Gazette*. "Let associations and combinations be everywhere set up to consult and recover our just rights." The Boston Town Meeting organized a "committee of correspondence . . . to state the rights of the colonists of this province . . . as men, as Christians . . . and publish the same to the several towns in the province and to the world."[13] Three weeks later, the committee issued a 7,000-word declaration that began:

> Gentlemen. We the Freeholders and other Inhabitants of Boston . . . can no longer conceal our impatience under a constant, unremitted, uniform aim to enslave us, or confide in an administration which threatens us with certain and inevitable destruction.[14]

Massachusetts Governor Thomas Hutchinson charged that the document

> would be sufficient to justify the colonies in revolting and forming independent states. . . . I know no line that can be drawn between the supreme authority of Parliament and the total independence of the colonies. It is impossible that there should be two independent legislatures in one and the same state . . . two legislative bodies will make two governments, as distinct as the kingdoms of England and Scotland before union.[15]

John Adams agreed with the governor's words, but not his sentiments. "It is difficult to draw a line of distinction between the universal authority of Parliament over the colonies . . . and no authority at all," Adams exclaimed. "If there be no such line, the consequence is either that the colonies are vassals of the Parliament or that they are totally independent. As it cannot be supposed to have been the intentions of the parties in the compact that we should be reduced to a state of vassalage, the conclusion is that it was their sense that we are thus independent."[16]

Hutchinson and Adams were both closer to the truth than they realized. When Virginia's House of Burgesses finally reconvened in March 1773—more than a year after its previous meeting—Henry, Richard Henry Lee, and Thomas Jefferson responded to the Adams document and formed an eleven-man committee of correspondence.

"Not thinking our old and leading members up to the point of forwardness and zeal which the times required," Thomas Jefferson recalled,

> Mr. Henry, Richard Henry Lee, Francis L. Lee . . . and myself agreed to meet in the evening in a private room of the Raleigh [Tavern], to consult

John Adams befriended Patrick Henry at the First
Continental Congress and later sent him his pamphlet
Thoughts on Government, *which became the basis*
for Virginia's constitution. (LIBRARY OF CONGRESS)

on the state of things. . . . We were all sensible that the most urgent of all measures was that of coming to an understanding with all the other colonies, to consider the British claims as a common cause to all, to produce a unity of action; and for this purpose that a committee of correspondence in each colony would be the best instrument for intercommunication; and that their first measure would probably be to propose a meeting of deputies from every colony at some central place, who should be charged with the direction of the measures which should be taken by all.[17]

Infuriated by the audacity of Henry and the others, Governor Dunmore dissolved the Assembly after only eleven days, but it was too late. The committees of correspondence that Henry and his counterparts across America had established became the mechanism for the colonies to act in concert if the mother country deprived Americans of more liberties.

They would not have to wait long.

Instead of rallying the support of powerful moneyed interests in the colonies, the English government persisted in driving them into the rebel camp. Early in 1773, East India Company shares plunged from 280 to 160 pence on the London Stock Exchange. The lingering Townshend Act tax on tea had cut American consumption so deeply that it pushed the company to the brink of bankruptcy, with 17 million tons of unsold tea spilling out of its British warehouses. So many members of Parliament owned East India Company shares, however, that they acted to save the company by exempting it from duties on tea landed in England for reshipment to America. In addition, Parliament gave the company a monopoly on tea sales in America, allowing it to bypass local wholesalers and retailers and sell directly to consumers through its own retail outlets at lower prices than independent retailers. With tea still one of America's most popular beverages, the loss of tea sales threatened to bankrupt hundreds of small, independent stores and merchants—many of them Tories with no thoughts of rebellion until now.

In September, the East India Company shipped a half-million pounds of tea to Boston, New York, Philadelphia, and Charleston. Outside Philadelphia, a crowd of 8,000 threatened to board the *Polly,* which carried 697 chests of tea, as it prepared to sail up the Delaware River on Christmas Day. It put about and sailed out to sea, while East India Company consignees resigned, thus ending further tea shipments to the city. In New York, leaflets warned harbor pilots against guiding tea ships into the harbor, and after the Sons of Liberty labeled the East India Company's consignees "enemies of America," they too resigned. New York Governor William Tryon, who had moved from North Carolina, warned the British Board of Trade that it would require "the protection of the point of the bayonet and muzzle of the cannon"[18] to land tea in New York. On December 2, the *London* arrived in Charleston, where a mass meeting produced results similar to those in Philadelphia and New York.

On December 16, the first of three tea ships arrived in Boston Harbor and tied up at the wharfs. Hundreds of protesters pushed their way into Old South Church to demand that the governor order the ships back to England. When, at the end of the day, word arrived of his refusal, shouts of

"To the wharf!" sent the crowd pouring into the streets towards the harbor. A group of forty or fifty disguised themselves amateurishly as Indians before boarding the three ships with blankets over their heads and coloring on their faces. Methodically, skillfully, they lifted tea chests from the holds with block and tackle, carefully split each open with axes, and dumped the tea and splintered chests into the water. They worked steadily until they had dumped all the tea—342 chests in all, valued at £9,659, or about $600,000 in today's dollars. They damaged nothing else aboard the ships, and there were no fights, no brutality, no injuries to the crew—nothing but calm, orderly discharging of tea. Just who participated and who witnessed the "Tea Party" from shore remains one of American history's tantalizing mysteries.

On December 17, silversmith Paul Revere, a courier for Boston's Sons of Liberty, rode to Philadelphia, spreading news of the "Boston Tea Party" in every town and village as he traveled—with dramatic effects. The colonies stopped drinking tea, ending forever the status of tea as America's primary nonalcoholic beverage.

London responded angrily to the Boston Tea Party, calling it vandalism. England's attorney general formally charged Boston's most outspoken political leaders—John Hancock and Samuel Adams, among others—with "the Crime of High Treason" and "High Misdemeanors" and ordered them brought to justice. Surprisingly, Virginia's leaders did not disagree. Having abandoned anti-British boycotts, they had consumed 80,000 pounds of tea in 1773 and planned drinking more in 1774. Bostonians, Washington concluded, were mad, and like other Virginians he condemned the Boston Tea Party as vandalism and wanton destruction of private property—an unholy disregard for property rights.

Although winter snows and bitter cold dampened Boston's enthusiasm for street protests, spring brought a resumption of disorders followed by reprises of the Boston Tea Party elsewhere along the coast. A mob disguised as Indians boarded a tea ship in New York in March and dumped its entire cargo into the water. In April, a tea ship tied up in Annapolis, only to a have a mob set fire to it and destroy its cargo. A ship attempting to land tea in Greenwich, New Jersey, met the same fate.

Infuriated by colonist insolence, George III ordered his ministry to punish Massachusetts in ways that would deter would-be rebels in other colonies. As ordered, Parliament responded with a series of "Coercive" measures, beginning with the Boston Port Bill that shut the city's harbor until Boston compensated the East India Company for its losses and the customs office for uncollected duties on destroyed tea. All Boston-bound food supplies would divert to Salem, Massachusetts, where British troops would oversee delivery into Boston and, if necessary, starve the city into submission.

The eloquent British parliamentarian Edmund Burke pleaded with his colleagues to

> reflect how you are to govern a people who think they ought to be free, and think they are not. Your scheme yields no revenue; it yields nothing but discontent, disorder, disobedience; and such is the state of America, that after wading up to your eyes in blood, you could only end just where you began; that is, to tax where no revenue is to be found.[19]

The House of Commons ignored Burke and passed more Coercive Acts. One of them annulled the Massachusetts Charter and colonial self-government and gave the king or royal governor sole power to appoint or remove colonial executive officers, judges, and law enforcement officers. To silence radicals, Parliament banned town meetings without the consent of the governor and his approval of every item on the agenda.

The first of the Coercive Acts seemed reasonable enough to those Virginians who had disapproved of the Boston Tea Party as vandalism. Bostonians had condoned the destruction of private property; it was only just that they compensate the owners for damages. Even the legalized quartering of British troops in homes, as well as taverns and empty buildings, seemed reasonable enough to Virginia's planter aristocracy as a necessary evil for maintaining law and order in rebellious Boston. But Virginia's collective nods of sanctimonious approval for the initial Coercive Acts turned into collective outrage when Parliament extended its punishment of Bostonians beyond Massachusetts to other colonies, including Virginia. With passage of the Quebec Act, Parliament ended self-government in Canada and extended Canadian boundaries to the Ohio River, thus stripping Virginia and many of its wealthiest and most prominent citizens—Washington, Henry, the Lees, and many others—of hundreds of thousands of acres and millions of pounds of investments in lands north of the Ohio River extending to the Great Lakes. The Quebec Act proved a colossal political error that pushed Britain's largest, wealthiest, and most heavily populated American colony firmly into the antiroyalist camp. Once fiercely loyal British subjects, Virginia's Tidewater aristocracy now faced the loss of vast amounts of wealth accumulated over generations if the Quebec Act went into effect. With few exceptions, they decided to pool their collective wealth and organize the tens of thousands of Virginians who depended on them economically into an army to protect their property from the British government.

Facing the loss of his Ohio properties, Henry raced to Williamsburg to organize the response. With Jefferson and other members of the committee of correspondence, Henry "cooked up a resolution . . . appointing the first day of June, on which the Boston Port Bill was to commence, for a day of fasting, humiliation and prayer to implore heaven to avert the evils of civil war, to inspire us with firmness in support of our rights, and to turn the hearts of the King and Parliament to moderation and justice."[20]

More important than the prayers it generated, Henry's resolution served as a flare that signaled Virginia's unity with other American colonies in their opposition to the Coercive Acts. Without support from the powerful Virginians, the other colonies would have been all but helpless to confront the powerful British empire. With Virginia, they could now resist the British with confidence of success.

"The reception of the truly patriotic resolves of the House of Burgesses of Virginia gladdens the hearts of all who are friends to liberty," Samuel Adams exulted to Richard Henry Lee. The *New Hampshire Gazette* was even more ecstatic: "Heaven itself seemed to have dictated it to the noble Virginians. O Americans, embrace this plan of union as your life. It will work out your political salvation."[21]

Chapter 6

We Must Fight!

With Virginia's support, the other colonial committees made plans for an intercolonial congress in Philadelphia in September 1774. In anticipation, the Massachusetts committee drew up a binding covenant for the colonies to stop importing British goods and end all business dealings with Britain effective October 1—unless Parliament reopened the port of Boston and repealed the Coercive Acts.

Henry urged Virginia's Assembly to approve the covenant. Railing at the king, his ministers, and Parliament for starving the people of Boston, he worked the gallery spectators into such a frenzy that "some of the most prominent . . . ran up into the cupola and doused the royal flag which was there suspended," according to Judge Spencer Roane.[1]

"He is by far the most powerful speaker I ever heard," Westmoreland planter George Mason declared.

> Every word he says not only engages but commands the attention; and your passions are no longer your own when he addresses them. But his eloquence is the smallest part of his merit. He is in my opinion the first man upon this continent, as well in abilities as public virtues, and had he lived in Rome . . . Mr. Henry's talents must have put him at the head of that glorious commonwealth.

Mason called Henry the "principal" author of the resolves and measures "intended for the preservation of our rights and liberties."[2]

Outside the assembly hall, Henry's words roused people to action across Virginia. Along the shores of Chesapeake Bay, Richard Henry Lee's neighbors, who had signed his Westmoreland Protests during the Stamp Act uprising, sent a huge supply of grain to Bostonians to ease the shortage created by the Boston Port Bill. The *Virginia Gazette* suggested a ban on horse racing and urged bettors to contribute moneys they would have spent on races to the relief of Boston. In Henry's native Hanover County, farmers and other freeholders rallied around him, declaring,

> We are free men; we have a right to be so. . . . Let it suffice to say, one for all, *we will never be taxed but by our own representatives*; this is the great badge of freedom, and British America hath been hitherto distinguished by it. . . . Whether the people there [at Boston] were warranted by justice when they destroyed the tea we know not; but this we know, that the parliament, by their proceedings, have made us and all North America parties. . . . If our sister colony of Massachusetts Bay is enslaved we cannot long remain free. . . . We recommend the adoption of such measures as may produce a hearty union of all our countrymen and sister colonies. UNITED WE STAND, DIVIDED WE FALL. . . .[3]

The British government responded by replacing the American-born civilian governor of Massachusetts, Thomas Hutchinson, with British General Thomas Gage, who marched into Boston with four divisions of troops and declared martial law.

On August 1, the members of what had been Virginia's House of Burgesses convened in Raleigh Tavern in Williamsburg and agreed to cease buying all British goods except medicine and to end all exports, including tobacco, to which Britons had become addicted. It also voted to end the slave trade, which, it said, "we consider most dangerous to virtue and welfare in this country. . . ."[4] The convention then elected seven delegates to attend the intercolonial congress in Philadelphia, with George Washington receiving the most votes, followed by Richard Henry Lee and Patrick

Henry. Thomas Jefferson failed to win a place among the delegates. To ensure a voice for conservative elders, the House named the venerable Edmund Pendleton of Caroline County, the Tidewater lawyer who had bitterly opposed Henry's Stamp Act resolutions ten years earlier. Before the convention adjourned, Washington pledged, "I will raise one thousand men, subsist them at my own expense, and march myself at their head for the relief of Boston."[5]

At Washington's invitation, Patrick Henry and Edmund Pendleton arrived at Mount Vernon on August 30 to rest up before proceeding together to Philadelphia the following day. Washington's neighbor George Mason—firmly in favor of a blanket boycott of trade with Britain—joined them for supper. After a midday dinner the following day, Washington, Henry, and Pendleton mounted their horses and said their farewells to Martha. According to Pendleton, she stood at the door "talking like a Spartan to her son on his going to battle: 'I hope you will all stand firm,' she said. 'I know George will.'"[6]

The trio took four days to cover the 150 miles to Philadelphia by horseback and boat—often riding in the cool, predawn hours before breakfast and stopping for food and rest in Annapolis, Maryland; New Castle, Delaware; and Christina Ferry (now Wilmington), Delaware. Although Philadelphia took little or no notice of most arriving delegates, some 500 dignitaries and a delegation of officers from every military company went out to greet the celebrated Colonel George Washington and escort him and his friends to the city line, where a company of smartly uniformed riflemen and a military band escorted them from the city line past cheering crowds into the center of the city and the elegant City Tavern for a banquet. Of all the delegates, Washington was the most renowned. Every child in America—and many in Britain—could recount his military adventures in the West—the blood-curdling ambush by the French and Indians near Fort Duquesne [now Pittsburgh], the slaughter of 1,000 colonial troops, Washington's daring escape through a hail of arrows and bullets, and his courage in leading survivors to safety.

When Washington and Henry arrived in Philadelphia, Richard Henry Lee arranged for them to stay at the palatial mansion of his brother-in-law, Dr. William Shippen Jr., America's foremost lecturer on anatomy. Although

*George Washington was named commander in chief
of the Continental Army by the Continental Congress
in 1775, but took command too late to prevent the
slaughter of American Patriots on Bunker Hill.*
(LIBRARY OF CONGRESS)

scheduled to convene on Thursday, September 1, Congress did not have a
quorum until the following Monday, but a banquet at City Tavern brought
many delegates face-to-face before then. It proved a deep disappointment to
both Henry and John Adams. "Fifty gentlemen, meeting together, all
strangers, are not acquainted with each other's language, ideas, views, de-
signs," Adams complained to his wife, Abigail. "They are therefore jealous
of each other—fearful, timid, skittish."[7] Henry was neither fearful nor
timid, nor skittish, but he was clearly uncomfortable—out of place, unable
to understand the thinking or accents of many delegates—and with good
reason. Without roads or public transport, establishment of cultural ties in

colonial America had been difficult at best and often impossible. Philadelphia lay more than three days' travel from New York, about ten days from Boston, and all but inaccessible overland from far-off towns such as Richmond or Charleston. There were few roads, and foul winter weather and spring rains isolated vast regions of the country for many months and made the South—and southerners—as foreign to most New Hampshiremen as China and the Chinese—and vice versa. In fact, only 60 percent of Americans had English origins. The rest were Dutch, French, German, Scottish, Scotch-Irish, Irish, even Swedish. Although English remained a common tongue after independence, German prevailed in much of Pennsylvania, Dutch along the Hudson River Valley in New York, French in Vermont and parts of New Hampshire and what would later become Maine. Author-schoolteacher Noah Webster compared the cacophony of languages to ancient Babel, and Benjamin Franklin had complained as early as 1750 that Germantown was engulfing Philadelphia. "Pennsylvania will in a few years become a German colony," he growled. "Instead of learning our language, we must learn theirs, or live as in a foreign country."[8]

With the Pennsylvania Assembly convening in the State House, the delegates to the intercolonial meeting met in Carpenters' Hall, the craftsmen's union headquarters and meeting hall, about two blocks to the east on Chestnut Street. Only Georgia failed to send a delegate. With Virginia's acquiescence a key to success, the delegates unanimously elected fifty-three-year-old Peyton Randolph, Speaker of the House of Burgesses, to chair the meeting. Though stout, Randolph idealized Virginia's Tidewater aristocracy, dressed elegantly with a powdered wig and just enough of "Old England" in his bearing to command respect from "commoners."

Of the procedural questions that delegates faced after Randolph called them to order, they quickly resolved two, dubbing themselves "Congress" (the press would label it the Continental Congress) and giving Randolph the title of "President." A third question on voting would prove more contentious and, indeed, would hound them and their successors for the next fifteen years: whether to vote as equals, with each colony having one vote, or as representatives of the people, with each delegation casting votes in proportion to the population of its state. The question puzzled the entire

Assembly. None had ever dealt with problems of a free republic. Assigning each colony an equal vote would allow eight or nine colonies with a collective minority of the people to dictate to the majority, while voting proportional to population would allow Virginia and Massachusetts to act in concert and dictate to the eleven other colonies. Delegates sat puzzled—indeed stunned by the grave injustices that each system might produce.

"None seemed willing to break the eventful silence," said Charles Thomson, who had been elected secretary of Congress, "until a grave looking member, in a plain dark suit of minister's gray, and unpowdered wig arose. All became fixed in attention on him. . . ."[9] It was Patrick Henry.

John Adams described Henry's inaugural address on America's national stage:

> Mr. Henry . . . said this was the first General Congress which had ever happened; and that no former congress could be a precedent; that we should have occasion for more general congresses, and therefore that a precedent ought to be established now; that it would be a great injustice if a little colony should have the same weight in the councils of America as a great one. . . .

According to Adams, Henry went on to proclaim,

> Government is dissolved. Where are your landmarks, your boundaries of colonies? We are in a state of nature, sir. . . . The distinctions between Virginians, Pennsylvanians, New Yorkers, and New Englanders, are no more. I am not a Virginian, I am an American. I propose that a scale should be laid down; that part of North America which was once Massachusetts Bay and that part which was once Virginia ought to be considered as having a weight. . . . I will submit, however; I am determined to submit, if I am overruled.[10]

Governor Samuel Ward of tiny Rhode Island objected to Henry's argument, pointing out that each county in Virginia sent two delegates to the House of Burgesses, regardless of any county's population or wealth. To

Henry's surprise, his ally Richard Henry Lee raised another objection to proportionate representation: Congress had no way to measure the population. New York's John Jay stepped in with a compromise: "To the virtue, spirit, and abilities of Virginia we owe much. I should always, therefore, from inclination as well as justice be for giving Virginia its full weight." Given the impossibility of obtaining a population count, however, Jay said Congress should give each colony an equal voice, but that the voting method not become a precedent until Congress was "able to procure proper materials for ascertaining the importance of each colony."[11]

Congress remained in session seven weeks, during which every delegate had to "show his oratory, his criticism, and his political abilities," John Adams complained to his wife, Abigail. Calling the proceedings "tedious beyond expression," he told her that if a motion were made that two plus two equaled five, delegates would debate it endlessly "with logic and rhetoric, law, history, politics and mathematics."[12] Because of Virginia's importance, at least two Virginia delegates served on every committee, with Henry serving on three—including one with John Adams and Richard Henry Lee to prepare a final address to the king. With so many of his colleagues quoting from it, Henry acquired a translation of *L'Esprit des lois*, or *The Spirit of Laws*, a monumental work by France's Baron de Montesquieu, whom John Adams and other Congress "intellects" cited as casually as a minister citing the Scriptures.[13]

On September 17, Congress endorsed the Suffolk Resolves adopted in Suffolk County, Massachusetts, which declared the Coercive Acts unconstitutional and urged the people of Massachusetts to withhold payment of all taxes until Britain repealed the Acts. The Suffolk Resolves (and Congress) urged the people to boycott British goods and form their own armed militia to end the need for British military protection against the Indians. On September 28, Pennsylvania delegate Joseph Galloway proposed a "Plan of a Proposed Union between Great Britain and the Colonies" to create a new American government, with a president-general appointed by the king and a grand council, as an "inferior and distinct branch" of Parliament.

After a New York delegate seconded Galloway, John Jay and South Carolina's Edward Rutledge proffered their support. A curious silence then gripped Congress, awaiting some opposition. With no one else apparently willing to challenge the proposal, Henry finally stood to denounce it, with what presaged his lifelong opposition to centralized government.

> The original constitution of the colonies was founded on the broadest and most generous base. The regulation of our trade was compensation enough for all the protection we ever experienced from England. We shall liberate our constituents from a corrupt House of Commons, but throw them into the arms of an American legislature that may be bribed by that nation which avows, in the face of the world, that bribery is a part of her system of government. Before we are obliged to pay taxes as they do, let us be as free as they; let us have our trade with all the world."[14]

Led by Henry's and Samuel Adams's fierce opposition, Congress rejected the plan by a single vote, and it later expunged the proposal from the record. "Had it been adopted," Henry's grandson William Wirt Henry commented later, "the independence of the colonies would have been indefinitely postponed. . . ."[15]

"He is a real half-Quaker," a spectator at the convention wrote of Henry to Robert Pleasants, Henry's Quaker friend in Virginia. Henry, he said, was "moderate and mild, and in religious matters a saint; but the very devil in politics—a son of thunder."[16]

Except for his denunciation of the Galloway proposal, Henry had no more nor less impact at the Continental Congress than his counterparts—largely because he was, for the first time in his life, in the metaphorical big pond of American politics, with some of America's best educated, best trained lawyers. Many had studied in Britain and debated with that nation's most brilliant scholars. To his credit, Henry did not display the meaningless rhetorical tricks and "string of learning" that mesmerized semiliterate mountain people in Hanover County, Virginia. Instead, he held his tongue and had the good sense and political instinct to begin studying Montesquieu's work on government.

On October 14, as Congress prepared its declaration and resolves, Paul Revere galloped to the door of Carpenters' Hall to announce that the Massachusetts House had met in Salem and declared itself a Provincial Congress. In effect, Massachusetts had staged a coup d'état, overthrowing royal rule and creating the first independent government in America. The Provincial Congress elected John Hancock its president and assumed all powers to govern the province, collect taxes, buy supplies, and raise a militia.

Stunned by the news, members of the Continental Congress did not know whether to cheer the boldness of Massachusetts assemblymen or lament their probable capture and slaughter by British troops. When delegates collected themselves, they issued a declaration supporting "the inhabitants of Massachusetts" and urging "all America . . . to support them in their opposition."[17] Congress then issued resolutions condemning the Coercive Acts and all the taxes imposed since 1763, along with the practice of dissolving assemblies and maintaining a standing army in colonial towns in peacetime. It issued ten resolutions proclaiming the rights of colonists, including the right to "life, liberty and property" and the right to control internal affairs (including taxes) through their own elected legislatures. Before adjourning, the delegates voted to form a Continental Association to boycott imports from Britain, end exports to Britain and its possessions, and to end the slave trade. The Association agreed to impose an economic boycott on any town, city, county, or colony that violated Association rules. On October 26, Congress prepared a petition for redress of grievances to the king and an address to the British and American peoples. Before adjourning, it resolved to reconvene on May 10, 1775, if Britain did not redress American grievances by then.

After signing the document, Patrick Henry, Richard Henry Lee, and George Washington saddled up for the long ride home. John Adams approached them to say good-bye and showed them a letter he had received from the mayor of Northampton, Massachusetts, saying, "We must fight if we can't otherwise rid ourselves of British taxation . . . enacted for us by the British parliament."

"By God," Henry interrupted, "I am of that man's mind. We must fight."

Richard Henry Lee disagreed: "We shall infallibly carry all our points; you will be completely relieved; all the offensive acts will be repealed; the army and fleet will be recalled, and Britain will give up her foolish project."

"Only Washington was in doubt," Adams noted.[18]

When Henry arrived home, his Hanover County neighbors asked him the prospects of reconciliation with Britain. Already furious at the intrusions of the British government in his life, Henry asserted that Britain "will drive us to extremities—no accommodation will take place—hostilities will soon commence—and a desperate and bloody touch it will be."[19] In his heart and soul, Patrick Henry had already declared war.

Chapter 7

"Give Me Liberty . . ."

Virginia was preparing for war when Henry rode home from the First Continental Congress in September 1774. "Every county is now arming a company of men whom they call an independent company," Royal Governor Lord Dunmore wrote to the secretary of state for the colonies on Christmas Eve. In fact, almost every state was arming or planning to do so. Maryland had resolved two weeks earlier to organize a militia to eliminate the need for protection by regular British troops. Delaware followed suit two weeks later, and in early January, George Washington took command of the hundred-man Fairfax Independent Company in Alexandria—Virginia's first such force.

When Henry reached Scotchtown after the Continental Congress, he learned that his wife had attempted suicide during his absence and had deteriorated into deep depression. His oldest daughter, Martha, and her husband, John Fontaine, who had been caring for the five younger Henry children, had brought the entire brood to Scotchtown for the Christmas holidays in hopes of lifting Sarah Henry's spirits. Henry had little time for his family, however. Stirred by fears of imminent British attack, he rode into Hanover town to call together the men of the county. He "addressed them in a very animated speech, pointing out the necessity of our having recourse to arms in defense of our rights, and recommending in strong terms that we should immediately form ourselves into a volunteer company."[1] Abetted by a few jugs of white lightning, Henry's emotional appeal sent the mountain men into a frenzy of patriotic fervor that left them pushing and shoving to volunteer in his company. After they'd finished signing up, they elected him their captain by unanimous vote, and Henry rode home to spend what remained of the Christmas holidays with his family. They proved to be melancholy days indeed. After plunging into an abyss of depression, Sarah Henry died early in the new year.

After burying his wife, Henry buried himself in nonstop political and military activities, drilling his volunteers and preparing for the Second Virginia Convention. Only six or seven other counties across the colony had managed to raise companies of any consequence. In fact, most Virginians agreed with Richard Henry Lee that the king and Parliament would respond favorably to the Continental Congress petition for redress—much as they had responded by repealing most of the Townshend Acts in 1770 in the aftermath of the Boston Massacre.

Indeed, all England seemed to support the American petition. When Parliament reconvened in January 1775, petitions from London, Bristol, Birmingham, Liverpool, Manchester, and almost every other trading city asked for restoration of normal relations with the colonies.

On January 12, however, George III dashed their hopes. After reading the petition of the Continental Congress, he responded with a broad, cynical smile, complimented its eloquence, and laid it aside. A fortnight later, he rejected it and demanded that Parliament halt trade with the colonies, provide army protection for Loyalists, and arrest colonist protesters as traitors. As the House of Commons debated passage of legislation to transform the king's pronouncements into law, Edmund Burke again pleaded with his colleagues to reconsider. "The use of force alone is but temporary," he protested. "It may subdue for a moment; but it does not remove the necessity of subduing again, and a nation is not governed which is perpetually being conquered."[2] Parliament relented only slightly after Burke's speech by offering a blanket pardon to repentant rebels—with the exception of such "principal Gentlemen who . . . are to be brought over to England . . . for an inquiry . . . into their conduct." Among them were George Washington,

Patrick Henry, John Hancock, Samuel Adams, John Adams, and other radicals the government believed were in "a traitorous conspiracy" against a monarch seated by "Divine Providence." As punishment for such a crime, British law dictated hanging by the neck and "while you are still living your bodies are to be taken down, your bowels torn out . . . your head then cut off, and your bodies divided each into four quarters. . . ."[3]

Although news had reached America that the king had smiled at the Continental Congress petition, word of his subsequent rejection and Parliament's trade embargo had yet to reach the former burgesses when they called for a Second Virginia Convention. They picked Richmond as their site rather than Williamsburg, where a buildup of British naval strength in nearby waters raised the menace of Lord Dunmore's arresting Henry, Richard Henry Lee, and other Virginia political leaders. A town of only 600 residents and 150 homes, Richmond had no assembly hall, as such. The largest seating area was in St. John's Anglican Church on Richmond Hill, with space in its pews for about 120 people.

On March 20, 1775, the delegates sidled into the pews—Washington, Jefferson, Richard Henry Lee and other renowned Virginians. Henry took a seat in the third pew on the gospel, or left, side of the church facing the front. Almost all wanted to believe rumors, born of the king's smile, that Parliament would repeal most of the Intolerable Acts and restore calm in America. Every delegate seemed in a good mood as the convention opened—every delegate but Henry. Confident again in his regional political pond, he reclaimed his Demosthenic airs and "in the sacred place of meeting, launched forth in solemn tones."[4] He proposed three resolutions, with the first two merely parroting the Maryland resolutions of the previous December: "That a well regulated militia, composed of gentlemen and yeomen, is the natural strength and only security of a free government; that such a militia in this colony would forever render it unnecessary for the mother country to keep among us, for the purpose of our defense, any standing army of mercenary soldiers . . . and would obviate the pretext of taxing us for their support."[5]

Henry's third resolution, however, broke new ground with nothing less than a declaration of war: "That this colony be immediately put into

St. John's Church in Richmond, Virginia, where Patrick Henry delivered his stirring speech ending, "Give me liberty, or give me death." (LIBRARY OF CONGRESS)

a state of defense, and . . . prepare a plan for embodying, arming, and disciplining such a number of men, as may be sufficient for that purpose."[6] Spectators standing at the rear of the church applauded, as Peyton Randolph, the president of the convention, stood at the front trying to bring his "congregation" to order.

Richard Henry Lee immediately seconded Henry, and in the debate that followed, many delegates insisted that peace was imminent and that Henry's resolutions were premature. "Washington was prominent, though silent," recalled Edmund Randolph, who had chosen to remain in America while his father, a staunch Tory, prepared to return to England. "His [Washington's] looks bespoke . . . a positive concert between him and Henry."[7]

When all the delegates had finished expressing their views, Henry stood to speak. A clergyman at the church described the scene:

Henry arose with an unearthly fire burning in his eye . . . this time with a majesty . . . and with all that self-possession by which he was so invariably distinguished . . . the tendons of his neck stood out white and rigid like whipcords. . . .[8]

Mr. President, it is natural to man to indulge in the illusions of hope. We are apt to shut our eyes against a painful truth—and listen to the song of that siren, till she transforms us into beasts. Is this the part of wise men engaged in a great and arduous struggle for liberty? . . .

Henry paused . . .

I know of no way to judge the future but by the past. And judging by the past, I wish to know what there has been in the conduct of the British ministry for the past ten years to justify the hopes with which these gentlemen have been pleased to solace themselves and the House? Is it that insidious smile with which our petition has been lately received? Trust it not, sir. . . . Suffer not yourselves to be betrayed with a kiss. Ask yourselves how this gracious reception of our petition comports with those warlike preparations which cover our waters and darken our land. Are fleets and armies necessary to a work of love and reconciliation? . . . Let us not, I beseech you, sir, deceive ourselves longer . . .

Henry's voice rose . . .

We have petitioned—we have remonstrated—we have supplicated—we have prostrated ourselves before the throne . . . we have been spurned, with contempt from the foot of the throne. There is no longer any room for hope. If we wish to be free . . . we must fight!
I repeat it, sir: We must fight![9]

Henry paused again, staring heavenwards at the roof beams of the church. The delegates sat in stunned silence, many believing they had heard a voice as from heaven uttering the words, 'We must fight,' as the doom of Fate . . . He stood silently, as if in prayer. The tension of his listeners building, awaiting an inevitable eruption.

Gentlemen may cry peace, but there is no peace. . . .

His voice grew louder. . . . The walls of the building and all within seemed to shake and rock in its tremendous vibrations. . . .

The war is actually begun! The next gale from the north will bring to our ears the clash of resounding arms!

. . . thunder. . . .

Our brethren are already in the field! Why stand we here idle? What is it the gentlemen wish? What would they have?

After a solemn pause, he stood . . . like an embodiment of helplessness . . . his form was bowed . . . a condemned galley slave . . . with fetters, awaiting his doom. . . .

Is life so dear, or peace so sweet, as to be purchased at the price of chains and slavery?

He raised his eyes and chained hands toward heaven and prayed . . .

Forbid it, Almighty God!

He then turned toward the timid loyalists . . . quaking at the penalties of treason . . . and bent his form yet nearer to the earth . . . with his hands still crossed . . . he seemed to be weighed down with . . . chains . . . transformed into hopeless . . . humiliation . . . under the iron heel of military despotism. . . .

I know not what course others may take, but as for me . . .

He arose proudly . . . the words hissed through his clenched teeth while his body was thrown back . . . every muscle and tendon was strained against the fetters which bound him, and, with his countenance distorted with agony and rage . . . his arms were hurled apart . . . the links of his chains were scattered

Interior of St. John's Church in Richmond, Virginia, where the Virginia House of Delegates met on March 23, 1775, and heard Patrick Henry deliver his stirring "liberty-or-death" cry for revolution against Britain. Henry stood in the third pew in the left-central section of the assembly. (LIBRARY OF CONGRESS)

to the winds . . . his countenance radiant . . . he stood erect and defiant . . . the sound of his voice . . . the loud, clear, triumphant notes . . .

Give me liberty! . . .

. . . the word 'liberty' echoed through the building . . . he let his left hand fall powerless to his side and clenched an ivory letter opener in his right hand firmly, as if holding a dagger . . . aimed at his breast. . . .

. . . or give me death.[10]

. . . a blow upon the left breast with the right hand . . . seemed to drive the dagger to the patriot's heart.[11]

The audience sat in stunned silence, unable to think, let alone speak or applaud. Patrick Henry's "blow upon the left breast," and, indeed, his "loud, clear triumphant notes," resounded beyond the walls of Richmond's Anglican church across the colony and continent—across the sea. "Henry was thought . . . to speak as man was never known to speak before," Edmund Randolph noted. "Patrick Henry, born in obscurity . . . rousing the genius of his country and binding a band of patriots together to hurl defiance at the tyranny of so formidable a nation as Great Britain."

After delegates had caught their collective breaths, the convention passed Henry's resolutions and appointed a committee to prepare a plan for "embodying, arming, and disciplining" the Virginia militia. On March 27, after only a week, the convention adjourned, but in every county across the state, men and boys sewed the words "Liberty or death" on their shirt fronts and rode to their county courthouses to join local militias and fight the British. By then, Virginians and the other American colonists were aware that King George and the British government had rejected the petition of the First Continental Congress. Lord Dartmouth, the secretary of state for colonial affairs, sent blanket orders to royal governors and commanding generals in America to use whatever means necessary to enforce the Coercive Acts in Massachusetts and "arrest the principal actors and abettors."[12]

On April 18, 1775, General Gage sent troops out of Boston to destroy a militia arsenal in Concord, while a detachment went to Lexington, where British spies reported that Samuel Adams and John Hancock were hiding after fleeing Boston. Patriot spies fanned out across the countryside to warn of the approach of British troops, with Paul Revere reaching Lexington at midnight—in time to warn Adams and Hancock and allow them to flee. As the British approached Lexington, militia captain John Parker positioned about 200 minutemen—almost half the town's population—in two lines on the green, one behind the other. They ranged in age from sixteen to sixty-five and included eight pairs of fathers and sons who stood side by side to face the dreaded Redcoats.

While the main British force marched to Concord five miles distant, Major John Pitcairn led a detachment of seven hundred troops into Lexington, convinced that "one active campaign, a smart action, and burning two or three of their towns will set everything to rights."[13] Pitcairn ordered the Patriots to remain where they were, lay down their arms, and prepare to surrender. When some of the minutemen broke ranks and ran for cover behind nearby stone walls, Pitcairn ordered his men to move against them. Amidst the confusion and shouting that followed, a shot rang out—"the shot heard around the world."

When the firing ceased, eight minutemen, including Parker, lay dead and ten lay wounded. The minutemen managed to wound only one British soldier and Pitcairn's horse, but they had triggered a revolution that would send the world's greatest empire into irreversible decline.

As the main British force in Concord searched in vain for Patriot arms, minutemen attacked a platoon of British soldiers guarding Concord's North Bridge. Realizing the Patriots had removed most of the arsenal, the British commander ordered his men to return to Lexington. On the way, however, they met a growing rain of sniper fire. Minuteman ranks had swelled into thousands. Musket barrels materialized behind every tree, every boulder, every stone wall. Facing annihilation unless they returned to Boston, the isolated platoon abandoned plans to search for Hancock and Adams and stepped up their pace to double time. Although General Lord Hugh Percy met them in Lexington with 1,000 more Redcoats, the minuteman force had grown to 4,000. They came from everywhere, with town after town sending 100, 200, or however many men they could muster to rally around their fellow countrymen. Had there been a supreme commander to organize them, they would have wiped out the British force. As it was, their relentless, albeit uncoordinated, assault left 73 British soldiers dead, 174 wounded, and 26 missing before the expedition returned to Boston. The Patriots suffered 49 dead, 42 wounded, and 5 missing. The decimated British troops wreaked revenge in every town, looting and burning houses, bayoneting anyone who stood in their way, civilian or military.

As the British troops retreated, a member of parliament asserted that Americans "would not fight," that "they would never dare face an English army, and did not possess any of the qualifications . . . to make a good soldier." In Boston, however, Lord Percy conceded,

Whosoever looks upon them as an irregular mob, will find himself much mistaken. They have men among them who knew very well what they are about, having been employed as rangers against the Indians and Canadians, and this country being much covered with wood and hill is very advantageous for their method of fighting.[14]

The Patriot propaganda machine that Samuel Adams had organized in and around Boston sent riders like Paul Revere across the colonies to herald the Lexington victory and heighten American Anglophobia with tales of alleged British atrocities. Besides accusing the British of setting fires to homes, shops, and barns in Lexington, Adams told newspapers that the British had

pillaged almost every house they passed, breaking and destroying doors, windows, glasses . . . and carrying off clothing and other valuable effects. It appeared to be their design to burn and destroy all before them. . . . But the savage barbarity exercised upon the bodies of our brethren who fell is almost incredible. Not content with shooting down the unarmed, aged, and infirm, they disregarded the cries of the wounded, killing them without mercy, and mangling their bodies in the most shocking manner.[15]

The propaganda had its desired effects, inflaming passions and provoking hundreds, at first, then thousands of colonists from farms, villages and cities across New England to gather their arms and rally to the side of the minuteman force outside Boston. As their numbers swelled to more than 10,000, they took up positions on the hills around Boston, thus confining the British troops in the city with Boston's civilian population.

The day after the fighting at Lexington, Virginia Governor Dunmore ordered a squadron of marines from a schooner in the James River to march into Williamsburg while the town slept and seize the contents of the Powder Horn, a curious, eight-sided militia arsenal with a cone-shaped roof, in which the local militia stored its gunpowder. By dawn the marines had loaded all fifteen half-barrels of powder on board the *Magdalen* and, in effect, left the local militia defenseless against assault by renegade Indians or rebel slaves. As word of the marine action spread through town, an angry mob formed in front of the governor's palace to demand return of the powder. In seclusion and unwilling to address a mob of commoners, Dunmore sent word that marines had seized the powder to put down an incipient slave rebellion. When the growing mob hooted down the governor's first emissary, he sent a second message threatening to free the slaves and organize them into an army that would "lay the town in ashes."[16]

As Dunmore menaced Williamsburg, Patrick Henry was at Scotchtown saddling up for the ride north to the Second Continental Congress on May 10. When he learned of the raid on the Powder Horn, he changed plans and rode to Hanover Courthouse to rally volunteers for an assault on Williamsburg and the governor.

"A blow must be struck at once," he shouted, "before an overwhelming force should enter the colony." Calling the governor's action at the Powder Horn a "fortunate circumstance," he predicted it would end the people's "habitual deference . . . towards the governor. . . . You may in vain mention . . . the duties on tea and so on. These things . . . do not affect them. But tell them of the robbery of the magazine and that the next step will be to disarm them, and they will then be ready to fly to arms to defend themselves."[17]

Before setting off with his company towards Williamsburg, Henry worked his men into a frenzy, telling them the moment had come "to decide whether they chose to live free . . . or become hewers of wood and drawers of water for these lordlings."[18] Telling them they were "striking the first blow in this colony in the great cause of American liberty," he urged them to move quickly, "that their enemies in this colony were now few and weak—that it would be easy for them, by a rapid and vigorous movement, to compel the restoration of the powder . . . or to make a reprisal on the king's revenues . . . which would fairly balance the account. . . ."[19]

As Henry's company advanced towards Williamsburg, Governor Dunmore ordered cannons emplaced on the green surrounding the palace and sent his wife and children to safety on the British man-of-war *Fowey*. Henry, meanwhile, dispatched a sixteen-man detachment to the royal treasurer's home to demand £330 in payment for the stolen military stores. If he refused, the men were to take him hostage. With Dunmore's cannons trained on the heart of Williamsburg and the *Fowey*'s guns ready to fire on Yorktown, the treasurer acceded to Henry's demands to save "the many innocent persons who would suffer by [Henry's] entrance into Williamsburg. . . ."[20] The money arrived at Henry's camp the following day, May 7, and he pledged to give it to the Virginia Assembly to buy more powder for the militia. Dunmore declared Henry a traitor and, with that knowledge, Henry let out a roar of defiance and ordered his troops to return to their farms in Hanover.

Although Henry's Powder Horn expedition drew no blood, it proved as effective in stirring the passions of the South against the British as the Boston Massacre had been in the North. Before he ended his adventure, his own force had grown to more than 150 men, while 5,000 other Virginians across the state streamed into their county courthouses to volunteer, wearing shirts emblazoned with the new state motto: Liberty or Death.

After returning to Scotchtown to fetch his wardrobe, Henry set off for the Second Continental Congress in Philadelphia to the cheers of his men who saluted him "with repeated huzzas."[21] He did not arrive until May 18, eight days after Congress had convened and too late to win committee appointments of any consequence. New faces were in the hall: Pennsylvania's Benjamin Franklin, John Hancock and Samuel Adams of Massachusetts, and George Clinton of New York, among others. Lyman Hall had come from Georgia, which had not sent a representative to the previous congress. Although Congress had invited "the Oppressed Inhabitants of Canada" to send delegates, none had appeared, and, by the time Henry took his seat, word reached Philadelphia that thousands of British troops were massing to sail for America. Congress acted swiftly, resolving on May 26 that "these colonies be immediately put into a state of defense." Five days later, a provincial congress in North Carolina declared independence from Britain.

On June 14, Congress voted to incorporate the Massachusetts troops besieging Boston into a new Continental Army and resolved to raise six companies of riflemen in Pennsylvania, Maryland, and Virginia to reinforce the troops in Boston. The following day, June 15, Congress elected

Virginia's George Washington as commander in chief of the Continental Army—a shrewd appointment that John Adams had engineered to ensure Virginia's continuing support of the war. With Washington its selection, Congress put what was largely a northern army in the hands of not only the most experienced military commander, but a Virginian, whose political influence would ensure southern backing for the war.

On June 16, Washington accepted command, declared his intention to serve without pay, and rode off to war—too late, however, to prevent a needless slaughter of American troops near Boston. After proclaiming martial law, the British spotted Patriots building a small fort atop Breed's Hill on the Charlestown peninsula across the harbor from Boston. British ships landed 2,400 troops onto the peninsula on June 17 and laid a barrage on the hilltop to protect Redcoats edging up the slope. A murderous rain of Patriot fire forced the British to retreat, however. A second attempt to scale the hill met with similar results. On the third attempt, the British threw off their heavy backpacks and charged up the hill, bayonets fixed. The firing from the top gradually diminished—and then ceased. The Americans had run out of powder. The British overran the hilltop, then assaulted and captured neighboring Bunker Hill. When they were done, 100 dead Americans and 267 wounded lay strewn across the two hilltops, but the assault had cost the British 1,045 casualties and elevated their American victims to martyrdom. Bunker Hill became a cause célèbre across the colonies for both Patriots and Loyalists.

Early in July, Congress adopted two important resolutions by Philadelphia's John Dickinson. The so-called Olive Branch Petition on July 5 reasserted American allegiance to King George III and petitioned him to prevent further hostile acts against colonists while negotiators formulated a plan for reconciliation. In the second resolution the following day— "Declaration of the Causes and Necessities of Taking Up Arms"—Congress rejected independence but asserted American willingness to die rather than be enslaved.

Chapter 8

"Don't Tread on Me"

When Congress adjourned on August 2, 1775, Patrick Henry and Thomas Jefferson all but galloped south to Williamsburg. Lord Dunmore had already fled the Governor's Palace to a British man-of-war and threatened to send his marines to crush opposition to British rule. Ten days later, on June 17, 1775, the colony's former burgesses ignored Dunmore's threats and assumed control of government, ending 175 years of British control. They voted to raise three regiments of 1,000 men each to defend the colony against British troops in the east and five companies of eighty-five men each to guard western borders against Indian attacks. Although Henry's followers nominated him commander in chief, veteran officers of the French and Indian War objected strongly to the selection of someone with no military rank or experience as their commander. Despite his immense popularity, Henry won election by only one vote over Hugh Mercer, an older Scotsman with battlefield experience in the French and Indian War. While Mercer stomped off angrily to join the Continental Army under Washington, William Woodford, another veteran of the French and Indian War, agreed to take command of the Second Regiment, while Henry took over the First Regiment, along with the title of commander in chief of Virginia forces. To prevent emergence of a military dictator, the Virginia Convention established a civilian Committee of

Safety, led by old Edmund Pendleton, with supreme command of the military.

Henry and the other former burgesses voted to print £350,000 in Virginia currency to establish an arms production plant in Fredericksburg near the northern Virginia iron mines. At Henry's insistence, the Convention gave troops complete freedom of worship and dissenting ministers the right to preach in the Virginia Army, thus bringing freedom of religion to a small corner of Britain's southern colonies for the first time.

When the Convention adjourned on August 26, Henry rode home to put his plantation and family affairs in order. After seeing his children safely ensconced in his daughter Martha's home, he returned to Williamsburg in September to take command of Virginia's armed forces. One thousand strong, with more drifting in every hour, the volunteers cheered his arrival and escorted him through town along Duke of Gloucester Street past the deserted Governor's Palace to the College of William and Mary. Among them were the fierce-looking Culpeper Minutemen, wearing buck-tailed hats, scalping knives and tomahawks in their belts, and green shirts emblazoned with Patrick Henry's words: Liberty or Death. The cornet, or standard-bearer, who led them carried a flag with a coiled rattlesnake poised to strike. Beneath it a motto warned, Don't Tread on Me.

"They look like a band of assassins," commented one merchant.

All the men from Henry's Piedmont hills seemed to be in the march, young and old. Clients he had defended in court marched with those he had opposed—along with Shelton's tavern regulars who had reeled to his fiddle. They were an odd mixture of wizened frontiersmen, farmers, planters, boys. . . . In the mix were Major Thomas Marshall and his son, Lieutenant John Marshall, the future secretary of state and chief justice of the United States. Student volunteers from William and Mary included James Monroe, the future president. His fearlessness and rifle skills earned him a quick promotion to lieutenant.

Henry's oldest son, eighteen-year-old John, rode alongside his father, ready to fight, but like so many other young volunteers, woefully untrained for anything other than shooting quail. Henry appointed his son a cornet of the First Virginia Regiment. Unfortunately, Henry was no better trained than his son or the rest of his men, and he remained in Williamsburg in

DON'T TREAD ON ME

One of many Revolutionary War "rattlesnake flags" symbolizing vigilance (it has no eyelids) and deadly bite when attacked. Some Virginia rattlesnake flags bore Patrick Henry's "Liberty or Death" slogan as well as "Don't Tread on Me."
(Library of Congress)

September to learn to be a soldier while the Continental Congress reconvened in Philadelphia. Historians still question how well Henry learned his lessons. The Committee of Safety, apparently, did not believe he learned them well enough to lead his troops into battle—that he was too indecisive, too friendly with his men, and unable or unwilling to impose the harsh discipline that produced precision soldierly responses.

"His studies had been directed to civil and not to military pursuits," one member of the Committee of Safety argued. "He is totally unacquainted with the art of war and has no knowledge of military discipline."[1] Indeed, Edmund Pendleton apologized to the experienced Colonel Woodford: "Believe me, sir the unlucky step of calling that gentleman from our councils, where he was useful, into the field . . . the duties of which he must . . . be an entire stranger to, has given me many an anxious and uneasy moment. In consequence of this mistaken step . . . we must be deprived of the service of some able officers, whose honor and former ranks will not suffer them to act under him in this juncture, when we so much need their services."[2]

Even George Washington, a staunch friend and admirer of Henry, seemed uneasy about sending Henry into the field as a regimental commander. "I think my country made a capital mistake when they took Henry out of the senate to place him in the field; and pity it is that he does not see this, and remove every difficulty by a voluntary resignation."[3]

Although Patrick Henry appointed experienced officers to train rank-and-file troops, he had no one to teach him the skills of command and battlefield strategy, and when the Committee of Safety decided to strike at Lord Dunmore, it sent the experienced Colonel Woodford and his troops instead of Henry.

From his ship off Norfolk, Lord Dunmore had wreaked vengeance on Virginians by sending marines to raid coastal towns and plantations, plunder supplies, and carry off slaves with promises of freedom for volunteering to fight alongside the British. Late in October, British marines were on their way to Hampton, with orders to pillage the town and burn it to the ground. Pendleton's Committee of Safety ordered Woodford to lead his 700-man regiment and the 500 Culpeper Minutemen to repel the British landing and establish an independent command post. Although Woodford succeeded, Henry was furious at having been ignored by the Committee of Safety and demanded that it relay all future orders through him.

A few days later, word arrived that King George had not only rejected the Olive Branch Petition, he had declared the colonies to be in open rebellion and ordered an armada of 500 British ships to sail for America with 20,000 British troops and 9,000 German mercenaries to crush colonial resistance. The armada divided into two fleets, with the larger part sailing to New York to establish the central British command for North America and divide the New England colonies from the mid-Atlantic and southern colonies. The smaller part of the fleet would carry Major General Lord Cornwallis toward Charleston, South Carolina, the largest port in the South and a primary link in America's vital tobacco and rice trade. Once he captured Charleston, he could then send some warships to blockade Wilmington, North Carolina, and another flotilla to block the entrance to Chesapeake Bay, thus shutting down the economy of Virginia without engaging the most powerful of the American colonies militarily.

With carte blanche from London to combat Virginia's rebellion from within, Lord Dunmore ordered marines to seize Norfolk, Virginia's largest town. With sentries posted at every corner, he offered residents the choice of swearing allegiance to the king or losing their homes and properties. He then proclaimed martial law in the entire colony and ordered all able-bodied men to report for duty in the British military or risk forfeiting their properties and possibly their lives as deserters. He offered all slaves, indentured servants, and criminals their freedom if they turned on their masters and joined the British army. "I hope it will oblige the rebels to disperse to take care of their properties," Dunmore gloated.

After lengthy strategy discussions, the Committee of Safety again ignored Henry and sent Woodford with 900 Virginia regulars and the Culpepper Minutemen to attack Norfolk. To deceive Dunmore, Major Thomas Marshall sent one of his servants to Dunmore's camp pretending to be a runaway with information indicating Woodford's troop strength to be far smaller than it actually was. On that intelligence, Dunford went into battle with only 200 regulars and 300 blacks and Tories. The result was a slaughter that left even the most battle-hardened frontiersmen retching at the blood-bath. Dunmore and the survivors fled to Norfolk and rowed to the safety of British frigates. Outraged, Dunmore plotted revenge, and, on January 1, 1776, he ordered his ships to fire on the Norfolk waterfront while marines landed and set the town ablaze, leaving 6,000 people homeless in the dead of winter—some of them loyal Tories. With Dunmore's ships patrolling the coast, every other town along Virginia's shoreline feared the same fate.

Frustrated again at not having been sent into action, Henry quarreled with Woodford, saying that, as a subordinate, he should have kept his commanding officer informed of all his movements. Woodford snapped back that he had received his orders from the Committee of Safety, had kept them informed, and assumed that they were in touch with Henry.

Just as the controversy reached explosive proportions, the Continental Congress intervened by incorporating the First and Second Virginia and four other regiments into the Continental Army. Congress put two experienced brigadier generals in overall command and relegated Henry to the command of only the First Regiment as a colonel. Insulted by his subordinate position and rank, he resigned from the military on February 28, 1776.

When they learned of his resignation, Henry's troops "went into mourning, and, under arms, waited on him at his lodgings," according to the *Virginia Gazette*. "Your withdrawing yourself from the service," they said in a letter to him, "fills us with the most poignant sorrow, as it at once deprives us of our father and General, yet . . . we are compelled to applaud your spirited resentment to the most glaring indignity."[4]

Henry comforted them by admitting, "I am unhappy to part with you. I leave the service, but I leave my heart with you. May God bless you, and give you success and safety, and make you the glorious instruments of saving our country."[5]

The controversy over Henry's resignation did not die, however. In a letter to the *Gazette*, one officer charged that Henry's political enemies

> strove to bury in obscurity his [Henry's] martial talents. . . . Virginia may truly boast, that in him she finds the able statesman, the soldier's father, the best of citizens, and liberty's dear friend. . . . The officers and soldiers, who know him, are riveted to his bosom: when he speaks, all is silence; when he orders, they cheerfully obey . . . [6]

Ninety officers signed a letter expressing the same sentiments, and, at a farewell dinner hosted by his officers, the endless toasts to his health left them so drunk, they "assembled in a tumultuous manner and demanded their discharge, and declared their unwillingness to serve under any other commander." Henry delayed his departure to put down the mutiny, visiting "several barracks and using every argument in his power with the soldiery to lay aside their imprudent resolution." Saying that "his honor alone" had motivated his resignation, Henry pledged that while he would no longer be able to serve his country in the military, he would serve "the glorious cause" as a private citizen.[7]

No satisfactory explanation exists for denying Henry's appointment to high command other than Pendleton's letters referring to lax discipline over his men. What Pendleton called laxity, however, Henry called liberty, believing that free men—neighbors all—needed only direction from their elected leader, not schoolhouse discipline. On the other hand, nothing in his few months of military service in Williamsburg gave him any claim over two experienced brigadiers general to supreme command of the eight Virginia regiments in the Continental Army. Henry did study some military science in Williamsburg—*The New Art of War, Treatise of Military Discipline*, and *The Manual Exercise*, with "the most up-to-date methods of infantry drill and tactics. . . ." But without any war experience, his textbook studies did not qualify him to risk men's lives and the fate of the Revolution in battle. With his forthright, humble letter to his troops, he all but admitted his lack of qualifications as a military commander and set about serving his state as a civilian leader instead. Indeed, he was destined to become one of the most important civilian leaders of the American Revolution.

After resigning his military commission, Henry returned to Scotchtown to gather his family about him once again, put his financial affairs in order, and, like other farmers—in or out of the military—attend to the spring planting. Within days of his return, however, his Hanover County followers elected him and his brother-in-law John Syme to the Fifth Virginia Convention.

On March 17, 1776, British troops began evacuating Boston, and Virginia's Convention prepared to declare independence from England, naming Henry to a committee to create a new government. What was Virginia to become? The short struggle against Britain had made it clear that most colonies would be unable to stand alone as independent countries and survive. But Virginia was not like most colonies. It was wealthier and more heavily populated than the other colonies, and huge by comparison—larger than every European nation except Russia and Turkey.

At the time of the First Continental Congress, Henry had studied Baron de Montesquieu's seminal work on government, *The Spirit of Laws*. The French political philosopher classed government into three categories: the republic, based on virtue; monarchy, based on honor; and despotism, based on fear. Liberty, Montesquieu wrote, was most likely to survive in small republics in which governors remain close to the governed and aware of their needs. "In a large republic," he warned, "the public good is sacrificed to a thousand views . . . In a small one, the interest of the public is perceived more easily, better understood. . . ."[8] Also essential to the survival of liberty, Montesquieu declared, was the separation of powers into executive, legislative, and judicial branches, with the powers of each branch held by different individuals, acting independently of those in other branches, to prevent collusion.

"The grand work of forming a constitution for Virginia is now before the convention . . . " Henry wrote to John Adams, the man he most respected among delegates from other states he had met at the Continental Congress. "Is not a confederacy of our states necessary? If that could be formed, and its objects for the present be only offensive and defensive, and guaranty respecting colonial rights, perhaps dispatch might be had." Adams sent Henry—"as a token of friendship"—a pamphlet he had written entitled *Thoughts on Government,*[9] with a plan for a democratic/republican style government, which Henry "read with great pleasure. . . ." In his letter of thanks, Henry warned Adams that unless Congress agreed on a plan for funding the Continental Army, "our mutual friend the General [Washington] will be hampered. . . ."[10]

"My Dear Sir," John Adams answered Henry,

I had this morning the pleasure of yours. . . . Happy Virginia, whose Constitution is to be framed by so masterly a builder! . . . I know of none so competent to the task as the author of the first Virginia resolutions against the Stamp Act, who will have the glory with posterity, of beginning and concluding this great revolution. . . . I esteem it an honor and a happiness that my opinion so often coincides with yours. . . . It has ever appeared to me that the natural course and order of things was this: for every colony to institute a government; for all the colonies to confederate and define the limits of the continental constitution; then to declare the colonies . . . confederated sovereign states; and last of all, to form treaties with foreign powers. But I fear we cannot proceed systematically, and that we shall be obliged to declare ourselves independent states before we confederate, and indeed before all the colonies have established their governments. . . . We all look up to Virginia for examples.[11]

After Henry published Adams's scheme of government in the *Virginia Gazette*, the Convention adopted most of it in principle, creating a bicameral legislature with a popularly elected lower house—the House of Delegates, or Assembly—and a Senate, or upper house, elected by members of the Assembly. The two houses were to elect a governor to serve as chief executive with consent of a privy council—also elected by the two houses. The two houses would also elect all other executives—treasurer, attorney general, and so forth. The governor would appoint all judges, with the advice and consent of the upper house.

The Virginia Convention made a few minor changes, most of them based on the deep fears of executive tyranny implanted by George III's treatment of the colonies and the arbitrary powers imparted to colonial governors as the king's personal representatives. It limited the governor's term in office to one year and the length of time he could serve to three successive terms. After a hiatus of four years, he could serve a maximum of three more one-year terms. He could not legislate or rule by decree. Only the House of Delegates could originate laws, which the Senate would have to approve or reject for them to take effect. Despite Henry's objections, the Convention denied the governor the right of veto and the right to dissolve the legislature.

The Convention rejected "every hint of power which might be stigmatized as being of royal origin," explained Edmund Randolph, then a delegate and later governor. "No member but Henry could with impunity to his popularity have contended as strenuously as he did for an executive veto. . . . Amongst other arguments he averred that a governor would be . . . unable to defend his office from usurpation by the legislature . . . and that he would be a dependent instead of a coordinate branch of power." In the end, however, "the Convention gave way to their horror of a powerful chief magistrate without waiting to reflect how much stronger a governor might be made for the benefit of the people."[12]

One addition Virginians made to the John Adams plan of government was mandatory voting, with fines for failing to vote. The convention limited voting privileges, however, to white, male freeholders with at least fifty acres of unimproved land, or twenty-five acres of improved land (cultivated, with a dwelling), or an improved lot in a town. Independence, in other words, did not change the "mental condition" of Americans, as an

English observer put it at the time. "Their deference for rank and for judicial and legislative authority continued nearly unimpaired," and early state constitutions such as Virginia's kept voting powers in the hands of property owners and Christians—despite inclusion of bills of rights that seemed to empower all citizens.[13]

As a preface to its framework for government, the Virginia Convention included a declaration of rights written by George Mason, who began with an affirmation that "all men are born equally free. . . ." After delegates complained that the phrase gave blacks equal claims to freedom, old Edmund Pendleton resolved the arguments with an eight-word amendment that "all men are created equally free and independent *when they enter into a state of society. . . .*"

Among other rights, the sixteen articles guaranteed the "inalienable right to enjoy life, liberty, and happiness, the freedom of the press, the right to a speedy and fair trial before a jury, and the freedom of elections." The sixteenth article asserted that "all men are entitled to the free exercise of religion. . . ." and would lead to separation of church and state in Virginia in 1786. The articles prohibited excessive bail and fines, cruel and unusual punishment, imprisonment except by law or jury judgments, inheritance of public offices, and a standing army.

On June 29, the Virginia Convention adopted one of the first written constitutions in the Americas and proclaimed that "the government of this country [Virginia] as formerly exercised under the Crown of Great Britain, is TOTALLY DISSOLVED." After George Mason placed Henry's name in nomination, the Convention elected Henry first governor of the newest, largest, and most powerful state in America, thus allowing him to fulfill his pledge to his troops to serve "the glorious cause" as a private citizen.[14]

Virginia's declaration of independence came three weeks after Richard Henry Lee, Virginia's delegate to the Continental Congress, proposed the sweeping resolution that the United Colonies "are, and of right ought to be, free and independent States." He also proposed that "a plan of confederation be prepared and transmitted to the respective colonies for their consideration and approbation."[15]

On July 2, Congress adopted Lee's resolution, and on July 4, it approved a Declaration of Independence written largely by Thomas Jeffer-

*Planter George Mason was among the first
members of Virginia's House of Burgesses
to support a boycott of British goods after
Parliament raised duties and sought to tax
American colonists.* (LIBRARY OF CONGRESS)

son and to which John Hancock appended his bold signature as president
of Congress. As Hancock was signing the Declaration, Patrick Henry was
taking his oath as first governor of the free and independent Commonwealth of Virginia. In an evident response to criticisms of his coarse ap-
parel, Henry laid aside his coarse country clothes before taking office.
Breaking with his past, he crowned his head with an unpowdered wig and
donned a costly black suit with knee breeches, overlaid by a scarlet cloak
and other adornments that befitted the highest office in the new and sovereign Commonwealth—including a costly, ornate carriage.

"He had been accused by the big-wigs of former times as being a coarse
and common man, and utterly destitute of dignity," explained his son-in-
law Judge Spencer Roane, "and perhaps he wished to show them that they

were mistaken."[16] He apparently succeeded. From that time on, his friends and enemies addressed him as "Your Excellency" or "Your Honor."

Almost all Virginians and, indeed, leaders in other states, hailed Henry's election. "Once happy under your military command," wrote the officers and men of the First and Second Regiments that he had once commanded, "we hope for more extensive blessings from your civil empire . . . our hearts are willing, and arms ready to maintain your authority as chief magistrate. . . . " Replying that "the remembrance of my former connection with you shall ever be dear to me," Henry urged them, "Go on, gentlemen, to finish the great work you have so nobly and successfully begun. Convince the tyrants again, that they shall bleed, that America will bleed to her last drop, 'ere their wicked schemes find success."[17]

Henry's Quaker friends were equally elated that "the representatives of the people have nobly declared all men equally free," and they proposed a plan for gradual emancipation of slaves. "I can but wish and hope," wrote Virginia's Quaker leader Robert Pleasants, "that great abilities and interest may be exerted toward a full . . . confirmation thereof."[18]

In New York, meanwhile, the 10,000 British troops General Howe had evacuated from Boston landed unopposed on Staten Island. Ten days later, 150 British transports sailed into New York Bay and landed 20,000 more British troops and 9,000 Hessian mercenaries. Meanwhile, a second British fleet sailed within sight of Charleston, South Carolina, and rained cannon fire over Fort Moultrie on Sullivan's Island at the entrance to Charleston Bay. Instead of destroying the fort, however, the cannon balls embedded themselves in the soft palmetto logs of the fort's walls and strengthened them—indeed, made them all but impenetrable. When the fort's cannons returned fire, the British fleet had no choice but to sail away ingloriously, leaving the South free of British occupation for the moment.

With fewer than 20,000 men to defend the sprawling New York area, Washington desperately needed help defending Long Island. On August 16, Patrick Henry's former troops—the 700 men of the First and Second Virginia regiments—broke camp in Williamsburg and marched northward through the oppressive summer heat, with the Culpeper Minutemen carrying their rattlesnake flag, to which they had added Henry's words, "Liberty or Death." They reached Washington's headquarters on Harlem Heights in less than a month—but they were too late. Twenty thousand British and Hessian troops had stormed ashore in Brooklyn on the southwestern edge of Long Island and overrun the Patriot force of 5,000 defenders, killing 1,500 and capturing the American army's entire food supply—along with two American generals. Only a thick fog allowed survivors to escape in the dark of night across the East River to New York Island (Manhattan) on August 29.

After the Battle of Long Island, the British high command freed one of the captured American generals—John Sullivan of New Hampshire—to go to Congress with a proposal for an informal peace conference. On September 6, Congress sent Benjamin Franklin, John Adams, and Edmund Rutledge of South Carolina to Staten Island to confer with Britain's military commanders General Sir William Howe and his brother Admiral Lord Richard Howe. After the usual preliminaries on September 11, the conference came to an abrupt end when the Howes insisted that the Americans renounce the Declaration of Independence as a condition for any further discussions.

Washington immediately posted the Connecticut militia to guard against a British landing at Kips Bay on the eastern shore of Manhattan Island and moved the main body of his troops to Harlem Heights, about six miles to the north.[19] Three days later, on the morning of September 15, five British ships in the East River began pounding American emplacements at Kips Bay with cannon fire. Within hours, 6,000 of the 8,000 Connecticut troops had fled. In disbelief, Washington galloped to the scene to rally the troops, but the slaughter on Long Island had left them so terrified they ignored Washington's orders. Officers and soldiers alike sprinted to the rear without firing a shot, leaving Washington and his aides exposed to possible capture.

"Good God," Washington cried out. "Are these the men with which I am to defend America?"[20]

As the British landed, Washington and his aides galloped off to safety, as British buglers mocked them with the call of hunters on a fox chase. "I never felt such a sensation before," said a Washington aide. "It seemed to crown our disgrace."[21]

Connecticut militiamen continued disappearing, reducing one regiment to only fourteen men, another to fewer than thirty. With his troop strength disintegrating, Washington withdrew from Manhattan northward towards White Plains, on the mainland in Westchester County—only to have another British force scatter the Continental Army in three directions. While some of his men moved northward into the Hudson River Highlands, Washington led a contingent of about 5,000 men in full flight across the Hudson to New Jersey.

Despite Washington's desperate situation, the Virginia state constitution left Henry without authority to help, and the lengthy debates that rent the House of Delegates over each decision left the state's military in limbo. As titular leader of America's largest, most powerful state, Henry decided to ignore the constitution and simply assume the powers he needed to act. Gambling that his popularity was too broad based for the House of Delegates to challenge him, he ordered men and materials sent to Washington, then issued orders to improve state defenses against British attacks in the East and South and Anglo-Indian raids in the West. He wrote to Washington of his decisions and received this reply: "Your correspondence will confer honor and satisfaction, and, whenever it is in my power, I shall write to you with pleasure."

Washington gave Henry details of his recent military defeat and the status of the army, calling "our defeat on Long Island . . . and the evacuation of New York . . . [acts] of prudence and necessity." He reported the troops "in some measure dispirited by these successive retreats," and he complained about "the evils of short enlistments," urging establishment of "a permanent body of forces." To help Henry defend Virginia, he suggested that Henry act to create

obstacles against the enemy's ships and tenders, which may go up your rivers in quest of provisions, or for the purpose of destroying your towns. If you have depended on batteries to prevent them without any other obstruction, a trial of the matter has taught us to believe that it will be altogether ineffectual. . . . I would strongly recommend row galleys . . . officered with brave and determined men . . . would be the most likely means of securing your towns and houses on navigable waters. . . .

He reminded Henry that he expected Virginia to furnish the Continental Army with fifteen battalions.[22]

Henry immediately acted on Washington's advice, winning Privy Council approval to arm six sloops to protect entrances to inland waterways and prevent British ships from sailing upstream to pillage river-front villages and plantations. Seeking more sweeping powers, he bullied the House of Delegates with vague threats of resignation to win appointment as chairman of a new Navy Board. He used his new authority to open six new shipyards and assemble a navy of seventy ships—refitting some captured British ships, but building many from scratch. In addition to 600 seamen, Henry's Virginia Navy recruited 300 marines to repel British hit-and-run assaults on coastal towns and plantations. Henry ordered the swiftest of the ships to slice through the British blockade at the entrance to Chesapeake Bay and carry tobacco to the West Indies to exchange for badly needed supplies such as gunpowder and salt.

As head of state, Henry invested himself with powers over the conduct of foreign affairs and established trade relations with the governors of Cuba and New Orleans, and through them the king of Spain. "I need not inform your excellency," he wrote to the governor of Cuba (and much the same to the governor of New Orleans), "that these states are now free and independent, capable of forming alliances and of making treaties.

> I think the connection might be mutually beneficial; for independent of the beef, pork, livestock, flour, staves, shingles, and several other articles with which we could supply your islands, we have vast quantities of skins, furs, hemp, and flax, which we could by an easy inland navigation, bring down the Mississippi to New Orleans from our back county, in exchange for your woolens, linens, wines, military stores, etc.[23]

At Henry's request, the Spanish king approved shipment to Virginia of "a quantity of goods" to Havana and from there to New Orleans, for overland shipment to Williamsburg.

With the House of Delegates unable or unwilling to stop him, Henry inserted himself into every area of Virginia's war effort, unilaterally ordering counties that had yet to supply troops to the Continental Army to muster twenty-six companies of militia. Washington had asked the states for eighty-eight battalions, of which Virginia and Massachusetts were to supply fifteen each, Pennsylvania twelve, and other states the rest, in proportion to their populations. Virginia, however, had not been able to assemble enough men and materials to protect its own territory, let alone contribute more troops to the Continental Army.

As Washington's army retreated across New Jersey, Henry acted to send reinforcements. "I have issued the necessary orders this morning that the Troops of Horse (six) shall be marched to join General Washington,"[24] Henry notified the War Office in Philadelphia.

Besides creating Virginia's Navy and raising troops for Washington's Continental Army, Henry took charge of procurement of war materiel for both Virginia's militia and the Continental Army. "There are now ten tons of lead, which are ready to be delivered for the use of the Continental Congress," he wrote to Richard Henry Lee and Virginia's other delegates in Congress.[25] And he informed John Hancock, the president of Congress, that "we have a gun factory at Fredericksburg."[26] Henry also ordered the evacuation of cattle and other food stores, as well as military supplies, from coastal areas, where British raiders might capture them, and he wrote to the governors of neighboring states such as Maryland and North Carolina to coordinate defense measures. Fearful that Tories in coastal towns might facilitate landings of British raiders, he set about "removing out of the country certain natives of Great Britain."[27]

Henry faced serious problems in the western reaches of Virginia, where Indian tribes had taken advantage of the conflict with Britain to attack white settlements and reclaim lands that settlers and various land companies had staked out in Kentucky and the Ohio Valley. One group of Kentucky settlers retaliated by massacring an entire peaceful Shawnee village—men, women, and children. The atrocity threatened to set the frontier ablaze just as Henry needed more troops to fight the British. Henry was furious, as he ordered militia commanders in two western counties

to embody fifty men . . . and order them to Kentucky . . . to ward off the stroke which may be expected. Have every gun in your county put into good order and get ready for action. Lead may be had from the mines. An order for 1 lb. for each man of your militia accompanies this; powder it is said is plenty among you. If it can't be had otherwise, send to Richmond for it.

Henry ordered "trusty scouts" into Shawnee country and told the militia commander to build "proper stockades or defenses to receive the more helpless part of the people." As he would later explain,

> I really blush for the occasion of this war with the Shawnees. I doubt not that you detest the vile assassins who have brought it on us at this critical time, when our whole force was wanted in another quarter. Tis a few wicked men who committed the murder. Why do not those among you of a contrary character drag them to justice? Shall this precedent establish the right of involving Virginia in war whenever anyone in the back country shall please?

As the war against the Shawnees dragged on, Henry told commanders, "I mean bringing the murderers of the Indians to justice," accusing them of being "traitors . . . agents for the enemy who have taken this method to find employment for the brave back woodsmen at home, and prevent their joining General Washington to strike a decisive stroke for independency. . . ."[28]

He had no sooner ordered troops west when he received another request from Washington for more troops. Working almost twenty-four hours a day, he managed to organize an officer corps and report to Congress that "one full battalion of troops of this state are under orders to march to Jersey."[29] With that, however, he all but collapsed, pushed to exhaustion in his dawn-to-dusk efforts to raise troops and locate military supplies. In addition, he contracted malaria and now had no choice but to go home to Scotchtown to recuperate. He remained bedridden for nearly six weeks—so sick at times that rumors of his death began to circulate. Not uncommon in an era when swarms of mosquitoes infested Virginia's wet lowlands, malaria produced periodic bouts of chills, fever, debilitating fatigue, and anemia. When they could get some, victims treated themselves with the bark of the cinchona tree, which contained quinine. Others relied on rum laced with garlic, red pepper, or other strong ingredients. Unable to tolerate alcohol, however, Henry simply suffered much of the time. His drink of choice was spring water, whose bacterial contamination often aggravated his condition.

Henry did not remain totally idle during his illness, however. Already interested in promoting higher education, he helped Hampden-Sydney Academy obtain a charter as a college—the first to serve Henry's beloved Piedmont. Named a founding trustee, he would hold his trusteeship the rest of his life and send six of his sons and many of their boys to study there.

The war followed Henry to Scotchtown when George Rogers Clark, a twenty-three-year-old Kentucky frontiersman, appeared at his door, saying he had been elected to the Virginia Convention by Kentucky settlers and needed 500 pounds of gunpowder to fight the Indians. Born and raised in Charlottesville, Clark had gone to the Kentucky wilderness as a surveyor for early settlers and metamorphosed into their political leader. When Clark arrived, Henry had already received intelligence reports of a British plan to incite a full-scale Indian war against colonists in the West and force Washington to dilute his army and fight on two fronts. Henry quickly approved Clark's request and sent him on to Williamsburg for Privy Council approval.

After six weeks of convalescence, Henry returned to Williamsburg in September 1776, this time bringing his two sisters, Anne and Elizabeth, to care for him and assume responsibilities as hostesses in the Governor's Palace. Within days, however, Henry longed for his children, and his daughter Martha brought twelve-year-old William and nine-year-old Anne, along with her own infant son Patrick Henry Fontaine, to enliven the governor's mansion with the shouts of children. Henry needed play as much as his children. Henry's two youngest, only five and seven, were staying with Henry's sister, Jane Meredith, at the time, and his oldest, John, had marched north with the First Virginia Regiment.

During Henry's absence, Thomas Jefferson had emerged as the foremost young political leader in the House. He succeeded in furthering Henry's agenda to expand individual liberties by repealing laws that forced dissenters to pay taxes to the Anglican church and made membership a prerequisite for voting. The Assembly also abolished fines for failure to attend church at least once a month—and the punishment of ten whip lashes for refusal to pay those fines. Jefferson was curiously unconcerned with military affairs, however, and left Virginia's coastline "naked and defenseless" after the Williamsburg regiments marched north to join the Continental Army. The House of Delegates, therefore, drew considerable comfort from Henry's return—so much so that they honored him by slicing off the western half of Pittsylvania County and renaming it Henry County. When the toasts had ended, however, Henry turned to neglected military affairs and learned of grim news from northern battlefields: Winter had enveloped the Northeast earlier than usual, and, with the powerful British army in close pursuit, Washington's men had fled westward across New Jersey through sheets of icy autumn rains towards the Delaware River. They barely made it to safety on the opposite bank in Pennsylvania. By early December, desertions had reduced his army to only about 3,000 men. Sickness left 500 of the 700 Virginians unfit for duty.

Rather than risk a water crossing, the British commander ordered 1,400 Hessians to remain in Trenton to keep a watch on the Americans on the opposite bank, while he led British troops to settle into comfortable winter quarters at nearby Princeton and await an opportunity in the spring to wipe out Washington's crippled army and end the Revolution. The British advance left New York and most of New Jersey in British hands—and the Redcoats almost in sight of the American rebel capital. On December 12, Congress fled Philadelphia for Baltimore and, all but conceding defeat in the struggle for independence, began debating terms of capitulation. The American Revolution seemed at an end.

Chapter 9

Hastening to Ruin

With Virginia all but helpless to repel a British assault, Henry proposed the unthinkable to the House of Delegates. "In December 1776," Thomas Jefferson recalled, "our circumstances being much distressed, it was proposed in the House of Delegates to create a dictator, invested with every power, legislative, executive and judiciary, civil and military, of life and of death, over our persons and over our properties."[1] In fact, it was Washington who had implanted the idea in Henry's mind, having urged "an indiscriminate draft" to raise troops for the Continental Army. Although the final bill did not go as far as Henry had hoped, it nonetheless enhanced his powers

> to raise additional battalions . . . direct their operations within this Commonwealth . . . order them to march to join and act in concert with the Continental Army, or the troops of any of the United American States, and to provide for their pay, supply of provisions, arms, and other necessaries . . . by drawing on the Treasurer for the money which may be necessary from time to time.

It also gave him powers to seize foodstuffs and supplies for the military.

The irony of the self-professed opponent of British tyranny seeking dictatorial powers was not lost on his political opponents. "Surely," he argued, "whether . . . called a dictator or governor . . . an officer armed with . . . enlarged . . . powers was necessary to restrain the unbridled fury of a licentious enemy. . . ."[2]

Hypocritical or not, Henry's political turnabout was nothing more than a statesman's adaptation to changing realities. Every contemporary leader of consequence—Washington, Jefferson, Madison and others—would stage equally dramatic reversals of their political positions.

If Henry had not seized power, the British army would have overrun Virginia by the time the legislature or even the Council could have agreed on an effective response under democratic rules of debate. Democratic rule, Henry recognized, was inappropriate in a wartime emergency.

"Self-preservation is paramount to all law," Jefferson agreed. "There are extreme cases where the laws become inadequate even to their own preservation, and where the universal resource is a dictator, or martial law."[3]

With supplies of food, arms, ammunition, and money all but exhausted, however, Henry's task—even with dictatorial powers—bordered on the impossible. "Virginia," he lamented,

> impoverished by defending the northern department, exhausted by the southern war, now finds the whole weight . . . on her shoulders. . . . Whilst we are continuing our utmost exertions to repair the mighty losses sustained in defending almost every state in the Union, we at length find ourselves invaded, and threatened with the whole weight of the American war.[4]

As the Continental Congress considered capitulation, Washington knew he needed a quick, dramatic strike against the British to revive American morale and save the Revolution. In the dead of night on December 25, he led 2,400 troops through a blinding snowstorm across the ice-choked Delaware River. At eight the next morning, they reached Trenton, New Jersey, and found the 1,400-man Hessian garrison still abed, dissuaded by the storm from posting their usual patrol. Shocked awake by the reality of their plight, the terrified Germans raced out into the snow in their nightclothes to secure cannon emplacements at the head of King Street and repel the approaching Americans. Before they could get there, a young Virginia captain, William Washington, a distant cousin of the commander in chief, and his eighteen-year-old lieutenant James Monroe, charged through a hail of rifle fire and seized the weapons. Both men fell wounded but held fast until Washington's Continentals forced the Hessians to surrender, taking more than 1,000 Hessian prisoners.

Washington's victory set off a wave of euphoria that temporarily bolstered troop morale and public support for the Revolution. With the new year, army ranks began to swell instead of shrink, and, after a subsequent Washington victory at Princeton left western New Jersey in Patriot hands, Congress returned to Philadelphia.

Washington's victory did not resonate in many parts of the South, however, where the war seemed too far removed to be of concern. "I am very sorry to inform you," Henry wrote to Washington, "that the recruiting business of late goes on so badly that there remains little prospect of filling the six new battalions from this state voted by the Assembly."[5]

In fact, enlistments had come to a halt, Henry admitted to Richard Henry Lee. He blamed the failure to enlist new recruits on fears that leaving home to fight in the army would leave their families and farms vulnerable to attack—either by Indians in the West, British marines along Chesapeake Bay, or renegade slaves across the state. "Our seacoasts are defenseless almost," Henry complained to Lee. "The people on the Eastern Shore are very uneasy . . . Arms . . . are wanted here most extremely. . . . Five swift sailing boats are gone for arms to the West Indies. . . . Our factories are making some."[6]

In the West, he reported that a peace agreement between Virginia and the Cherokee nation had proved ineffective. "A fellow called the 'Dragging Canoe' has seceded from the Cherokees and 400 warriors have followed his fortune, lying in the woods and making war with us . . . Orders were issued a few days since for destroying Pluggy's Town [an Indian settlement]. Three hundred militia are ordered . . . from Fort Pitt."[7] In fact, the British had provoked the increased attacks by supplying Indians west of the Ohio River with arms and promises that they could keep any plunder and land they seized, along with all the scalps they could harvest.

Despite setbacks in the West, the Assembly sustained Henry's conduct of the war and, on May 29, 1777, unanimously elected him to a second term as governor. A few days later, Henry left abruptly for Hanover, where his uncle and namesake, Reverend Patrick Henry, had died suddenly. While there, however, the wedding of his sister Elizabeth mitigated his sadness—especially after he met Dorothea Dandridge, the eighteen-year-old daughter of his former neighbor in Hanover, Nathaniel West Dandridge, Martha Washington's cousin. When Henry had practiced law at Hanover Courthouse, Dolly, as her family called her, had been but a child. Only slightly older than his oldest daughter, she had now matured into a magnificent young woman, and forty-one-year-old Patrick Henry fell irretrievably in love. Although he did not know it, his son John, who was serving with Virginia's regiments in the North, also loved Dolly and had asked her father for her hand.

When Patrick Henry returned to Williamsburg in early July to begin his second term as governor, the vision of the beautiful Dorothea Dandridge haunted his every minute, and after only a few weeks, he rode back to Hanover and asked her father's permission to marry her. When he—and she—accepted, he sent the news to his entire family, including his son John, who had won a promotion to artillery captain in General Horatio Gates's Northern Army, near Albany, New York. In an era when fathers decided whom their daughters would marry, Dorothea's father evidently thought a sitting governor a better prospect for his daughter that a governor's son who might soon die in battle.

By the time Henry returned to Williamsburg, the British government had increased British forces in America to 48,000 and ordered North American commanders—General Sir William Howe in New York and General John Burgoyne in Canada—to crush the insurrection or face dismissal and disgrace. Howe and Burgoyne planned a three-pronged strategy to capture the rebel capital of Philadelphia and isolate New England from the rest of the colonies by gaining control of the Hudson River Valley from New York City to the Canadian frontier. While Howe led one force south to capture Philadelphia, a second force was to sail northward on the Hudson River to rendezvous in Albany with a third British army under

Burgoyne, which was then sweeping southward from Canada along Lake Champlain and Lake George.

Burgoyne's campaign started well, with 8,000 British and Hessian troops and Indian warriors overrunning the shores of Lake Champlain and capturing Fort Ticonderoga, Mount Defiance, and Fort Anne. Hopelessly outmanned, outgunned, and out of ammunition, the Patriots under British-born General Horatio Gates were helpless to slow Burgoyne's advance—until they reached Saratoga, about forty miles north of Albany. Suddenly, wagon loads of ammunition, arms, clothing, and tons of other materiel rolled into camp. Under a secret aid agreement, French ships had landed 200 field artillery pieces at Portsmouth, New Hampshire, along with thousands of muskets, kegs of powder, and enough blankets, clothes, and shoes to re-supply 90 percent of the Northern Army. Farmers—by the dozens at first, then by the hundreds—joined the wagon train of arms and stayed to fight to keep the British from overrunning their lands. By early October, the American army had swelled to 17,000, and new weapons were still arriving.

Unlike Gates, Burgoyne could not count on resupply or replacements. He put his troops on half rations and resolved to break through the American line that barred the road to Albany and the Hudson River link to New York. Unaccustomed to fighting in the North American wilderness, however, the British and Hessians advanced in traditional linear formation and marched straight into a slaughterhouse. General Daniel Morgan's riflemen lay hidden behind trees and boulders on the slopes of Bemis Heights, near Saratoga, New York, and let loose a hailstorm of bullets that toppled the Redcoats by the score as they marched forward relentlessly, row after row, stepping over their fallen comrades before dropping under the ceaseless fire. At the end of the day, Burgoyne had lost about 600 men—the Patriots half that number.

The Redcoats attacked again the next day, only to meet with another slaughter that cost them 700 troops captured, wounded, or killed. The Americans lost 150 men. On October 13, Burgoyne's army hoisted the white flag, and, after their commander signed the appropriate documents of surrender, 4,000 Redcoats began the slow trek to internment camps near Boston to await ships to carry them back to England.

Gates's victory elated the nation—and, evidently, the French government, which added to America's national euphoria by formally recognizing the United States as an independent nation. While the nation celebrated, Patrick Henry and Dorothea Dandridge took advantage of the festive mood in Williamsburg to wed. Both brought a variety of assets to their marriage—she a dowry of twelve slaves to add to his thirty; he, five children for her to raise—three of them young enough to require her particular attention: ten-year-old Anne, eight-year-old Betsy, and six-year-old Edward. All three grew to adore her, and in return for her evident love for his children, Henry grew to be "perhaps the best husband in the world," according to his brother-in-law Samuel Meredith.[8] With his marriage, Henry's assets now included his huge estate at Scotchtown, four farms totaling about 10,000 acres in the western part of the state, 10,000 acres in Kentucky and forty-two slaves, including Dolly's twelve dower slaves. Faced with the joyous prospects of a new life with a new wife, Henry decided to sell Scotchtown and "move away from all objects reminding me" of Sarah's madness and death. The sale yielded £5,000—enough to leave him independently wealthy for the moment.

After carrying his bride into the Governor's Palace in Williamsburg, Henry proclaimed a day of thanksgiving to celebrate French recognition of American independence, beginning with a military parade, artillery salutes, and "three huzzas from all present." Church bells rang, and Henry ordered a mug of rum for every soldier in town. Nine months later, Dolly gave birth to their first child.

After the guns fell silent at Saratoga, Patrick Henry's son, Captain John Henry, who had distinguished himself as an artillery commander, staggered between the hundreds of dead on the battlefield—many of them men he had commanded; some of them close friends. Already distraught over the marriage of the girl he loved to his father, he went "raving mad" as he walked among the fallen and finally broke his sword into pieces, and wandered off to no-one-knew-where.[9] Efforts to find him by his distraught father proved useless.

As Burgoyne's army marched to defeat in Saratoga, Howe's army of 15,000 British troops was sailing from New York into undefended Chesapeake Bay and landed on its northern shore near Philadelphia. Washington miscalculated British army strength and concentrated his power at the center of the lines along the east bank of Brandywine Creek, which blocked the road to Philadelphia. British general Lord Cornwallis, however, slipped away to the northwest with 8,000 troops and looped around and behind Washington's lines. As Redcoats closed in from three directions, Patriot troops fled in panic, losing about 1,000 men during the retreat. On September 19, Congress fled west to Lancaster, Pennsylvania, and a week later, General Howe and the British army marched into Philadelphia, believing they had ended the American Revolution.

Washington's humiliating defeat provoked angry grumbling in Congress that he was incompetent and should be replaced. A barrage of anonymous letters to Congress and the press praised Gates's success at Saratoga and denounced Washington's loss of the national capital. Washington was furious at the comparison, confiding in Henry that "I was left to fight two battles . . . to save Philadelphia with less numbers than composed the army of my antagonist, whilst the world has given us at least double.

> This impression, though mortifying in some points of view, I have been obliged to encourage, because, next to being strong, it is best to be thought so by the enemy . . . How different the case in the northern department! There the states of New York and New England resolving to crush Burgoyne, continued pouring in their troops, till the surrender of that army; at which time not less than fourteen thousand militia . . . were actually in Gates's camp . . . in many instances supplied with provisions of their own carrying.[10]

Regardless of the reasons for the different battlefield performances, the results convinced Congress to create a Board of War with supreme powers over Washington and the military, and it named Gates president and Gates's friend, Irish Colonel Thomas Conway, as Inspector General. Bitter over Washington's refusal to appoint him a major general, Conway used his newfound authority to plot Washington's ouster. While disparaging Washington and his generals with anonymous letters to Congress, he enlisted

Gates into the plot by appealing to the Englishman's ambitions and heaping scorn on Washington. "Heaven has been determined to save your country," Conway flattered Gates, "or a weak general and bad counselors would have ruined it."[11]

Another member of Conway's plot tried enlisting the iconic Patrick Henry: "The northern army has shown us what Americans are capable of doing with a general at their head," the anonymous critic wrote to Henry. Calling himself "one of your Philadelphia friends," he charged that "a Gates, a Lee, or a Conway[12] would, in a few weeks, render them an irresistible body of men." Warning Henry that "the letter must be thrown in the fire," he nonetheless urged Henry that "some of its comments ought to be made public, in order to awaken, enlighten, and alarm our country."[13]

In what may have been one of the most significant and least known decisions in his life and, indeed, of the Revolutionary War, Henry sent the letter by express rider to his friend Washington at Valley Forge, Pennsylvania, where Washington had settled his army in winter quarters after the British occupation of Philadelphia.

"I am sorry there should be one man who counts himself my friend who is not yours," Henry wrote to Washington.

> The censures aimed at you are unjust. . . . But there may possibly be some scheme or party forming to your prejudice. . . . Believe me, sir, I have too high a sense of the obligations America has to you to abet or countenance so unworthy a proceeding. . . . I really cannot tell who is the writer of this letter. . . . The handwriting is altogether strange to me. . . . But I will not conceal any thing from you by which you may be affected; for I really think your personal welfare and the happiness of America are intimately connected.[14]

Washington was equally emotional in thanking Henry, explaining that the anonymous letter "is not the only secret, insidious attempt that has been made to wound my reputation. There have been others equally base, cruel, and ungenerous . . . All I can say is that [America] has ever had, and I trust she will ever have, my honest exertions to promote her interest. I cannot hope that my services have been the best; but my heart tells me they have been the best I can render."[15]

The anonymous letter to Henry had, in fact, been written by the Surgeon General of the Continental Army, Dr. Benjamin Rush, the renowned Philadelphia physician who had signed the Declaration of Independence. When he assumed his army post, he found medical services disorganized (as were all services in the new army), but lacked the administrative skills to build an effective organization. Rather than admit his own failure, he complained to Washington of mismanagement by Director General Dr. William Shippen—Richard Henry Lee's brother-in-law. Beset by battle-field crises, Washington dismissed Rush's complaints and provoked the doctor's angry efforts to promote the general's ouster.

In his letter to Henry, Washington confided,

> My caution to avoid any thing which could injure the service prevented me from communicating but to a very few of my friends the intrigues of a faction which I know was formed against me, since it might serve to publish our internal dissensions; but their own restless zeal to advance their views has too clearly betrayed them and make concealment on my part fruitless. . . . General Gates was to be exalted on the ruin of my reputation and influence . . . and General Conway, I know, was a very active and malignant partisan, but I have reason to believe that their machinations have recoiled most sensibly upon themselves.[16]

Overall responsibility for the cabal to displace Washington remains unclear. Although Conway was arch-facilitator and Gates and Rush were evident co-conspirators, the plot may well have originated in the War Ministry in London, which generated most British espionage plots. The cabal began to collapse after Gates sent Major General Marquis de Lafayette—a close and loyal aide to Washington—on a quixotic mission to take command of the Northern Army in Albany in mid-February 1778. Once there, he was to mount an improbable expedition in the dead of winter to seize Canada from the British. When Lafayette arrived in Albany, however, there were too few troops and no money, arms, ammunition, or other supplies for the expedition. Neither the area commanders nor the commissary were aware that Gates had authorized a mission to Canada. "I have been deceived by the Board of War," Lafayette wrote to Washington. "It would be madness to undertake this operation."[17]

With Lafayette's revelations, the Conway Cabal, as it came to be called, collapsed. Congress ordered Conway demoted and transferred to an insignificant post along the Hudson River valley; Gates and the Board of War resigned, with Gates returning to his former post as commander of the Northern Army. Congress restored Washington to supreme command, giving him dictatorial powers and abandoning the concept of directing the war by committee.

Washington would never forget Henry's loyalty. "I can only thank you again, in language of the most undissembled gratitude, for your friendship," Washington wrote after crushing the cabal.

Henry proved his loyalty to Washington and the Revolution in other ways during the Continental Army's winter at Valley Forge. On a wooded plateau some twenty miles northwest of Philadelphia, Valley Forge gave Washington's small army the advantage of elevation if it had to defend itself against a larger enemy. Washington ordered his men to raise a city of huts, which—even in the bitter winter that followed—might have been tolerable had the Quartermaster General provided clothes, blankets, foods, and other supplies that Washington had ordered. "The soldiers lived in misery," according to Lafayette. "They lacked for clothes, hats, shirts, shoes, their legs and feet black from frostbite—we often had to amputate. . . . The army often went whole days without provisions. . . . The misery prevented new enlistments."[18]

By Christmas, desertions, disease, exposure to subzero temperatures, starvation, and thirst—for there were no springs on the Valley Forge plateau—had reduced Washington's Continental Army of 11,000 men to 5,000. Some froze to death; those who survived were too weak to fight. When Washington's pleas for supplies went unheeded by Quartermaster General Thomas Mifflin, he pleaded with Congress and the governors of every state for help.

"It is not easy to give you a just and accurate idea of the sufferings of the troops," Washington wrote to Patrick Henry at the end of 1777.

I fear I shall wound your feelings by telling you that on the 23rd [of December], I had in camp not less than 2,898 men unfit for duty by reason of their being bare foot and otherwise naked. . . . I can not but hope that every measure will be pursued . . . to keep them supplied from time to time. No pains, no efforts can be too great for this purpose. The articles of shoes, stockings, blankets demand the most particular attention. . . .[19]

Henry responded immediately, seizing nine wagonloads of clothing and blankets to meet the needs of Virginia's troops at Valley Forge. He promised Washington that "added to this supply, £15,000 worth of woolens etc. proper for the soldiers will set out from Petersburg in a few days. These last are procured under an act of Assembly empowering me to seize necessaries for our troops wherever they may be found." He said he had issued orders "to both Carolinas" for blankets and clothes and pledged that "nothing possible for me to effect will be left undone in getting whatever the troops are in want of." He also obtained and sent on to Washington enough funds to pay every Virginia soldier an attractive bonus for reenlisting. He was unable, however, to send Washington any additional troops, saying that he had sent two battalions south to support the Georgians and Carolinians. "Add to all this our Indian wars and marine service, almost total want of necessaries . . . deserters . . . small pox . . . there remains little prospect of filling the six new battalions from this state."[20]

As Henry was dealing with the crisis at Valley Forge, George Rogers Clark returned from the West with a plan to defeat both the Indians and their British sponsors. Rather than a frontal attack in Indiana and eastern Illinois, Clark proposed a surprise attack with a small force of irregulars on the rear of the British fort at far-off Kaskaskia, on the western border of the Illinois territory by the Mississippi River. If successful, he would then move eastward across Illinois, while a second force advanced from the east to trap the British in a vice and force them to flee northward to Canada. Impressed by Clark's daring and assuredness, Henry commissioned him a lieutenant colonel and scratched up enough money and supplies for him to recruit 175 men and set off for the West.

In the weeks that followed, Virginia's officers at Valley Forge informed Henry that some supplies he had sent via the Quartermaster General had never reached camp. In addition, they wrote of having found large stores of food and clothing in nearby towns that had not been sent to camp. Henry wrote to the Virginia delegation in Congress demanding an explanation. "I found upon enquiry," he wrote sternly, "that eight or ten thousand hogs and several thousand fine beeves might have been had very lately in a few counties convenient to the camp." He told the congressmen that he had commissioned three merchants "to purchase beef, or pork, to the amount of ten thousand pounds and drive it to camp in the most expeditious manner, and advanced them the cash. I have also directed Colonel Simpson to seize two thousand bushels of salt on the eastern shore . . . and reserve a thousand more to answer further orders that may become necessary." He said he hoped that "these several steps" would ease the immediate crisis among Virginia regiments at Valley Forge. "But Gentlemen," he scolded,

> I cannot forbear some reflections on this occasion, which I beg you will be pleased to lay before Congress . . . It is with the deepest concern that the business of supplying provisions for the grand army is seen to fall into a state of uncertainty and confusion. And while the [Virginia] executive hath been more than once called upon to make up for deficiencies in that department, no reform is seen to take place . . . no animadversions [adverse criticisms] that I know of, have been made upon the conduct of those whose business it was to forward it to the army . . . this country abounds with the provisions for which the army is said to be almost starving . . . the perilous situation of the American Army will be relieved when a reform takes place . . . from mismanagement in which have flowed evils threatening the existence of American liberty.[21]

To Henry's consternation, his letter produced no response. Indeed, a month later, he received this astonishing letter from Washington:

> For several days past we have experienced little less than a famine in camp, and have had much cause to dread a general mutiny and dispersion. . . . From every appearance there has been heretofore so astonishing a deficiency in providing that unless the most vigorous and effectual measures

are at once everywhere adopted, the language is not too strong to declare that we shall not be able to make another campaign.

Isolated in his Valley Forge headquarters, Washington said he had no way of knowing whether the sought-after provisions had fallen into "improper hands" or whether "a diminution of resources and increased difficulties in the means of procuring" had caused the shortages. "I address myself to you," he wrote to Henry, "convinced that our alarming distresses will engage your most serious consideration and that the full force of that zeal and vigor you have manifested upon every other occasion will now operate for our relief."[22]

Arriving, as it did, after his own letter to Congress and the shipment of ample supplies from Virginia to Valley Forge, Washington's letter outraged Henry. "I am really shocked at the management of Congress," he vented to Richard Henry Lee. "Good God! Our fate committed to a man utterly unable to perform the task assigned to him! . . . I grieve at it . . . I am really so harassed by the great load of continental business thrown on me lately that I am ready to sink under my burden."[23]

Fortunately, Henry did not sink under his burden. His relentless letters spurred Washington's aides to look into the activities of Quartermaster General Mifflin. A Philadelphia-area merchant before the Revolution, he had sought to profit from his office by waylaying supplies bound for Valley Forge into his own warehouses, where he sold them to the highest bidders. When Washington confronted him, he resigned and Congress reassigned him to an obscure military post where he could do no harm. Washington persuaded his trusted friend, Rhode Island Major General Nathanael Greene—also a merchant in private life—to accept the Quartermaster General's post. Within days, Valley Forge had a surplus of clothing, food, and other supplies.

Elated over resolution of the supply problem, Henry sent Washington "a stock of good rum, wine, sugar and such other articles as his Excellency may think needful . . . to the preservation of [Washington's] health." A grateful Washington thanked Henry, saying the "agreeable present" had found him "in a humor to do it all manner of justice."[24]

On May 1, 1778, an aide rode into Washington's headquarters at Valley Forge with a letter from Benjamin Franklin in Paris that the French government had signed two treaties with the United States: the first, a treaty of amity and commerce, the second a treaty of alliance pledging direct French military aid to the United States once England declared war against France.

At Valley Forge, Washington proclaimed an official day of "public celebration," beginning with religious services and followed by "military parades, marchings, the firings of cannon and musketry."[25] Patrick Henry rejoiced at the news and predicted an early end to the war news: "I look at the past condition of America as at a dreadful precipice from which we have escaped by means of the generous French, to whom I will be everlastingly bound by the most heartfelt gratitude."[26]

Within weeks, Washington and his army left Valley Forge to attack the British and end the young republic's longest and coldest winter, but worse was yet to come.

Chapter 10

Obliged to Fly

The announcement of the French alliance with America spurred renewed British efforts to reconcile differences with the Americans. When, however, Lord Carlisle arrived in America with a three-man commission to negotiate with Congress, Henry grew incensed that Congress might end the Revolution short of independence. He warned Richard Henry Lee that Britain "can never be cordial with us. Baffled, defeated, disgraced by her colonies, she will ever meditate revenge. We can find no safety but in her ruin, or at least her extreme humiliation. . . .

"For God's sake, my dear sir," Henry pleaded with his friend, "quit not the councils of your country until you see us forever disjoined from Great Britain. Excuse my freedom. I know your love to our country, and this is my motive."

With Henry's warning resounding through the chamber, members of Congress refused even to receive—let alone negotiate with—the British commissioners and declared any individual or group who came to terms with Carlisle's commission an enemy of the United States. The only issues open to discussion with England, Congress asserted, was withdrawal of British troops and American independence. Should Britain "persist in her present career of barbarity, we will take such exemplary vengeance as shall deter others from a like conduct."[1]

Lord Carlisle tried bypassing Congress with a "Manifesto and Proclamation to the American People" threatening "to desolate" the country if Americans rejected his offer to negotiate. "Under such circumstances," Carlisle warned, "the laws of self-preservation must direct the conduct of Great Britain." Carlisle offered to negotiate with the "Provincial Assemblies" and promised a general pardon to all who ended their rebellion. When an aide to Lord Carlisle delivered the offer of a general pardon to Williamsburg, Henry called it "calculated to mislead and divide the good people of this country" and ordered the aide "to depart this state . . . with the dispatches and to inform him [Lord Carlisle] that, in future, any person making a like attempt shall be secured as an enemy to America."[2]

With no confederation yet in place, Henry, as head of a sovereign state, undertook to establish formal diplomatic relations with both France and Spain, appointing one of Richard Henry Lee's brothers—William Lee—as Virginia agent to France. Lee was able to purchase almost V£220,000 in artillery, arms, and ammunition from the French ministry of war using the state's own printed money—the "Virginia pound." Henry also made an unsuccessful application to the Spanish governor of New Orleans for a loan.

With the western part of the state still under siege, land values in the West plunged, and two of Henry's friends shared an opportunity with him to buy 30,000 acres for V£15,000 in depressed Virginia pounds. In effect, Henry and his partners paid the equivalent of V£3,333 for the lands, with each partner taking outright ownership of his share. Henry's 10,000 acres straddled Leatherwood Creek, a tributary of Smith River, in Henry County, near present-day Martinsville.

On May 29, 1778, Virginia's Assembly reelected him governor for a third term by acclamation, with no other name even placed in nomination. As he had after election to his first term, Henry fell ill after taking the oath of office and remained bedridden for more than a month. Still distraught over the disappearance of his son John after the Battle of Saratoga, Henry sent Washington an emotional letter asking his help in finding the boy. In accord with Henry's request, Washington burned the letter and began a discreet search. Months later, in September 1778, Washington forwarded to Patrick Henry "a letter for Capt. Henry, whose ill state of health obliged him to quit the service. . . ."[3] Shortly afterwards, Dolly assuaged some of Henry's concerns over his son by giving birth to her first and his seventh child, a girl they named Dorothea—the first child of a sitting governor to be born in a governor's mansion in America. It was customary to name firstborn girls for their mothers, just as parents named firstborn boys for their fathers.

A month after baby Dorothea's birth, Washington again wrote to Henry that "I was informed (upon further enquiry after him) that he had got no further than Elizabeth town in the Jerseys and was there rather distressed for want of money, having been indisposed at that place for sometime." Washington said that the commanding officer in Elizabeth "readily understood to furnish what money he wanted and in other respect help him."[4] John eventually found his way home, and his father lopped off 1,000 acres from his 10,000-acre Leatherwood plantation for the boy to farm on his own, giving him seven of the forty-two slaves at Leatherwood.

On June 17, the British declared war on France, and when a French fleet set sail for America with troops to support Patriot forces, the British evacuated Philadelphia to consolidate their forces in New York. On June 18, 3,000 Redcoats boarded ships and sailed down the Delaware River to the Atlantic and the sea route to New York, while the remaining troops began the overland trek northward through New Jersey. With their artillery, military equipment, and baggage train of 1,500 carriages stretching twelve miles, the columns provided just the sort of slow-moving target Washington had been seeking. Instead of direct confrontation, his army could trail the British convoy and harass them with deadly sniping from the sides and rear. He did not believe the Continental Army was large enough or strong enough to defeat the British army in direct, head-to-head confrontations, but he was certain his Americans could weaken and demoralize the British with constant harassment. Attrition and exhaustion, he believed, would eventually force them to abandon the field and sail home to Britain.

With the beginning of the summer campaign, Washington issued his usual call to Congress and states for more men and materiel. He faced constant depletion of his forces because of the short enlistment periods—often as little as thirty days—that many states had been forced to offer as incentives for army service. Farmers, especially, had to leave the army and

*Dorothea Henry, Patrick Henry's first child
by his second wife, also named Dorothea and
to whom her daughter was said to bear a close
resemblance.* (FROM A NINETEENTH-CENTURY
PHOTOGRAPH OF A PAINTING)

return to their fields in spring and fall to plant and harvest crops to sustain
their families. "Public service seems to have taken its flight from Virginia,"
Henry lamented to Richard Henry Lee, "for the quota of our troops is not
half made up, and no chance seems to remain for completing it.

> The Assembly voted three hundred and fifty horse and two thousand
> men to be forthwith raised, and to join the grand [Continental] army.
> Great bounties are offered, but I fear the only effect will be to expose our
> state to contempt, for I believe no soldiers will enlist. . . . Let not Con-
> gress rely on Virginia for soldiers.[5]

Even with near-dictatorial powers, Henry found he could not force Virginians to do his bidding and march off to battle. "I ordered fifty men to be raised," complained one captain to Governor Henry, "only ten appeared." He said that militia members fail even to appear at musters, saying that "they can afford to pay . . . the trifling fine of five shillings . . . by earning more at home. . . . With such a set of men, it is impossible to render any service to country or county."[6]

Most Virginians owned small properties far from the centers of political power. Few expected independence to affect their lives. Almost all believed that the same powerful Tidewater planters who had taxed them before the war as burgesses under British rule had called for independence only to protect their own interests from British taxation, and would reclaim their seats after independence and tax them just as heavily as before.

As the British evacuated Philadelphia, a week of heavy rains combined with searing summer heat and suffocating humidity to slow the huge British convoy to six miles a day. On June 26, the exhausted Redcoats encamped at Monmouth Courthouse (now Freehold), New Jersey, with the Patriots only six miles behind. Two small forces of 1,000 men each had been stalking the British, and Washington ordered a 4,000-man brigade under English-born General Charles Lee to attack the center of the British line from the rear, while the two smaller forces under "Mad" Anthony Wayne and the Marquis de Lafayette sliced into the British flanks. Washington would hold the main army, three miles back. If the attack succeeded, his army would join the battle; if the British proved too powerful, the main army would cover an orderly retreat by the forward brigade. After the attack began, Washington sent his aide Colonel Alexander Hamilton to reconnoiter. To Hamilton's astonishment, Lee's force was retreating in chaos, leaving Lafayette's column trapped behind enemy lines. Outraged at Hamilton's report, Washington galloped into Lee's camp shouting "till the leaves shook on the trees."[7]

"You damned poltroon [coward]," he barked at Lee, then ordered him to the rear and took command himself. He galloped into the midst of the retreating troops, shifting his mount to the right, to the left, turning full circle and rearing up—gradually herding the men into line.

"Stand fast, my boys!" he shouted. "The southern troops are advancing to support you!"[8] As Washington's men drove the British back, "Mad" Anthony Wayne lived up to his sobriquet by ordering an insane charge into the British flank that opened the way for Lafayette's men to escape capture. With cannon blasts still blazing overhead, Washington reformed the lines and led a huge frontal attack. Great horseman that he was, he charged heroically atop his huge horse, calling to his men, inspiring them to follow. With a surge of energy, the Continentals repelled a British cavalry charge and sent enemy forces reeling back toward Monmouth Courthouse.

"General Washington was never greater in battle than in this action," Lafayette recalled. "His presence stopped the retreat; his strategy secured the victory. His stately appearance on horseback, his calm, his dignified courage . . . provoked a wave of enthusiasm among the troops."[9]

Before Washington could seal his victory, darkness set in and ended the day's fighting. As Washington and his exhausted troops slept, the British quietly slipped away to Sandy Hook, a spit of land on the northern New Jersey shore at the entrance to New York Bay. Transports carried them away to New York and deprived the Americans of a clear-cut victory. Although Monmouth was not decisive, the Americans nonetheless claimed victory, with Washington writing to his brother John that Monmouth had "turned out to be a glorious and happy day. . . ."[10]

Washington wrote to Henry as if to America's head of state: "I take the earliest opportunity of congratulating you on the success of our arms over the British on the 28th June near Monmouth Court House."

The enemy left 245 dead upon the field and 4 officers . . . but we found, besides, several graves and burial holes, in which they had deposited their dead before they were obliged to quit the ground. . . . I think I may without exaggeration assert that they will lose near one thousand men in this way before they quit Jersey, and that their army will be diminished two thousand by killed, wounded, desertion, and fatigue.[11]

As Henry rejoiced over Washington's victory, he received exhilarating news from the West. George Rogers Clark had sailed down the Ohio River with his small force disguised in Indian garb—buckskins, moccasins, and tomahawks. Leaving their craft at the junction with the Wabash River, they marched 120 miles overland through the wilderness to Kaskaskia for six days—two of them without food—and caught the British by surprise at night. Wading along the Mississippi River mud flats, they entered a gate left open for small river craft to float into the fort. Slipping into the British commander's quarters as he slept, they surprised him in his bed and, with a knife at his throat, he surrendered the fort "without a drop of bloodshed."

In the weeks that followed, Clark's force moved across the territory, capturing the fort at Cahokia, more than 200 miles north along the Mississippi, then crossing back through Illinois to Indiana to capture the British fort at Vincennes and nearby territories inhabited by French immigrants from Canada. Henry acted swiftly to bolster Clark's forces, sending another expedition under Colonel Evan Shelby to attack a force of Tories and Indians and crush British hopes of inciting an Indian war in the West. Henry promoted Clark to commander in chief of the Virginia troops in the County of Illinois, and ordered him "to spare no pains to conciliate the affections of the French and Indians."

> Let them see and feel the advantages of being fellow citizens and freemen. Guard most carefully against every infringement of their property, particularly with respect to land. . . . Strict and severe discipline with your soldiers may be essential to preserve from injury those whom they were sent to protect and conciliate. . . . I send you herewith some copies of the . . . [Virginia] Bill of Rights, together with the French alliance . . . to show our new friends the ground upon which they are to stand and the support to be expected from their countrymen of France. . . . I think it possible that they may be brought to expel their British masters and become fellow citizens of a free state.[12]

Clark's winning ways won him the allegiance of enough settlers and Indians to secure the territory for Virginia, which named it, simply, Illinois County. Still suffering the stings of his rejection as commander in chief of Virginia's armies, Henry trumpeted the news of his and Clark's superbly successful grand strategy and military triumph to the Virginia Assembly and to the Continental Congress:

It appears that his success has equaled the most sanguine expectations. He has . . . struck such terror into the Indian tribes between that settlement and the lakes that no less than five of them . . . bound themselves with promises to be peaceful in the future. The great Blackbird, the Chappowow chief, has also sent a belt of peace to Colonel Clark, influenced . . . by the dread of Detroit's being reduced by American arms.[13]

Henry took advantage of the Virginia Assembly's ebullient mood to win legislation that banned importation of slaves, thus resolving, in part, a moral dilemma that remained a continuing burden for him: his embrace of individual freedom and his continuing ownership of slaves. The ban on slave importation salved his conscience somewhat and accomplished a major priority of his social agenda to stem the growth of slavery.

As Clark and his army moved to challenge other British pockets of resistance, the House of Delegates appointed Colonel John Todd chief administrator of the new County of Illinois. "You will take care to cultivate and conciliate the affections of the French and Indians," Henry ordered Todd.

You are on all occasions to inculcate on the people the value of liberty and the difference between the state of free citizens of this commonwealth and that slavery to which Illinois was destined. . . . Let it be your constant attention to see that the inhabitants have justice administered to them for any injuries received from the troops. . . . You will also discourage every attempt to violate the property of the Indians, particularly in their lands.[14]

While managing the western campaign, Henry also provided George Washington with intelligence reports on campaigns in the western Carolinas, where Virginia militia were fighting Indians, and in southeastern Georgia, where they were battling a British advance from Florida. "My last accounts from the South are unfavorable," he reported to Washington, in mid-March 1779:

Georgia is said to be in full possession of the enemy, and South Carolina in great danger. One thousand militia are ordered thither from our southern counties. . . . About five hundred militia are ordered down the Tennessee River to chastise some new settlements of renegade Cherokees that infest our southwestern frontier and prevent our navigation on that river. . . . Fort Natchez and Morishac are again in the enemy's hands; and from thence they infest and ruin our trade on the Mississippi.[15]

On July 4, 1778, a French fleet under General Vice Admiral Charles-Henri Comte d'Estaing sailed into Delaware Bay near Philadelphia with twelve ships of the line, five frigates, and an invasion force of 4,000.

At the time, Washington's army was marching northward through New Jersey in the aftermath of the Battle of Monmouth. He sent word to the French commander to sail up the New Jersey coast to Sandy Hook and seal the entrance to New York Bay, thus trapping the British fleet in New York Harbor and the British army on Manhattan Island. Washington, meanwhile, led his army to Paramus, New Jersey, across the Hudson River from New York. His initial plan was to attack New York from the west, while d'Estaing's ships sailed in from the south, but the French ships drew too much water to cross the sandbars into New York Harbor, and, as the British ships bobbed tantalizingly in the waters beyond cannon range, d'Estaing had to abandon the planned assault. "It is terrible to be within sight of your object," he fretted, "and yet be unable to attain it."[16]

Washington was ready with an alternative strategy, however: a joint, land-sea attack on the 6,000-man British fortification at Newport, Rhode Island—the last British stronghold in New England. D'Estaing agreed and sailed eastward. With cannons ablaze and marines firing from the top rails, the French frigates sprinted through the narrow channels that rimmed Newport and other islands of Narragansett Bay, capturing, burning, or ramming every British vessel they could find. The British themselves set fire to three of their frigates to prevent their capture by the French. Just as the French began celebrating their first victory in America, however, a cry from a crow's nest heralded the approach of the British fleet, which had followed the French up from New York, laying just out of sight beyond the horizon. The French frigates needed all night to maneuver out of the tight channels, but by morning on August 10, they lay in position to repel a British attack. Then the winds shifted, and, seeing an opportunity to destroy the British fleet, d'Estaing sailed out to sea to attack.

As the powerful French fleet approached, the British came about and sailed back towards New York with the French in pursuit under full canvas. The chase continued all day and night and most of the next day, with the French closing in by the hour. At the end of the second day, the British fleet had no choice but to come about and engage, but before the titanic battle could begin, the sea began churning angrily. Violent waves and winds gripped both fleets and tossed their ships about, spinning them in different directions, out of control, rolling and pitching violently, ripping sails and snapping masts like twigs. The gale roared relentlessly through the night. By morning both fleets lay crippled, barely able to steer, let alone engage in battle. D'Estaing's flagship had lost its masts and rudder and bobbed about helplessly. A second man-of-war had lost two of its three masts, and a third was out of sight beyond the horizon or at the bottom of the sea. A British ship closed in to sink the crippled French ships, but the bigger French guns held it off, and the British abandoned the attack and limped off to safety in New York. The French fleet managed to reach Boston for refitting before sailing off to the French West Indies and reopening American waters to British depredations. Taking full advantage of the French departure, a British fleet with 3,500 marines sailed to Georgia and captured Savannah.

Unlike the American North, the approach of winter weather in the milder climate of the South did not force British forces to retire to winter quarters as early or for as long. As Henry had reported to Washington, British troops in Florida had pushed northward and captured most of Georgia by mid-March. By May, they had overrun the entire state and reached the outskirts of Charleston. To the horror of farmers and plantation owners, the British freed indentured servants and slaves who were willing to swear allegiance to Britain and, if able, fight the rebels.

As Henry's third and last permissible term in office approached an end, he made preparations to move his family west to his Leatherwood plantation—far from the dangers of attack by British forces on the coast. Before he could leave office, however, the war took a turn for the worse: On May 10, a British fleet sailed into Hampton Roads and set fire to what was left of Norfolk, along with Portsmouth and nearby Suffolk. The threat of further British incursions sent Virginia's government fleeing inland to Richmond. "The troops which landed," Henry reported to the Assembly, "burnt, plundered, and destroyed Suffolk, committing various barbarities."[17]

On June 6, however, Henry had no choice but to put the cares of office behind him when the Assembly elected Thomas Jefferson to succeed him as governor. The Virginia Assembly tried to draft Henry into serving a fourth term until he rebuked them for violating the state constitution. He remained so popular, however, that less than three weeks after his retirement, the House of Delegates voted to send him to Congress. By then, however, he and his family had left for Leatherneck in far off Henry County, where his "tedious illness" made his attendance in Congress impossible.[18]

High on a hill in the Blue Ridge Mountains at the center of Henry County, Leatherwood's "manor house" boasted magnificent views of the surrounding country, but its size and condition devastated Henry's wife, Dorothea. In sharp contrast to the Governor's Palace, their new home was a two-room brick structure that Henry described as "a sort of camp." Henry's entourage numbered more than fifty people, including his wife and baby and five of his six children by his first wife. His oldest child, Martha, came with her husband, John Fontaine, and their three children. Although he had sold a few slaves to buy various properties, the new properties he bought came with resident slaves, and he now owned seventy-five slaves, along with thirty-three horses, seventy-nine cattle, and enough hogs and sheep to provide adequate supplies of meat and wool for the coming years.

Henry, of course, was perfectly content camping in the wilderness, but his family had grown too used to the luxurious surroundings of the Governor's Palace and Scotchtown, and his wife—already pregnant with her second child—had never tasted frontier life. Within days, however, the slaves helped Henry, his oldest son, William, and his son-in-law John Fontaine convert the interior of the house into a relatively comfortable dwelling, and, in the weeks that followed, they added a wing to the main house and several freestanding outbuildings—a kitchen, washhouse, storehouse, stable, grist mill, distillery, an overseer's house, slave cabins, and, of course, a "necessary." A separate spinning house with looms would provide the Henry family and their servants with clothes and blankets. Refusing to wear manufactured clothes from England, Henry would wear homespun or American-made clothing in public for the rest of the war and, indeed, the rest of his life.

With the house complete, Dolly gave birth to her second child and Henry's eighth—another daughter, whom they named Sarah. Somewhat fearful for his family's safety, Henry, William, and John Fontaine set out on horseback to explore the huge property and search out squatters. The most mild-mannered squatters agreed to leave after they harvested their small crops in the fall—and the rest agreed to leave after Henry and the boys confronted them with cocked rifles and a squad of his most ferocious looking slaves. After expelling the squatters, Henry surveyed neighboring lands and quickly added nearly 4,000 more acres to his original 10,000 and planted tobacco, corn, and wheat.

Henry and the boys also rode across the hills to meet their widely dispersed neighbors—most of them owners of small farms under 1,000 acres each. Unlike owners of large Tidewater plantations in the east, most hill-country farmers worked their own lands, helped only, perhaps, by one or two slaves picked up at bargain prices at auction. Instead of incentives such as extra clothes and food with which Tidewater planters usually induced slaves to work harder, most hill-country farmers saw slaves as workhorses to be driven by the whip. The ubiquitous "crack" of the whip heard across the South earned the region's farmers the pejorative nickname of "cracker." The brutality of mountain life in the South spawned an atmosphere of violence and lawlessness that lasted into the last half of the twentieth century.

Living as they did in the county that bore his name, the farmers of Henry County thought it only right to elect Patrick Henry to the Assembly, and, after nearly a year's retirement, Henry returned to the House of Delegates for the spring session in May 1780. By then, the British had captured Charleston in what was the worst defeat of the war for the Americans since the Battle of Long Island. Attacking with 14,000 troops, the British captured the 5,400-man American army and its commanding general Benjamin Lincoln. Among the captured troops were 1,400 Virginians from the First, Second, and Third Virginia regiments, under the command of General William Woodford, Henry's former rival in

Williamsburg. As the British swept northward, they added to the terrors of military conquest and plunder by freeing an estimated 30,000 slaves—one-sixth of South Carolina's entire slave population—and at least that number of indentured servants. As the Assembly debated measures to defend Virginia against invasion, another attack of malarial fever forced Henry to return home on June 7, after only two weeks in the capital.

Although George Washington warned Governor Jefferson of a possible British attack on the Virginia coast, Jefferson decided that, with the fall of Charleston, the British armies to the south posed a greater menace, and he sent 2,500 militiamen to the Carolinas. Meanwhile, Washington sent General Gates to take command of the Southern Army, and ignoring intelligence reports of a possible trap, Gates ordered his force to move against the British supply base at Camden, South Carolina. As the Americans approached Camden from the north on the morning of August 16, 2,400 British infantrymen under Major General Lord Cornwallis attacked from the south, while a company of ferocious British dragoons under the legendary Colonel Banastre Tarleton, galloped in from the rear. Tarleton's cavalry slaughtered nearly 900 Americans and captured 1,000.

With the American Southern Army in full retreat, Washington replaced Gates with Rhode Island's Major General Nathanael Greene, who shifted the direction of his army's retreat to the west—deep into the wilderness to stretch British supply lines too thin to follow. Greene's army retreated to within fifty miles of Henry's Leatherwood plantation. Knowing Henry was still Virginia's most influential figure, Greene sent Henry, as well as Governor Jefferson, an urgent appeal for help. "Our force is so inferior, that every exertion in the State of Virginia is necessary to help us," he wrote to Jefferson. "I have taken the liberty to write to Mr. Henry to collect fourteen or fifteen hundred volunteers to aid us."[19]

Henry and his son rode about the country, impassioning men to volunteer with a terrifying warning that the British were freeing and arming slaves to slaughter patriot farmers. As the cry went out that Patrick Henry needed men, nearly 2,500 Virginians streamed southward to bolster Greene's army and force Cornwallis to retreat into South Carolina, where he retired to winter quarters in Winnsborough, about 125 miles northwest of Charleston. The Cornwallis retreat ended the threat to Henry County and to

Patrick Henry's family, and, from then on, whenever Henry returned home, he made certain that if his wife was not already pregnant from his last visit, she most certainly would be by the time he left.

Apart from his evident passion to propagate, three factors spurred the phenomenal growth of his family: For one thing, the normally high infant mortality rate that decimated most families in eighteenth-century America—especially in the wilderness—would, for whatever reason, spare all but two of Henry's children.[20] But another factor that impelled the growth of Henry's family was his and Dorothea's deep and genuine love of children. Both of them adored youngsters. He loved playing with them, telling them stories, strutting about playing his fiddle as they danced and jumped and sang in circles around him. His daughter Elizabeth remembered him as a "great laugher," who taught his boys to ride, fish, and hunt. When they were small, he often took them riding on his own horse, with one boy behind him and the other riding in front. And a third factor that helped produce a big family was his genuine love of his wife. Unlike many planters, he had no liaisons with slaves or, for that matter, with any woman other than his wife. Somewhat unusual for his times, he embraced a strict moral code that kept him true to his marriage vows and away from drink and gambling.

In January 1781, Governor Thomas Jefferson paid the price of ignoring George Washington's advice to protect Virginia's waters, when 2,200 British troops under a new British commander—Brigadier General Benedict Arnold—sailed up the James River unopposed and burned Richmond.

To the south, however, General Nathanael Greene—bolstered by Henry's Virginia volunteers—set out with 3,600 men into South Carolina to harass Cornwallis. Although his force was too small to attack Cornwallis's main camp at Winnsborough, Greene sent Daniel Morgan, the heroic commander at Saratoga, with 800 riflemen to attack British supply lines. Cornwallis riposted by sending Tarleton and his fearsome dragoons to destroy Morgan's force. Morgan retreated northward, all but disappearing across a meadow called Cowpens, near the North Carolina border. When Tarleton spotted what seemed to be the American rear guard retreating at the far end of the meadow, he sent his colossal thoroughbreds thundering

*Brigadier General Benedict Arnold sold the plans
of West Point defenses to the British and deserted
to join the British army against his former
comrades, leading a British force that burned
Richmond, Virginia.* (LIBRARY OF CONGRESS)

across the tall grass—into the jaws of a trap. At Morgan's signal, his infantrymen and horsemen charged from the surrounding forest and shrubs into Tarleton's flanks and rear, whooping and shrieking as they set upon the hitherto unconquerable English cavalry with bullets and bayonets. "We made a sort of half circuit at full speed," an American officer exulted, "[and] came upon the rear of the British line, shouting and charging like madmen. We were in among them with bayonets."[21]

The British force panicked, their horses rearing and spinning, hooves flying, riders hurled to the ground, stumbling to their feet hysterically, and fleeing in all directions. Professionals all in traditional warfare, none had experienced what would later be called guerilla tactics. "Give them one more fire and the day is ours," Morgan cried out to his men. And indeed it was.[22] Hundreds of Redcoat horsemen—the perpetrators of the

Camden massacre—dropped their rifles and fell to the ground on their faces, some in fetal positions, others with their arms spread-eagled as they sobbed for mercy. Morgan all but eliminated Tarleton's 1,000-man cavalry as a factor in the South Carolina campaign, killing 329 and capturing 600 at a cost of fewer than 75 American lives.

Infuriated by the humiliation, Cornwallis pursued the elusive Morgan into North Carolina, where the American general linked up with Greene's main force at Guilford (present day Greensboro), about thirty miles south of the Virginia border. In the battle that followed, Cornwallis won the field, but lost nearly one-third of his men and had to retreat to his coastal base at Wilmington to let survivors lick their collective wounds.

Greene returned to South Carolina and, in the months that followed, his army captured one after another of the British posts across the state, gradually narrowing the British presence to the confines of Charleston.

In the meantime, Cornwallis grew convinced that control of the Carolinas would not be possible until he conquered Virginia, and, with his own troops refreshed and Tarleton's cavalry remanned and refurbished, he set out with 7,000 men to capture Richmond. Washington sent Lafayette with 1,000 regulars to defend the state capital, but the Frenchman's tiny force was no match for the huge British army. As Governor Jefferson and the rest of the Virginia government fled westward to Charlottesville, Lafayette and his band of Americans abandoned Richmond and retreated into the outlying forests. On May 23, 1781, the British seized the Virginia capital and, with Lafayette in full flight northward, Tarleton led a new, but no less fearsome, troop of horse westward unopposed to try to capture Jefferson and the rest of the Virginia government and end the war in that colony. In Henry's former home county of Hanover, they burst into one house in the middle of the night, found his half brother John Syme Jr., and took him prisoner. The following day, the horsemen thundered into Charlottesville and captured seven assemblymen before they could rise from their desks. Alerted by a breathless young Patriot officer, Captain Jack Jouett, Henry and the others fled over a narrow mountain pass into the Blue Ridge mountains, where frontiersmen and back-country hunters could use their long rifles to block any further British advance. Legend has it that Henry and two other legislatures stopped at a farmer's house for

food and drink, only to be rebuffed by the farmer's wife when they identified themselves as legislators fleeing the British.

"My husband and sons are just gone to Charlottesville to fight for you,"
she shouted, "and you're running away? Ride on—you'll have nothing
here."

"But we were obliged to fly," Henry snapped at the old lady. "It would
not do for the legislature to be broken up by the enemy. Here is Mr.
Speaker Benjamin Harrison; you don't think he would have fled had it
not been necessary?"

"I always thought a great deal of Mr. Harrison till now," the woman
barked, "but he'd no business to run from the enemy."

Harrison then pointed out Patrick Henry and said that he had fled
with them.

"Well," the woman concluded, "if that's Patrick Henry then it must be
all right. Come in."[23]

As Harrison and Henry bickered in the back country, Tarleton's horsemen rode into Charlottesville, sending Jefferson in full flight to his aerie
at Monticello, where he sent his wife and two daughters to safety in another town. As he and two colleagues hurriedly sorted official papers to
take with them, Jouett galloped to the door to warn that Tarleton's men
were but five minutes away at the foot of the mountain. Jefferson barely
escaped capture by riding off through the woods on the opposite side of
the hill.

As Tarleton's dragoons terrified local farms, Cornwallis pushed Lafa-
yette's little force northward to within sight of the Rappahannock River and
Fredericksburg, where the sudden arrival of General "Mad" Anthony
Wayne and 1,300 Pennsylvanians halted the British advance. After Wayne
replenished, reclothed, and rearmed Lafayette's little army, the combined
American force crossed the Rappahannock to attack. Far from his sources of
supplies—his men exhausted in the stifling Virginia heat and humidity—
Cornwallis had no choice but to begin a measured retreat to Chesapeake
Bay and the safety of his ships.

Out of his depth in military matters, Jefferson decided to turn over his
office "to abler hands" as he neared the end of his second term. He told
Washington he believed that "a military chief" would bring "more energy,

promptitude and effect for the defense of the state."[24] The Assembly elected General Thomas Nelson, the owner of a large Tidewater plantation, to replace Jefferson and opened "an inquiry . . . into the conduct of the Executive of this state for the last twelve months."[25]

Although Edmund Randolph scoffed at the inquiry as "the usual antidote for public distress," Henry voted with the majority of the Assembly to investigate allegations that Thomas Jefferson had failed to make "some exertions which he might have made for the defense of the county."[26] Outraged by the proposed inquiry, Jefferson would never forgive Henry, although he admitted quite openly that his unwillingness to seek reelection stemmed directly from his inability to perform his gubernatorial duties properly at the time of the British invasion.

By June 22, Cornwallis's retreat toward the sea left Richmond back in American hands, with Lafayette's force following hard on the English rear guard, sniping first at one flank, then the other, and pouncing on foraging parties. At Richmond, 1,600 militiamen joined his force, and, as volunteers from plantations pillaged by Tarleton swarmed into camp, Lafayette's army swelled to more than 5,000 men—still too small for a direct engagement, but large enough for bolder strokes. With every step beyond Richmond, Lafayette sent patrols into the surrounding forests to channel the English vanguard onto the cape between the York and James rivers. He sent patrols to the opposite banks to prevent the British from leaving the cape, while his vanguard struck incessantly at the British rear and forced them inexorably toward Yorktown, at the end of the cape overlooking Chesapeake Bay.

In the North, meanwhile, an army of nearly 7,000 French troops at Newport, Rhode Island, marched southward to join Washington's 8,000-man Continental Army. On August 30, a French fleet of warships entered Chesapeake Bay and surrounded the cape at Yorktown to prevent any British escape by water. Two weeks later, the combined allied force marched into Williamsburg, and four weeks later, the American Continental Army charged through enemy redoubts. As shell bursts reduced British fortifications to rubble, Cornwallis made a vain counterattack, but on October 17, he sent a message to Washington proposing "a cessation of hostilities."

Thomas Jefferson. His disastrous one-year term as Virginia governor saw the British army overrun the state, burn the capital at Richmond, and chase the government to the safety of the Blue Ridge Mountains. Henry's subsequent criticism of Jefferson's stewardship provoked bitter recriminations by Jefferson. (LIBRARY OF CONGRESS)

Two days later, Cornwallis, Washington, and Rochambeau, among others, signed the articles of capitulation.[27]

In the euphoria that followed, the Virginia Assembly not only laid aside its Jefferson inquiry, it passed a resolution of "sincere thanks . . . to our former Governor . . . for his impartial, upright and attentive administration whilst in office . . . and mean, by thus publicly avowing their opinion, to obviate and remove all unmerited censure."[28] The resolution did little to soothe Jefferson, or to calm his fierce anger towards Henry, whom he described to all who would listen, "as being all tongue without either head or heart."[29]

Unlike Jefferson, George Mason called Patrick Henry one of the greatest heroes of the Revolution for having sounded the first clarion call for independence with his impassioned cry for "liberty or death." It was Henry, Mason declared, who was first to rouse the people to revolution. "I congratulate you most sincerely," Mason wrote to Henry after Yorktown, "on the accomplishment of what I know was the warmest wish of your heart, the establishment of American independence and the liberty of our country. We are now to rank among the nations of the world; but whether our independence shall prove a blessing or a curse must depend upon our own wisdom or folly, virtue or wickedness."[30]

Chapter 11

A Belgian Hare

When the Virginia legislature reconvened in Richmond, British depredations had left fewer than 300 homes standing, and the depleted population was unable to offer legislators many services. In sharp contrast to the magnificent House of Burgesses in Williamsburg, the legislature convened in a small frame building, with members paid next to nothing. It was not much fun; most delegates had to lodge in uncomfortably tight quarters and were often in foul moods. Nonetheless, they heaped encomiums, along with their thanks and good wishes, on the heroes of the Revolution—Washington, Lafayette, Greene, French King Louis XVI, and endless other American and French personages both in and out of the military. They also conducted some essential business, electing as governor the Tidewater aristocrat and long-time burgess Benjamin Harrison, a cousin of Martha Washington. The government was bankrupt and paper money was worthless, so the legislators restricted use of outstanding paper money to payment of 1781 taxes or the purchase of new, government-issued "specie certificates" that would yield 6 percent a year in coins or other specie.

To replenish the state treasury, the Assembly imposed a variety of crushing new taxes: a 1 percent property tax on land, a flat two-shilling tax (about $6 today) on every horse and mule, a three-penny tax (about 75 cents today) on each head of cattle, a five-shilling tax (about $15 today) per wheel on pleasure carriages, and a whopping fifty-pound tax on every billiard table (about $3,000 today!) to discourage (or perhaps exploit) gambling. Taverns had to pay five pounds ($300) for their licenses and every master had to pay a ten-shilling ($30) capitation tax for every slave and every white male over twenty-one in his employ or under his control as an indentured servant. Without specie, however, payment of most taxes became all but moot, and the government agreed to accept the equivalent in tobacco or hemp for half the taxes due. As angry Piedmont farmers had sensed throughout the war, the same men who had taxed them as burgesses under the royal colonial government had returned to tax them as assemblymen under the independent government of Virginia. Only their titles had changed.

A week after the legislature reconvened, Henry's malarial fever overwhelmed him again, and he returned to Leatherwood. When he arrived, he found that Dolly had given birth to her third child, a daughter she had named Martha Catherina—Henry's ninth child. Despite her husband's debilitating illness, the ever-patient Dolly persevered, managing the household of thirty-two slaves and thirty-four indentured workers, tending to her huge collection of children and step children, and nursing her sick husband—all without complaint.

For the next eighteen months, his illness kept him either in his sickroom or close to home,* and few acts of consequence were passed in the legislature during that time, according to Henry's grandson.

Although the Assembly met as scheduled, it was little more than a social club. The Assembly's wealthy planters still ruled their huge plantations like private fiefdoms and the rest of the state as mere extensions of their lands. They had joined the Revolution because they had had the most to lose from British taxation and other government intrusions in the way they ran their properties and the state. Now they ruled again and had no intention of allowing the state to intrude where they had repulsed the British government.

---

*Documents relating to Henry reveal nothing about his activities during the eighteen-month period that begins with his serious illness. Although he disappears from the pages of history, the most likely explanation is the simplest—that he remained at home, tending his farm when he was well enough, but always out of public scrutiny.

"During the visit I made I saw this estimable assembly quiet not five minutes together," said a surprised German visitor to Richmond. "It sits, but this is not a just expression, for those members show themselves in every possible position rather than that of sitting still. . . . In the ante-room, they amuse themselves zealously with talk of horse-races, run-away Negroes, yesterday's play . . . according to each man's caprice."[1]

Other state legislatures were no more active or constructive than Virginia's, however. After decades of ever more restrictive British laws, Americans were fed up with government telling them how to live and what to do with their earnings. They had heeded Henry's call and risked death for "liberty"—and when they won their liberties, they expected government to stay out of their lives—as, indeed, did Henry. He envisioned postrevolutionary America developing into a vast agrarian society, with farmers able to live as independent, self-sufficient property owners, free from the tyranny of big government.

What Henry called liberty, however, George Washington called anarchy, as he pleaded in vain during seven years of war for enactment of federal laws to empower Congress to force men to fight and to tax citizens to pay the costs of war. He envisioned an orderly postrevolutionary America under a strong central government empowered to control every citizen's baser instincts. To Washington's dismay, the Confederation Congress proved as ineffectual as its predecessor Continental Congress. After the British and Americans signed a preliminary peace treaty on April 15, 1783, Congress faced war debts of more than $50 million, plus interest. Although its members recommended a 5 percent tariff on imports as a partial solution, the Articles of Confederation required approval from the legislatures of every state to put it into effect.

Henry had just returned to the Virginia Assembly for the first time in more than a year when the Assembly faced a vote on the national tariff. Still the unquestioned leader in the Assembly, he found himself caught by surprise by the impending vote. Not having studied the issues, he urged his followers to vote as his friend Washington had recommended—that is, for the tax. After the vote, however, he developed second thoughts about granting Congress any taxing powers and, a few days later, he asked the Assembly to rescind its vote and add restrictions. He suggested a 5 percent tariff limited to twenty-five years, with receipts earmarked to pay wartime debts.

Henry's "enmity to everything which may give influence to Congress and infringe on individual liberties put him in opposition to any permanent national government tax," Thomas Jefferson explained. After rebelling for more than twenty years against taxation by London's Parliament, Henry said he was not about to grant those powers to Congress. On the other hand, he recognized that none of the states would be able to engage in international trade until Congress repaid their collective war debts and that "ruin was inevitable unless something was done to give Congress a compulsory process for the delinquent states."[2]

So the question for Henry and other American leaders was how to repay national government debts without giving the national government taxing powers. It was an impossible question that leaders of every state tried to answer, knowing that there was no answer. Henry had never before been so indecisive—at a loss for words for one of the few times in his political career. After Washington sent a circular letter urging the states to strengthen the powers of the Confederation Congress, Henry recognized there was no other solution. Yielding to Washington's argument, he sacrificed his political beliefs in the interests of the national economy and told James Madison to "sketch out some plan for giving greater power to the federal government" and that he would support it in the Assembly. "A bold example set by Virginia," he declared, "would have influence on the other states." Madison wrote to Jefferson that Henry had been "strenuous for invigorating the federal government."[3]

Although shocked by Henry's political turnabout, the Assembly voted as he asked—in favor of the import duty, which, unlike a property or income tax, had a noncompulsory complexion in that no one is obligated to buy imported goods. To his and the Assembly's dismay, however, the New York legislature refused to accept it in its present form and set the process of saving the Confederation back to the beginning. Without approval by all the states, Congress could not levy the tax, and it remained without funds to pay current expenses, let alone the nation's debts. Henry's political sacrifice had been meaningless.

Henry's turnabout on the national tax, however, was but the first political shock he had prepared for Virginia's legislators. The next shock came when he called for reopening trade with Britain, and a third came with his call to permit Tories who had fled the state to return and reclaim their properties. A barrage of catcalls greeted his trade proposal, but Henry returned fire with accusations of insensitivity. He argued that most Virginians had suffered devastating economic hardships, "struggling through a perilous war, cut off from commerce so long that they were naked and unclothed. Why should we fetter commerce?" he asked, insisting that renewal of trade with Britain would "bless the land of plenty."[4]

Henry's proposal to allow the return of Tories provoked even more consternation. His close friend Judge John Tyler asked how he, "above all other men" could think of inviting "into our family an enemy from whose insults you have suffered so severely?"[5] Henry was ready, with one of his most eloquent speeches, saying he was willing to sacrifice his personal resentments and "all private wrongs . . . on the altar of my country's good."

"We have, sir, an extensive country without population," he explained, adopting the dramatic pose that had won him such renown:

> People form the strength and constitute the wealth of a nation. . . . Fill up the measure of your population as speedily as you can . . . and I venture to prophesy there are those among the living who will see this favored land among the most powerful on earth. . . .
>
> But, sir, you must have men!
>
> Open your doors, sir . . . Let . . . liberty stretch forth her fair hand toward the people of the old world—tell them to come, and bid them welcome—and you will see . . . your wildernesses will be cleared and settled, your deserts will smile, your ranks will be filled . . .

Henry scoffed at fears of Tory uprisings, insisting that relations with "those deluded people" had changed with the king's acknowledgment of American independence. "The quarrel is over," he affirmed. "Peace hath returned and found us a free people. Let us have the magnanimity to lay aside our antipathies and prejudices and consider the subject in a political light. They are an enterprising, moneyed people. They will be serviceable in taking off the surplus produce of our lands and supplying us with necessaries during the infant state of our manufactures." He then looked at Judge Tyler:

"Afraid of them?" Henry sneered. "Shall we who have laid the proud British lion at our feet now be afraid of his whelps?"[6]

Henry's remarkable oration won passage of both resolves, but some assemblymen stalked out angrily when he presented a fourth proposal—to subsidize marriages between whites and Indians to encourage "the friendship and confidence of the latter, whereby . . . their hostile inroads be prevented." Henry proposed a £10 bounty to every white man or woman marrying an Indian and settling in Virginia, along with a £5 bonus for each child born of such marriages. He also suggested tax exemptions on the livestock of mixed couples and free education for their minor children. Among the few to support Henry's proposal was John Marshall, America's future U.S. Chief Justice, who called it "advantageous to this country," but conceded to the all-but-empty chamber that "our prejudices . . . operate too powerfully."[7]

Although few transcripts exist, Henry sometimes relied on "such a volume of wit and humor" in his oratory, that, according to Judge Tyler, "the house would be in an uproar of laughter, and even set his opponents altogether in a perfect convulsion."[8] His wit and humor proved of little avail, however, in promoting intermarriage of whites and Indians.

Although his chronic illness made attendance difficult, Henry made token appearances in the Assembly in the spring of 1783, arriving after its opening and leaving before its adjournment to return to Leatherwood in time for the birth of Dolly's first son—Patrick Henry Jr.—his tenth child and fourth by Dolly. He made the weeklong ride back to Richmond for the fall session of 1783 and spring and fall sessions of 1784, and he used his still-enormous prestige and influence to obtain significant government support for improving river navigation and education. As an inveterate speculator in lands, he stood to gain—and did—from canal-building projects that tied the Staunton and Dan rivers to the Roanoke, which flows to Albemarle Sound and the Atlantic Ocean. Henry's Leatherwood plantation sat only twelve miles from the headwaters of the Dan. He also proposed a canal to connect Suffolk, on an inlet off Hampton Roads, to the Great Dismal Swamp. He and nine other investors, including George Washington, had purchased 40,000 acres of the area's marshland with which they intended harvesting timber, draining swamps, and developing land into a rich agricultural area.

In the fall of 1784, however, Henry alienated younger members of the House by bewailing the large number of abandoned churches in Virginia—the result of church-state separation following disestablishment of the Church of England. Railing against growing licentiousness, Henry proposed a new tax to support Christian churches, and a law making Christianity "the established religion of this Commonwealth; and all denominations of Christians demeaning themselves peaceably and faithfully, shall enjoy equal privileges, civil and religious." Although former Anglicans—now de-Anglicized as "Episcopalians"—supported Henry, younger delegates joined Presbyterians and Baptists in voting him down. Even ardent former Anglicans such as George Washington and John Marshall voted against Henry. Indeed, his proposal provoked reintroduction and passage of Thomas Jefferson's "Bill for Establishing Religious Freedom," which ended Virginia's state-church ties forever.

Henry's proposal also provoked a movement among ambitious young Assembly rebels to displace him and seize control of the House. Led by thirty-three-year-old James Madison of Orange, the rebels devised a scheme to flatter Henry into relinquishing power by putting him back into the governor's chair, where the state constitution would render him all but powerless to influence legislation. Without the temporary wartime authority that the Assembly had given him, they believed the ailing fifty-two-year-old governor would be helpless to prevent a new, younger generation linked to Jefferson from taking control of state government. Madison badly underestimated Patrick Henry's political staying power.

Barely five feet tall, Madison suffered chronic intestinal problems and "a constitutional liability to sudden attacks, somewhat resembling epilepsy. . . ."[9] Too frail and sickly for military service, he had spent three years of the war in Congress and led the unsuccessful struggle for interstate unity and congressional powers to levy taxes for national defense. Madison, however, served as the eyes and ears in Congress for Thomas Jefferson,

*James Madison. A Federalist at the Constitutional
Convention, he won election to the House of
Representatives only after agreeing to support
Patrick Henry's Antifederalist demands for a Bill
of Rights guaranteeing freedom of speech,
freedom of the press and other individual liberties.*
(LIBRARY OF CONGRESS)

whose ambitions were fixed on higher office. He called Madison "a pillar of
support."[10] Because of Madison's ties to Jefferson, however, Henry saw the
little man as a potentially dangerous political enemy and prepared to
counter his every move in the Virginia Assembly.

As the Assembly session approached its end, Virginia erupted in a frenzy
of excitement with the return of the Marquis de Lafayette for a farewell
tour of America. He had sailed home to France after Yorktown and been
unable to participate in the celebrations that had followed the signing of
the peace treaty with Britain. After touring the New England states, he
boarded the French frigate *Nymphe* in Boston harbor and enjoyed a restful
sail to Virginia for a reunion with Washington in Richmond. After landing

at Yorktown and touring the site of his heroic charge, he banqueted at Williamsburg and rode to Richmond the next day for a huge reception, where he stunned staid Virginians by embracing his former commander. Arm in arm, they strode into Trowser's Tavern to the cheers of the state's leading citizens, including governor-elect Henry, who announced he would name his next son Fayette. The Assembly voted to commission marble statues of Washington and Lafayette for Richmond's capitol.[11]

Although a constitutional figurehead, Henry remained the most revered patriot in America after Washington and Virginia's most powerful leader—indeed, one of America's most powerful leaders—and he knew it. So his return to the governorship would not, as Madison and his young friends had hoped, diminish Henry's control over the Assembly. Indeed, the governorship would offer many unforeseen advantages: On the personal side of his life, he could spend more time with his wife, children, and grandchildren, free of the exhausting day-to-day political struggles of the Assembly floor and the periodic three-hundred-mile round-trip rides to and from his Leatherwood home. On the political side, he could speak out on important issues, knowing that each utterance would command public attention whenever he signed legislation, welcomed important visitors, and greeted Virginia's notables at official functions with his lovely Dolly at his side. He had every intention of using his matchless rhetoric to bully, shame, or blackmail the Assembly into passing his legislative agenda. As Washington put it, Patrick Henry "has only to say, let this be law, and it is law."[12]

As his first term neared its end, Dolly bore him an eleventh child—another son, whom they named Fayette, in keeping with his promise to the marquis. A collection of *Sonnets and Other Poems* on the shelf of a Henry descendant contained this couplet to commemorate the arrival of Fayette Henry:

> *The Belgian hare could nothing to you show,*
> *Prolific Patrick—what a family man!*[13]

To add to his own brood—and his immeasurable joy in the company of children—his daughter Martha came to stay with her three boys, ages six, nine, and ten.

Although Henry's bill to subsidize mixed marriages with Indians evaporated into the legislative ether, his ceaseless pronouncements sustained his position as Virginia's most powerful political figure. To their immense frustration, Madison and the young Assembly rebels found it impossible to dislodge him. Indeed, his first days back in the governor's seat saw him reassert some of his wartime powers as head of state, as he ignored Virginia's constitutional limitations and issued executive orders to right what he considered Virginia's worst social wrongs.

On January 6, 1785, he put an end to settler incursions into Indian territory by "commanding all the commissioners, surveyors, and other persons to suspend the taking possession or surveying of any lands on the northwest side of the Ohio or below the mouth of the river Tennessee . . . [and] forthwith to withdraw therefrom." In an effort to make punishments fit crimes, he ordered the Mayor of Richmond to halt blanket executions and build a prison to hold perpetrators of lesser crimes. "With respect to some of them," he asserted, "the punishment of death seems disproportionate to the crime."[14]

In addition to righting wrongs, Henry set about rebuilding Virginia's military and establishing trade relations with other states and foreign countries. He asked the American consul in Paris "to procure . . . arms, powder, flints, and cartridge papers . . . and military stores" for a militia of about 50,000 men, and he wrote to the governors of other states suggesting that they appoint representatives to meet with Virginia's representatives "for the purpose of framing such regulations of trade . . . to promote the general interest."[15]

Henry's return to the governorship elated his old political ally Richard Henry Lee in the Confederation Congress, who wrote to restore "the same political relation under which our former correspondence was conducted. If it shall prove as agreeable to you to revive it . . . I shall be happy in contributing my part."

Admitting that their correspondence would not be as "interesting" as it had been during the Revolutionary War, Lee nonetheless warned Henry of an impending Spanish threat to Virginia's trade. Spain, he said, was "intent upon possessing the exclusive navigation of the Mississippi."[16]

Unlike the luxurious Governor's Palace in Williamsburg, the Governor's residence in Richmond was a simple two-story house with but two rooms on the ground floor—hardly adequate for Henry's wife, his eight children, and the army of relatives that marched through his house each year. Henry found a large home to rent on a plantation twelve miles west of Richmond across the James River in Salisbury, where, according to his son-in-law, Judge Spencer Roane, "They lived as genteely, and associated with polished society, as that of any governor before or since has ever done." Although his governor's salary did not provide enough funds to live as "genteely" as he wanted, he had realized enough cash from the sale of his Scotchtown plantation to allow him and his family to live in comfort. Roane said Henry and his wife "entertained as much company as others, and in as genteel a style."[17] Apart from allowing the Henrys to live together full time, living in the Richmond area restored Dolly's ties to her family and friends in Virginia's aristocracy and elevated her to the pinnacle of Virginia's society as First Lady—especially after George Washington came to dine and spend the night at Salisbury during his Richmond visit. Although Henry offered guests their choice of wine and alcoholic drinks, he never drank or smoked—indeed, despised both to the point where he prohibited his slaves from drinking or smoking.

"My complaints are many," he chuckled, "but it is gratifying to know that not one of them was caused by vice or any excess." His grandson confirmed that Henry "was very abstemious in his diet and used no stimulants."[18] While Henry served George Washington his favorite Madeira wine, Henry himself toasted his old friend with a glass of so-called "small beer," a low-alcohol beer that he drank on festive occasions instead of his usual spring water.

Dolly hosted regular public dinners for "the leading men of the Revolution," including George Mason, George Wythe, Richard Henry Lee, and others. To Dolly's delight, Richmond also gave the Henrys opportunities to present his two unmarried daughters to the most eligible bachelors in the state. The end of the war and its designation as the state capital had spurred a rapid growth of the once tiny village, with more than 1,000 new homes already built and an array of new government buildings under

The new capitol at Richmond, Virginia, built from 1785–1788 and designed by Thomas Jefferson, who copied plans of a Roman temple, the Maison Carée, *in Nîmes, France.* (LIBRARY OF CONGRESS)

construction—including an ostentatious all-marble capitol designed by Jefferson. A copy of a Roman temple in Nîmes, France, he crowned it with a grandiose portico, complete with six Corinthian columns.

In 1785, death struck Henry's family repeatedly and relentlessly, claiming his mother, his older brother William, and his last surviving aunt. "Thus is the last generation clearing the way for us, as we must shortly do for the next," he wrote in a somber letter to console his wife's cousin, Martha Washington's brother, Judge Bartholomew Dandridge, who was also nearing his end. Henry had no sooner posted his letter, when he learned that his sister Anne's husband, Colonel William Christian, had died fighting Indians in Kentucky. Death's staggering blows chased Henry back to the church of his childhood for solace, and he soon became a fervent parishioner. "Would to God," he wrote to Anne, "I could say something to give relief to the dearest of women and sisters. . . . While I am endeavoring to comfort you, I want a comforter myself."[19]

Ironically, Christian's death was an indirect result of the very congressional impotence and insolvency that Henry had sought unsuccessfully to resolve with the vote on the national tax. Without funds, Congress could not raise an army to defend American frontiers. After learning of Christian's death, Henry sent angry letters to the president of Congress and Virginia's delegates, demanding that Congress fulfill its obligations to protect American frontiers. Their replies indicated their impotence as they explained that states not exposed to Indian attacks opposed spending money to defend those that were.

Indeed, Congress did not even have money to pay troops for services rendered during the Revolutionary War. After the signing of the peace agreement with Britain in 1783, streams of soldiers had poured into Philadelphia demanding their long overdue back pay and bonuses—and threatening to open fire on the State House where Congress was sitting. With no money to pay the men, Congress fled—first, to Princeton, New Jersey, then Annapolis, and finally to New York. From his home in Mount Vernon, George Washington warned that "unless powers are given to Congress for the general purpose of the Federal Union, we shall soon mold into dust and become contemptible in the eyes of Europe."[20]

Washington's prediction became reality two years later. With their exports subject to each state's particular duties and trade restrictions, Britain and the rest of Europe simply stopped trading with Americans rather than navigate the complexities of sending goods across multiple state lines. America's foreign trade dropped 25 percent, farm income 20 percent. The decline gained momentum in 1786, when Spanish authorities fulfilled Lee's warning to Henry and closed the Mississippi River to American shipping. With no roads across the Appalachians for western farmers to transport grain to eastern markets, the Spanish closure of the Mississippi left them with no outlets for their crops. As creditor suits and tax liens multiplied, foreclosures cost hundreds of farmers their homes, livestock, lands, and tools of their trade. When auction proceeds were too little to cover debts, hysterical wives and terrified children watched helplessly as sheriffs' deputies dragged farmers off to debtors' prisons, where they languished indefinitely, unable to earn money to pay their creditors and without the tools to do so even if they won release.

Across the nation, enraged farmers—many of them Revolutionary War veterans—took up their rifles and pitchforks to defend their properties, firing at sheriffs who ventured too near. Reassembling their wartime companies, they attacked debtors' prisons, courthouses, and county clerk's offices. A mob of Virginia farmers shouting "Liberty or Death" burned down the county courthouses in King William and New Kent counties, near Richmond. Maryland farmers echoed the battle cries and burned down the Charles County courthouse. New Hampshire farmers marched to the state capital at Exeter, surrounded the legislature, and demanded forgiveness of all debts and the return of all seized properties to former owners. In North Carolina, western farmers seceded, creating their own State of Franklin— later Tennessee—and farmers in southwestern Virginia were poised to follow suit until Patrick Henry rode out to calm them with pledges to fight for reform.

As in the North, state capitals in the South were far removed from constituents in the West, where settlers faced greater dangers and lived on less productive lands but were assessed the same high taxes as eastern farmers. To prevent secession and possible war with hostile new western states, the normally impotent Confederation Congress enacted the most significant legislation—indeed, the only significant legislation—of its short existence: the Northwest Ordinance of 1787, under which Pennsylvania and other states joined Virginia in ceding their western territories north of the Ohio River to the Confederation. Virginia had ceded its lands north and west of the Ohio River in 1781.

The Northwest Ordinance provided for progressively free self-government in the new Northwest Territory until the population grew to 60,000. Congress would then divide the territory into at least three, but not more than five, self-governing states, which would join the Confederation on an equal footing with other states. Most astonishingly, the Ordinance included a bill of rights called "The Articles of Compact," which guaranteed individual rights to life, property, religious freedom, and education, and prohibited slavery for only the third time in American history. Vermont and Massachusetts had prohibited slavery earlier, in 1777 and 1783, respectively.

Although the Northwest Ordinance removed settlers north of the Ohio River from the tax rolls of America's thirteen states, it did little to calm tax protesters who remained within the boundaries of those states. With Henry's protest against British taxes still fresh in their memories, farmers across America sewed his wartime motto, Liberty or Death, on their shirt fronts to protest taxes that produced no visible benefits. None were more outraged than those whose lands lay on or near disputed state lines, where both states tried to tax them. A bitter dispute between Virginia and Maryland over their common boundary along the Potomac River taxed both the patience and pockets of traders, merchants, and farmers—and threatened to explode into outright war. Maryland claimed its boundary lay on the Virginia shoreline, and it taxed Virginia's river trade along with some planters such as Washington, whose fishery stretched nets into the river to trap herring, shad, and other fish that swam upstream to spawn. Virginia reciprocated, claiming its boundary lay on Maryland's shoreline and taxing all Maryland trade entering Chesapeake Bay.

"Different states have . . . views that sooner or later must involve the country in all the horrors of civil war," Secretary of War Henry Knox warned George Washington. "We are entirely destitute of those traits which should stamp us *one nation*."[21] Richard Henry Lee urged calling a convention "for the sole purpose of revising the Confederation" to permit Congress to act "with more energy, effect and vigor."[22]

It was Washington—retired from government at his Mount Vernon plantation—who brought Virginia and Maryland to the negotiating table with a scheme to establish joint jurisdiction over the commercial shipping channel in Chesapeake Bay and the lower Potomac River. He proposed that they join in a project he had conceived to link the Ohio River and

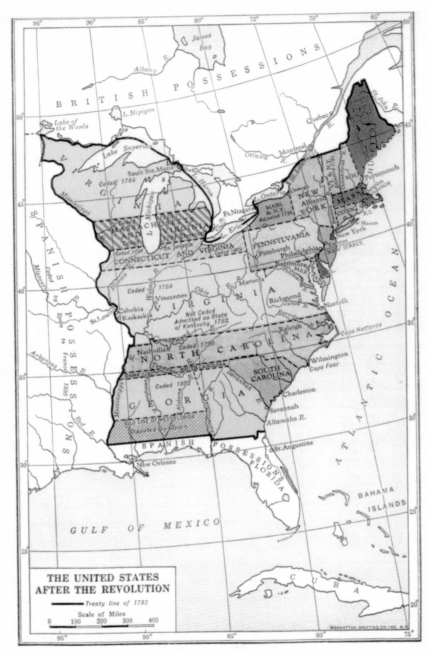

The United States in 1783.

Great Lakes with Chesapeake Bay with a system of canals and portage roads connecting the headwaters of the Potomac and James rivers to the Monongahela River, which runs into the Ohio at Pittsburgh. The waterway would generate huge revenues for both states and solve the conflict with Spain over Mississippi River navigation rights by allowing the wealth of the West—furs, ore, timber, and grain—to flow over the Appalachian Mountains to Atlantic ports for transport to Europe and the West Indies. Although Washington, Henry, and members of the Virginia and Maryland legislatures stood to profit handsomely from speculations they had made along the proposed waterway, the entire nation—and especially Henry's constituents on western farms—would also reap enormous benefits from the increased trade that would come with access to world markets. Washington invited Henry, George Mason, and James Madison, then serving in the Virginia House of Delegates, to join representatives from Maryland at Mount Vernon in March to discuss the project. Henry had to decline because of ill health, but other conferees agreed to a commercial union, with uniform commercial regulations, uniform currency, and pledges to hold annual conferences to review interstate commercial relations. The two states established two private companies, with George Washington as president of both, to build the inland waterway—the Potomac Company and James River Company. Henry and the Virginia Assembly voted to vest George Washington with fifty shares of the first and one hundred shares of the second, which he, in turn, placed in a public trust and later bequeathed to Congress to found a national university. George Washington University was the result.

Maryland's Assembly not only approved commercial union with Virginia, it invited Delaware to attend the next conference in Annapolis in September 1786. Elated by the goodwill generated at Mount Vernon, Madison asked Virginia's Assembly to invite all the states to send representatives to the next conference, which was to meet in Annapolis.

By the spring of 1786, America's economic slump had turned into a deep depression, with imports from Britain dropping an additional 30 percent from the previous year and exports falling 6 percent. Farm revenues had plunged 20 percent and sent tax delinquencies soaring, along with property confiscations for nonpayment of taxes. In western Massachusetts, farmers rebelled when former captain Daniel Shays, a farmer struggling to keep his property, convinced neighbors that legislators in Boston were colluding with judges and lawyers across the state to raise taxes to exorbitantly high levels and foreclose when farmers found it impossible to pay. With that, he shouted what some feared would provoke a second American Revolution: "Close down the courts!"

Echoing his call, farmers marched to courthouses in Cambridge, Concord, Worcester, Northampton, Taunton, and Great Barrington—and shut down the civil courts. Hailed by farmers across the nation, the shutdowns frightened courts into ending foreclosures in Massachusetts. Determined to expand his success, Shays led a force of 500 men to Springfield, where 1,000 more farmers joined him. After shutting down the State Supreme Court, they marched to the federal arsenal, intent on seizing arms, ammunition, and artillery. In Boston, meanwhile, the governor organized a 4,000-man private militia to march against Shays. Before they arrived at Springfield, however, soldiers at the arsenal unleashed a few artillery blasts that fell short of the approaching farmers but amply demonstrated the advantages of cannonballs over pitchforks.

Arriving militiamen chased the farmers to their homes and captured most of their leaders, although Shays fled to safety in what was then the independent republic of Vermont. In defeat, however, Shays's army scored a resounding victory when farmers across the state went to the polls and voted the governor and three-fourths of the legislature out of office. The new, pro-farmer legislature declared a tax holiday for a year, reduced taxes thereafter, released imprisoned debtors to go back to work, and exempted clothing, household possessions, and tools of trade from seizure in future debt proceedings.

Fears that Shays's Rebellion would ignite a national uprising spurred Congress to propose revisions in the Articles of Confederation to strengthen the national government's powers, but one state or another stood firm against every proposal. Later, when delegates from only five states—New York, New Jersey, Delaware, Pennsylvania, and Virginia—showed up for the opening gavel at the Annapolis Convention, they adjourned immediately, calling for a broader convention. Delegates from four other states had been on their way, but the convention had adjourned when they arrived.

With the Confederation disintegrating at an ever-accelerating rate, growing numbers of Revolutionary War leaders joined George Washington in calling for strengthening the national government. Although Patrick Henry originally agreed with Washington, he changed his mind abruptly—and, as it turned out, permanently—because of an incomprehensible misstep by New York's John Jay, whom Congress had appointed secretary for foreign affairs. After a year of negotiation, Spanish envoy Don Diego de Gardoqui suggested a treaty under which the United States would "forbear" navigation of the Mississippi River for twenty-five years in exchange for Spain's opening key ports in Spain as European gateways for American trade.

Jay asked Congress to change his instructions to allow him to give up American navigation rights on the Mississippi and Congress agreed. Jay's changed instructions, however, provoked a chorus of angry protests from irate southerners, whose state borders extended to the Mississippi River (see Map 2, page 176). Henry was even more irate—more so because Jay had violated his original instructions from Congress "not to relinquish or cede . . . to the government of Spain the right of the United States to the free navigation of the river Mississippi. . . ."[23] Indeed, Congress had ordered him "to stipulate the right of the United States to . . . the free navigation of the Mississippi. . . ."[24] With the river closed to American navigation, Spanish-licensed river boatmen would be able to impose exorbitant freight rates and make farming in the West so unprofitable that farmers would have to sell their lands to speculators.

Congressmen from northern states with ports on the Atlantic, however, cheered the Jay-Gardoqui agreement, which gave East Coast merchants and shipowners free access to European markets. Congress voted seven (northern states) to five (southern states) in favor of the new instructions for Jay, but short of the nine-state majority needed under the Articles of Confederation to ratify foreign treaties. The vote left southerners and westerners irate at the willingness of northern states to sacrifice the interests of other regions of the Confederation for the right price. Although legally powerless as governor, Henry remained a colossus among patriots—and, as he explained, "I exerted myself . . . to get petitions both to Congress and the Assembly to oppose the scheme." More than that, Henry's limited interest in a stronger national government turned as hostile as it had been in 1775, when he called for revolution against the British government in Richmond's St. John's Church. "Mr. Henry," said Federalist John Marshall, "has been heard to say that he would rather part with the Confederation than relinquish the navigation of the Mississippi."[25]

Equally irate was Virginia's young delegate to Congress, James Monroe, the hero of the Battle of Trenton who had replaced Madison in Philadelphia. "The object in the occlusion of the Mississippi," Monroe vented in a letter to Henry,

> is to break up so far as this will do it the settlements on western waters, prevent any in future, and to thereby keep the States southward as they now are. . . . In short, it is a system of policy which has for its object the keeping the weight of government and population in this [northeast] quarter, and is pursued by a set of men so flagitious, unprincipled and determined in their pursuits, as to satisfy me beyond a doubt they have extended their views to the dismemberment of the government . . . [26]

Outraged settlers in Kentucky talked of forming a militia to march against the Spanish in New Orleans; others threatened to reassert loyalty to the English king and invite British troops to reclaim the West and guarantee settler access to the Mississippi. "To sell us and make us vassals to the merciless Spaniards," one Kentuckian raged in the *Maryland Journal*, "is a grievance not to be born."

> Preparations are now making here . . . to drive the Spaniards from the settlements at the mouth of the Mississippi. In case we are not countenanced and succored by the United States . . . our allegiance will be thrown off, and some other power applied to. Great Britain stands ready, with open arms to receive and support us. They have already offered to open their resources for our supplies. When once reunited to them, farewell—a long farewell to all your boasted greatness.[27]

The threats of secession in the West emboldened New Englanders to call for establishment of a northern confederacy. "The five states of New England, closely confederated, have nothing to fear," proclaimed a correspondent in the *Boston Independent Chronicle*. "Let then our General Assembly immediately recall their delegates from . . . Congress, as being a useless and expensive establishment. Send proposals for instituting a new . . . nation of New England, and leave the rest of the continent to pursue their own imbecile and disjointed plans. . . . "[28]

With the Confederation facing political and economic collapse, delegates had gone to Annapolis to prevent fragile interstate ties from snapping. Without a quorum of states, however, they were impotent even to make recommendations. New York's Alexander Hamilton proposed a new and more forceful call to convention in Philadelphia, in May 1787, to discuss not only commercial relations, but "to render the constitution of the Federal Government adequate to the exigencies of the Union."[29] It was perhaps the last hope for saving the Union.

Chapter 12

Seeds of Discontent

Towards the end of Henry's second year as governor, he and Dolly hosted the capital's most joyous receptions since pre-Revolution Williamsburg days: the marriage of his two daughters. Anne married a prominent lawyer, Spencer Roane, while seventeen-year-old Betsey married Philip Aylett, a handsome, extremely wealthy nineteen-year-old who spent most of his days enjoying his family's apparently limitless supply of money. A hard-drinking card player, Aylett nonetheless became a devoted husband and father—and an effective legislator in the Virginia House of Delegates. Roane became a distinguished judge, winning appointment to the Virginia Supreme Court and eventually serving as its chief justice.

Henry is said to have given each daughter the same fatherly advice in letters that reflected his own married life. "My Dear Daughter," he began:

> You have just entered into that state which is replete with happiness or misery. . . . You are allied to a man of honor, of talents, and of an open, generous disposition. You have, therefore, in your power, all the essential ingredients of happiness. It cannot be marred if you now reflect upon that system of conduct which you ought invariably to pursue.

Asserting that wealth did not produce "matrimonial happiness," Henry gave his daughters several maxims to "impress upon your mind," the first of which was "never to attempt to control your husband, by opposition, by displeasure, or any other mark of anger." Calling "mutual politeness essential to that harmony which should never be once broken . . . between man and wife," he warned that any differences between husband and wife are

the greatest calamity . . . that are to be most studiously guarded against . . . The love of a husband can only be retained by the high opinion which he entertains of his wife's goodness of heart, of her amiable disposition, of the sweetness of her temper, of her prudence, of her devotion to him. Let nothing upon any occasion lessen that opinion. Has your husband stayed out longer than you expected? When he returns, receive him as the partner of your heart. Has he disappointed you? Never evince discontent. . . . Does he . . . invite company without informing you of it? . . . Receive them with a pleasing countenance . . . give to your husband and to your company a hearty welcome.

He urged each of his girls to "cultivate your mind by the perusal of those books which instruct while they amuse." He urged them to avoid novels and plays, which, he said "tend to vitiate the taste. History, geography, poetry, moral essays, biography, travels, sermons, and other well-written religious productions will . . . enlarge your understanding, to render you a more agreeable companion and to exalt your virtue."[1]

After his daughters' weddings, Henry stunned the Virginia political world by announcing his decision not to seek a third term as governor. "I shall resign my office next month and retire," he explained to his sister Anne Christian, "my wife and self being heartily tired of the bustle we live in here. I shall go to Hanover to land I am likely to get . . . or if that fails, towards Leatherwood again. My wife has five very fine and promising children. I rejoice to hear yours are so. Pray, my dearest sister, let me know how I may serve you or them. . . . God bless and preserve you, ever beloved sister."[2]

Several factors had combined to provoke his resignation: fatigue with "the bustle" of Richmond life was but one of them. Money had become a prime consideration after the marriages of his two older daughters. After providing them each with a dowry of £1,000, he found himself in the same position as most "wealthy" Virginia planters—land rich and cash poor. All but phobic about falling in debt, he faced just that if he depended on only his governor's salary for another year to support his wife and five small children—and pay maintenance and entertainment expenses of the governor's mansion. In addition, he had two older sons by his first marriage—fifteen-year-old Edward and his older brother, William, in his early twenties—whom he planned to send to college. To do so, he would have to turn his farms into profitable enterprises and resume practicing law.

Recognizing that a permanent move to Leatherwood would cut his ties to the state's political hub and isolate Dolly, he found a 1,700-acre plantation with twenty-seven slaves called Pleasant Grove in Prince Edward County. Only about eighty miles southwest of Richmond overlooking the Appomattox River tobacco country, it was near Hampden-Sydney College, the college he had helped found and where he planned to send his sons. To pay for the property, he hammered out an agreement to provide the equivalent of about $100,000 (today's dollars) in goods and services. According to his records, payment included several slaves, some lands he had bought in and around Richmond, his own legal services, two horses, and a barrel of rum. Within a year he added nearly 600 more acres to expand farm output. On a hill near the Appomattox River, the two-story house faced the world through a stately, two-story portico supported by tall Grecian columns.

On February 21, 1787, the Confederation Congress recommended that the states send delegates to a convention "for the sole and express purpose of revising the Articles of Confederation . . . "[3] Henry had only just settled into his new home when he received a letter from his long-time friend from their days in the House of Burgesses: the new governor Edmund Randolph. "I most sincerely wish your presence at the federal convention," Randolph wrote.

> From the experience of your late administration, you must be persuaded that every day dawns with perils to the United States. To whom, then, can they resort for assistance with firmer expectation than to those who

first kindled the Revolution? In this respectable character you are now called upon by your country. You will therefore pardon me for expressing a fear that the neglect of the present moment may terminate in the destruction of Confederate America.[4]

As he had when he refused to run for a third term as governor, Henry again shocked the nation by refusing to go to the Constitutional Convention—without even offering a reason for his refusal. Next to Washington, he had received the most votes in the Assembly—ahead of Randolph himself and such legendary figures as George Mason, George Wythe, and John Blair. Washington tried to convince Henry to change his mind, as did James Madison. Both met with outright rejections. "I am entirely convinced," Madison wrote to Washington,

> the hopes of carrying this state into a proper federal system will be demolished. Many of our most federal leading men are extremely soured with what has already passed. Mr. Henry, who has been hitherto the champion of the federal cause, has become a cold advocate, and, in the event of an actual sacrifice of the Mississippi by Congress, will unquestionably go over to the opposite side.[5]

In fact, Henry had already gone "over to the opposite side." Indeed, the Jay-Gardoqui affair had so infuriated him that he questioned whether the states should abolish rather than strengthen the Confederation. If the all-but-impotent Confederation had come so close to stripping Virginia's western farmers of their "natural rights" to ship goods to market, he reasoned that a strengthened national government could succeed where the Confederation had failed. He now argued that Virginia remained America's largest, richest, most heavily populated state, stretching from the Atlantic Ocean to the Mississippi River and northward to the Ohio River. As such, he saw no benefits in ceding her sovereignty and uniting with other states into a huge, unwieldy federal system. Whenever necessary or to her advantage, Virginia could, whenever she saw fit, join in a common defense against attack by foreign powers and participate in joint ventures like the Potomac Company.

Although he remained open to the idea of reforming the Confederation, he believed that the convention in Philadelphia was a fraud. Its delegates were all men of great wealth who exploited the economies of their states and, he believed, would collude to dominate the economy of the entire continent—at the expense of western farmers. "Mr. Henry's disgust exceeds all measure," Madison reported to Washington. By not attending the convention, Madison surmised, Henry would remain aloof from the proceedings and free "to combat or espouse the result of it."⁶

Henry was not the only American leader who refused an invitation to the convention. Richard Henry Lee, like Henry, a father of independence who had proposed the resolution for independence at the Continental Congress, also declined. George Washington, who had initiated the process of constitutional reform, also refused—changing his mind only after influential friends warned him that his refusal would doom the convention to failure and provoke the very anarchy he sought to prevent.

Although the Jay-Gardoqui negotiation was Henry's overriding political motive for not going to Philadelphia, Henry also faced financial problems. The combined tobacco production of his Prince Edward and Leatherwood plantations was not yielding enough revenue to support him and his family in the midst of the economic downturn. He simply could not afford to spend several months wining and dining with the nation's wealthiest men in Philadelphia. He could barely support his family—let alone send his boys to college—unless he resumed his law practice, and that would require his full-time attention.

Beginning on May 25, 1787, fifty-five delegates from twelve of the thirteen states met in the Pennsylvania State House in Philadelphia without the man who had sounded the clarion call for independence and become the symbol of liberty to almost all Americans. His absence was notable; his name was on everyone's lips, and his spirit seemed to hover about in the sweltering summer atmosphere of the convention hall. Although absent in person, Henry remained in continual contact with confederates at the convention who opposed a strong national government, and Madison conceded that "the refusal of Mr. Henry to join in the task of revising the Confederation is ominous."⁷

From the first, the conflicts that threatened the nation with anarchy were evident in delegate relationships—or lack of relationships—in the convention hall: the regional conflicts between North, South, East and West; the commercial conflicts between agrarian and urban interests; the political conflicts between large and small states. Indeed, Rhode Island, the smallest state, refused to send a delegate to the convention.

As one of the primary organizers of the convention, however, James Madison presented an optimistic front: "There never was an assembly of men," he boasted, "who were more devoted . . . to the object of devising and proposing a constitutional system which would . . . best secure the permanent liberty and happiness of their country."[8] Henry mocked Madison by asserting that there had never been an assembly of men who were more devoted to preserving and enhancing their own wealth. For as Henry noted, the delegates at Philadelphia were the wealthiest, most powerful and best educated men in America. None represented the less affluent farm regions in the western parts of the twelve states. Twenty-one held college degrees; twenty-nine were lawyers or judges, and nearly all held political offices or had served on Revolutionary War committees. With Washington presiding, they would sit five to six hours a day, six days a week, from May 25 until September 17, 1787, except for a nine-day adjournment between July 29 and August 6, to let a committee arrange and edit the resolutions into a readable draft constitution.

Convention rules gave each state one vote, determined by a majority of delegates from that state. Of all rules adopted, the two most important were the secrecy rule, to protect delegates from political reprisals for speaking or voting their consciences or private interests, and a rule allowing delegates to reconsider previous issues and change their votes. Although the convention allowed James Madison to take notes of the proceedings, he would keep the notes secret for his entire life. Among other reasons, he sought to prevent political enemies of the delegates—and the Constitution—from quoting elements of speeches out of context. Madison outlived all other delegates, surviving until 1836, forty-eight years after the convention.

Recognizing both the stature of Washington as the most unifying figure in the Confederation and the status of Virginia as its most powerful state, delegates elected him president. Although he did not participate in debate, at least three dozen of the fifty-five delegates had served under him in the Revolutionary War. All knew his views, which became paramount in the proceedings. Indeed, he had sent all the governors and other state leaders an outline of the kind of government he favored. It came as no surprise then that, after the initial election of officers and adoption of rules, Washington recognized immediately Virginia Governor Edmund Randolph to present the "Virginia Plan" of government, which fleshed out Washington's own outline for a new national government.

Born to a long line of English noblemen who had served as king's attorneys, Edmund Randolph had attended the College of William and Mary and studied law under his father, who fled to England with his close friend Lord Dunmore when the Revolution began. Twenty-two years old at the time, Edmund enlisted in the Continental Army, becoming an aide to Washington before returning to Virginia as State Attorney General, then mayor of Williamsburg until he succeeded Henry as Governor. After discussions with Henry, Randolph had gone to Philadelphia agreeing to seek only minor revisions of the Articles of Confederation, but, overwhelmed by the powerful personalities in his delegation, he reluctantly agreed, as governor of his state, to present the far-reaching Virginia Plan favored by Washington.

Instead of "revising the Articles of Confederation," as instructed by Congress, the Virginia Plan called for scrapping the Articles and creating a new form of government. It was nothing short of a bloodless coup d'état—a second American revolution without firing a shot.[9] Knowing the plan would meet with opposition, but unwilling to split with Washington, Randolph sought to retain links to all political factions and "expressed his regret that it should fall to him . . . to open the great subject of their mission. But," he said, "his colleagues had imposed this task on him."[10]

The Virginia Plan proposed fifteen resolutions which, among other things, called for replacing the unicameral Confederation Congress with "a *national* government consisting of a *supreme* Legislative, Executive and Judiciary." The national legislature would have an upper and lower house and be the most powerful branch of government, with sole power to elect

*Governor Edmund Randolph of Virginia refused to
endorse and sign the Constitution at the Constitutional
Convention in Philadelphia—only to change his position
at the Virginia ratification convention the following year
and vote for ratification. After George Washington won
election as President he appointed Randolph the first
U.S. Attorney General.* (LIBRARY OF CONGRESS)

both the executive and the judges of a supreme court. The people would
elect the lower house, with the number of delegates proportionate to the
number of "free inhabitants" in each state. The Lower house would elect
members of the upper house from nominees chosen by the legislatures of
each state. Most astonishing, the new Congress would have the very powers that Henry despised most about the British government—namely, "to
negative all laws passed by the several states . . . and to call forth the force
of the Union against any member of the Union failing to fulfill its duty
under the articles thereof."[11]

The Virginia Plan was nothing less than Washington's revenge for congressional failure to provide him and his troops with adequate funding

during the Revolutionary War. Under the Virginia Plan, the laws of Congress would be supreme and Congress would be free to use military force to enforce them. Washington believed that "the primary cause of all our disorders lies in the different state governments, and in the . . . incompatibility in the laws of different states and disrespect to those of the general government." The result, he declared, had left "this great country weak, inefficient and disgraceful . . . almost to the final dissolution of it. . . . "[12]

Delegates responded to the Virginia Plan with shocked silence. In effect, the plan called for the overthrow of the legally constituted American government. It would not only create an entirely new form of government, it would strip the states of their sovereignty. Outraged delegates from North and South denounced the plan, calling its presentation out of order and a violation of the mandate of Congress limiting the convention's role to *revising* the existing Articles of Confederation. "The act of Congress recommending the Convention," said South Carolina's Charles Cotesworth Pinckney, a Revolutionary War hero and prominent attorney, did not "authorize a discussion of a system founded on different principles" from the Federal Constitution [Articles of Confederation]." His cousin Charles Pinckney—a young Charleston attorney—demanded to know whether Randolph's plan was meant "to abolish state government altogether."[13]

In the days that followed, all semblances of collegiality disappeared, with southerners demanding that slaves (who had no vote and went uncounted when apportioning representatives in state assemblies) be counted in determining proportionate representation in the lower house. Small states rejected the concept of proportionate representation, arguing that two or three states with the largest populations—Virginia, Pennsylvania, and Massachusetts—could dominate the entire Union. They argued for perpetuation of the one-state, one-vote rule of the Confederation Congress. Delegates from large states countered that the one-state, one-vote rule would allow a handful of small states with only a minority of the nation's population to dictate to the majority.

As the debate raged, delegates grew increasingly mean-spirited, with some northerners even mocking the accents of delegates from the deep South, to which southerners countered by pretending they could not understand Boston's delegates and asking them to repeat themselves. When

Pennsylvania's abolitionists demanded an end to slavery, South Carolina's delegates threatened to walk out, and early in July, two of New York's three delegates did leave—stomping out in an angry protest against attempts to crush state sovereignty. Faced with a breakup of the Convention—and the Confederation itself—calmer heads prevailed, and the remaining delegates went to work to find compromises for their outstanding disputes. In the end they decided on proportionate representation in the lower house and state parity in the upper house. They gave the lower house sole power to originate appropriations legislation, thus keeping control over the nation's money—and, therefore, all government activities—in the hands of the electorate. As for slaves, northerners objected to counting nonvoting slaves in the population because it would give the owners of Virginia's huge Tidewater plantations inordinate political powers. George Mason, whose plantation was almost adjacent to Washington's Mount Vernon, argued that the inclusion of slaves in the population count would give them an indirect influence in legislation and that "such a system would provide no less carefully for the rights and happiness of the lowest than of the highest orders of citizens."[14] As southerners cheered his disingenuous position, Connecticut's Oliver Ellsworth responded tartly, "Mr. Mason has himself about three hundred slaves and lives in Virginia, where it is found by prudent management they can breed and raise slaves faster than they want for their own use and could supply the deficiency in Georgia and South Carolina."[15] To prevent a walkout by southerners, the convention compromised by allotting lower house votes based on the total free population of each state and three-fifths of the slave population. Spurred by messages from Patrick Henry, the South demanded another concession from the North, making it necessary for the upper house to confirm foreign treaties by a two-thirds vote instead of a simple majority. Southerners had not forgotten how northern states in Congress had almost ceded Mississippi River navigation rights to Spain two years earlier. Only the two-thirds requirement of the Confederation Congress had prevented the treaty from becoming law.

With each passing day, delegates found something new to dispute, until Washington lost all patience and collared delegates outside the meeting hall—at the City Tavern and at dinners in private homes—and demanded that they reach a compromise. As he later put it, "Every state has some objection. That which is most pleasing to one is obnoxious to another and vice versa. If then the union of the whole is a desirable object, the parts which compose it must yield a little in order to accomplish it." The reading of a statement by the aging Benjamin Franklin made the same point more humorously. The impasse, he said, reminded him of the Anglican leader who explained to the Pope, that "the only difference between our churches lies in the certainty of their doctrines—that the Church of Rome is infallible and the Church of England is never in the wrong."[16]

On July 29, the Convention recessed to allow a committee to combine the resolutions that had been approved into a cohesive finished document. When the convention reconvened on August 6, South Carolina's John Rutledge—another war hero and lawyer—read it aloud, beginning with the preamble:

"We the people of the States of New Hampshire, Massachusetts, Rhode Island and Providence Plantations, Connecticut [he read the names of all thirteen states] . . . do hereby declare and establish the following Constitution for the Government ourselves and our posterity."[17] The language put some delegates to sleep, but aroused others to renewed debate, with a core group of rabid abolitionists from the Quaker state of Pennsylvania reiterating demands for an end to the slave trade. South Carolina threatened to reject the document "if it prohibits the slave trade . . . If the states be all left at liberty on the subject, South Carolina may perhaps by degrees do of herself what is wished."[18] To keep the deep South in the Union, the North agreed not to interfere with the importation of slaves for twenty years, but almost every delegate found other elements of the Constitution unacceptable, with some predicting civil war when it went to the state legislatures for ratification. The delegates found something to debate until the very last day— most importantly, George Mason's demands for a bill of rights to guarantee individual rights and limits on national government powers.

In the end, Washington brought the convention to heel, warning, "There are seeds of discontent in every part of the Union ready to produce disorders if . . . the present convention should not be able to devise a more vigorous and energetic government."[19]

On September 12, a "Committee on Stile," for which Pennsylvania's Gouverneur Morris had exercised his brilliant writing skills, presented the convention with copies of the final draft of the Constitution, linking it through its preamble to the Declaration of Independence.

> WE, THE PEOPLE OF THE UNITED STATES, IN ORDER TO FORM a more perfect union, establish justice, insure domestic tranquility, provide for the common defence, promote the general welfare, and secure the blessings of liberty to ourselves and our posterity, do ordain and establish this Constitution for the United States of America.

What followed were seven Articles, with the first three defining the shape and powers of the national legislature, the executive, and the judiciary, and the methods of selection and qualifications for serving (and removal) in each. It gave Congress, inter alia, powers to raise taxes and levy duties, borrow money, regulate foreign and interstate commerce, maintain a standing army and navy, and declare war. The president was to be commander in chief of the military and have diplomatic powers to send and receive ambassadors and make treaties. It stripped the states of rights to deal with foreign powers. Article IV forced the states to recognize each other's laws and to give all citizens the rights of citizenship in every state. The same Article also provided for admission of new states and guaranteed "a republican form of government" in every state. Article V provided for amending the Constitution, and Article VI ranked laws by category. The Constitution and U.S. laws and treaties ranked highest as "the supreme law of the land," and local laws ranked lowest, with little or no consequence for the rest of the nation. Article VII required approval by ratification conventions in nine states for the Constitution to take effect in those states and create a new national government.

As president of the convention, Washington was first to sign—only to have Virginia Governor Randolph disrupt proceedings by calling the document a "fetus of monarchy" and saying it was "impossible . . . to put my name to the instrument." George Washington's neighbor, planter George Mason, was more dramatic: "I would sooner chop off my right hand," said the normally soft-spoken Virginian, "than put it to the Constitution as it now stands." Echoing his political ally Patrick Henry, Mason criticized "the dangerous power and structure of the government" under the Constitution and predicted it would end "either in monarchy or a tyrannical aristocracy. . . . This Constitution has been formed without the knowledge or idea of the people. . . . It is improper to say to the people, 'Take this or nothing.'" Mason had maintained contact with Henry during the convention and cited Henry's repeated demands for another, second convention "to know more of the sense of the people and . . . provide a system more consonant to it. As the Constitution now stands I can neither support it or give it my vote in Virginia, and I cannot sign here what I cannot support there."[20]

Although Patrick Henry had not set foot in Philadelphia, the lion of liberty's roar against governmental tyranny echoed across the land.

On the Wings of the Tempest

On September 17, 1787, thirty-nine of the forty-two delegates signed the Constitution, but Gouverneur Morris's brilliant language skills altered the last paragraph of the document to ignore the less-than-unanimous delegate vote with the misleading phrase, "Done in Convention by the unanimous consent of the states present." Less than two weeks later, the document reached the Confederation Congress, where at Patrick Henry's urging, Virginia delegate Richard Henry Lee objected to taxation by a national government without the consent of the states. After conferring with Henry, he also demanded that the Constitution "be bottomed upon a . . . Bill of Rights guaranteeing freedom of religion, freedom of the press, the right to trial by jury in criminal and civil cases, the right to free assembly, protection against unreasonable search and seizures."[1] Congress rejected his motion, saying it had no authority to change the Constitution—only to transmit it to the states, with or without a recommendation. It chose the latter, sending a copy to each state legislature for submission "to a convention of delegates chosen in each state by the people thereof." Richard Henry Lee warned Patrick Henry that "the most essential danger" of the Constitution was "its tendency to a consolidated government instead of a union of confederated states. The history of the world and reason concur in proving that so extensive a territory as the United States . . . never was or can be governed in freedom under the former idea . . . "[2]

With Patrick Henry, George Mason, Richard Henry Lee, and Edmund Randolph opposed to ratification, there seemed little hope that Virginia would ratify, and without Virginia there would be no effective union even with all twelve of the other states. For Washington, the failure to win ratification in his home state would be particularly humiliating, and, from the moment he arrived home in Mount Vernon he set to work against that eventuality.

"In the first moments after my return," he wrote to Patrick Henry and three other former Virginia governors, "I take the liberty of sending you a copy of the Constitution which the Federal Convention has submitted to the people of these states. . . ."

> I wish the Constitution . . . had been made more perfect, but I sincerely believe it is the best that could be obtained at this time—and as a constitutional door is opened for amendment hereafter—the adoption of it under present circumstances of the Union is in my opinion desirable. . . . The political concerns of this country are . . . suspended by a thread. . . . If nothing had been agreed upon . . . anarchy would soon have ensued— the seeds being ripely sown in every soil.[3]

Hoping to build support for the Constitution in his home state, Washington sent the same letter to former Virginia governor Benjamin Harrison and to Thomas Jefferson, whom Congress had appointed American minister in Paris.

Henry was in a foul mood when he received Washington's letter. Indeed, while Washington and the others had been in Philadelphia, Henry's deteriorating finances had forced him to sell more land to pay for costly improvements at the plantation he bought in Prince Edward County. When he and Dolly arrived, they had found the house in decay, with but one fireplace and, worse, without a "necessary," or outhouse. He was in no mood to study a constitution, let alone one that created a powerful national government. After reading it, he did his best to contain his rage as he scribbled his reply to Washington:

I have to lament that I cannot bring my mind in accord with the proposed Constitution. The concern I feel on this account is really greater than I am able to express. Perhaps mature reflection may furnish me reasons to change my present sentiments into a conformity with the opinion of those personages for whom I have the highest reverence. Be that as it may, I beg you will be persuaded of the unalterable regard and attachment with which I ever shall be, dear sir, your obliged and very humble servant.[4]

In fact, Henry had so many objections that he had neither the time nor the patience to enumerate them—nor the will to enter into a fruitless debate that risked alienating a man whom he admired deeply. Henry's objections, however, were legion. Predicting tyranny as inevitable, he railed at the failure of the Constitution to limit national government powers. "Congress," he predicted, "will have an unlimited, unbounded command over the soul of this commonwealth," with powers to pass any laws it deemed "necessary and proper," as stated in Article 1, Section 8. The president would have all but free rein to exercise whatever he defined as "executive power." The Constitution offered no specifics. And, Henry concluded, the judiciary had all but supreme power over every court in the land and could hear cases without juries—a right guaranteed in the English-speaking world since 1215, when King John had signed the Magna Carta.

Nor did the Constitution provide term limits for the president, members of Congress, or the judiciary. All could serve indefinitely and collude to create a tyranny. Henry feared the president and senate could collude with foreign governments to sell American territory or territorial rights as Congress had almost done with Spain during the Jay-Gardoqui negotiations. Henry also objected to granting the national government powers to maintain a standing army, to impose taxes without the consent of the states, to "negative" state laws, and to enforce federal laws with troops. Calling "the sword and the purse" the two greatest powers of government, he raged that "the junction of these without limitation in the same hands is . . . despotism," and demanded that the federal government share these powers with the states.

Among his other objections: the Constitution stripped states of their sovereignty and failed to protect individual rights to freedom of speech, freedom of religion, freedom of the press, trial by jury in civil cases, redress of grievances, and freedom of assembly to protest government actions. Virginia's Declaration of Rights guaranteed them all, he declared, but the Constitution would give the new national government the power to "negative" the state's guarantees of liberty. Henry argued that the Constitution would establish a national government with powers to impose the very tyranny from which Americans had freed themselves in their revolution against Britain. With these and so many more objections, Henry thought it useless to respond to Washington with anything but the short—and honest—note he actually sent. His objections were indeed "really greater than I am able to express."[5]

With poor prospects for a profitable crop, Henry set out to rebuild his law practice, riding the seven-odd miles to the Prince Edward County Courthouse each day to find prospective clients—and trumpet his objections to the proposed Constitution to everyone he met. As he extended the reach of his practice to other counties, one of his political opponents denigrated him by describing his clients as:

> horse thieves and murderers . . . who have lost him much of the great reputation he enjoyed in the neighborhood. . . . I am told that he will travel hundreds of miles for a handsome fee to plead for criminals, and that his powers of oratory are so great he generally succeeds . . . that a man in his neighborhood has been heard to say he should have no apprehension of being detected horse stealing, for that Governor Henry, or Colonel Henry, as he is sometimes called, would for £50 clear him.[6]

Henry had little choice in selecting clients, however. On the relatively lawless frontier, the sale of a horse easily provoked disputes and such disputes just as easily provoked musket fire. In any event, criminal law gave Henry the opportunity to win or lose by ignoring fine points of law and appealing to jury emotions. "As a criminal lawyer," his son-in-law Judge Spencer Roane explained,

> his eloquence had the fairest scope. He was the perfect master of the passions of his auditory, whether in the tragic or the comic line. The tones of

his voice, to say nothing of his manners and gestures, were insinuated into the feelings of his hearers in a manner that baffled all description. It seemed to operate by mere sympathy, and by his tones alone it seemed that he could make you cry or laugh at pleasure; yet his gesture came powerfully in aid, and if necessary would approach almost to the ridiculous.[7]

Roane cited one case of an unsavory defendant on trial for what was a clear-cut case of murder. Henry, however, turned the attention of the jury from the defendant to the defendant's elderly parents.

He presented . . . old Holland and his wife . . . asked what must be the feelings of this venerable pair at this moment and what the consequences to them of a mistaken verdict affecting the life of their son. He caused the jury to lose sight of the murder they were trying, and weep with old Holland and his wife, whom he painted, and perhaps proved to be, very respectable. . . . After a retirement of a half or quarter of an hour, the jury brought in a verdict of *not guilty!*[8]

It was only after the judge chastised them and reminded them that they could bring in a verdict other than the death penalty that they modified their verdict to one of manslaughter.

While Henry struggled to restore his family's financial health, he remained the most popular figure among his neighbors, who were struggling as much as he and obviously admired his willingness to travel far and wide to defend the helpless. Asked to serve as their delegate in the Assembly, he agreed and won election unopposed.

In Henry's absence, Richard Henry Lee had taken the lead in organizing the nation's anticonstitutionalists, or "Antifederalists," as they came to be called. He published a widely read series of *Letters of the Federal Farmer to the Republican*, warning that the new federal government "may command the whole or any part of the subjects' property . . . by means of taxes."[9]

Although Federalists despised taxation as much as Antifederalists, most Federalist leaders were wealthy merchants and planters for whom the economic benefits of normalized international and interstate trade under a strong national government would more than offset the cost of added taxes.

Antifederalists, on the other hand, represented owners of small farms that yielded too little to survive any added taxes. Fearing that a federal tax would combine with state taxes to force thousands of families off their lands, Lee proposed amending the Constitution to make federal taxes subject to approval by state legislatures. Lee also demanded passage of Henry's bill of rights "to restrain and regulate the great powers given to rulers:

> That the rights of conscience in matters of religion ought not be violated—
> that the freedom of the press shall be secured—That trial by jury . . . shall
> be held sacred—That standing armies in times of peace are dangerous to
> liberty . . . That the elections should be free and frequent; That . . . justice
> be secured by the independency of judges; That excessive bail, excessive
> fines, or cruel and unusual punishments, shall not be demanded or in-
> flicted; That the right of the people to assemble, for the purpose of peti-
> tioning the legislature, shall not be prevented; That the citizens shall not be
> exposed to unreasonable searches, seizure of their personas, houses, papers
> or property.[10]

Washington accused Lee and other opponents of the Constitution of using "every art that could inflame the passions or touch the interests of men" to defeat ratification. "The ignorant are told that should the proposed government obtain, their lands would be taken from them and their property disposed of, and all ranks are informed that the prohibition of the navigation of the Mississippi (their favorite subject) will be a certain consequence of the adoption of the Constitution."[11]

In Paris, meanwhile, Jefferson joined the debate, taking a middle road: "Were I in America," he wrote to John Adams, "I would advocate it warmly till nine [states] should have adopted it and then as warmly take the other side to convince the other four that they ought not to come into it till the declaration of rights is annexed to it."[12] In a subsequent letter to Washington, Jefferson was more specific, saying,

> There are two things . . . which I dislike strongly . . . the want of a decla-
> ration of rights . . . and the perpetual re-eligibility of the President. . . .
> This I fear will make that an office for life first, and then hereditary. I was

much an enemy to monarchy before I came to Europe. I am ten thousand times more so since I see what they are. There is scarcely an evil known in these countries which may not be traced to their king as its source. . . . I can further say with safety there is not a crowned head in Europe whose talents or merit would entitle him to be elected a vestryman by the people in my parish in America. However . . . I look forward to the general adoption of the new constitution . . . as necessary for us under present circumstances.[13]

A month after refusing to sign the Constitution, Governor Randolph published a letter in the form of a pamphlet addressed to the Speaker of the Virginia House of Delegates giving his reasons: the lack of presidential term limits, the lack of restrictions on judicial powers, and the failure to draw "a line between the powers of Congress and individual states . . . so as to leave no clash of jurisdiction or dangerous disputes . . . "[14]

With the publication of his pamphlet, Randolph joined Richard Henry Lee, George Mason, Patrick Henry, and the Antifederalists, who favored retention of a confederation made up of relatively small, independent republics, tied to each other only in the maintenance of a common defense. Hard off their experience with British rule, the majority of ordinary Americans harbored Antifederalist fears that a powerful national government would strip them of individual liberties. Arrayed against them however, were the enormously wealthy and influential Federalists, led by the redoubtable "Father of Our Country," George Washington. Although Washington made a show of remaining aloof from the political fray, he made his views known through James Madison and other champions of a strong national government. Only such a government, they argued, could pay the nation's debts and end the farmer tax riots raging across the nation. As Washington put it, "There is no alternative between the adoption of it [the Constitution] and anarchy. . . ."[15]

When Henry returned to the Virginia Assembly, he moved to block the call to a ratification convention. "No man is more federal than I," he protested, hoping to seduce pro-constitution delegates into joining his camp. Like George Mason, he opposed calling a ratification convention until amendments were added to the document to guarantee individual and states' rights. He warned that a ratification convention, as proposed, would have no power to amend—only to accept or reject—unless the Assembly gave it the power of proposing amendments. Mason seconded Henry's proposal, but the Assembly voted them down. As in other states, voting restrictions based on property ownership prevented Virginia's Antifederalists from converting their popular majority into a majority of Assembly delegates. Although Henry failed to block the call to convention, he had enough allies in the Assembly to delay elections to the convention until March and the actual convention until June 2, by which time, he hoped, other states might well have rejected the Constitution and rendered Virginia's ratification vote moot.

"The refusal of our governor and Colonel Mason to subscribe to the proceedings of the convention," Washington warned, "will have a bad effect in this state." Accusing them of "alarming" voters, he said that "some things are . . . addressed to the fears of the people and will no doubt have their effect."[16] Madison wrote to Jefferson in Paris and accused Henry of seeking "a partition of the Union into several confederacies." He said he feared that Henry would convince the Virginia ratification convention to vote against ratification and for a second constitutional convention to limit the new government's powers.

In fact, the objections of Lee, Mason and Henry were already having their effects far beyond Virginia. "Beware! Beware!" warned the *Massachusetts Centinel*. "You are forging chains for yourself and your children—your liberties are at stake."[17] Philadelphia's *Independent Gazetteer* predicted that the Constitution would create "a permanent ARISTOCRACY,"[18] while the *Freeman's Journal*, another Philadelphia newspaper, warned of congressional powers "to lay and collect taxes."[19]

The Antifederalist campaign gradually swayed public opinion against ratification of the Constitution, but Federalists controlled most state legislatures, and, one by one, they called ratification conventions. By February 6, 1788, conventions in six states had ratified the Constitution: Delaware, Pennsylvania, New Jersey, Georgia, Connecticut, and Massachusetts. The three smallest states—Delaware, New Jersey, and Connecticut—had favored ratification because of the military protection offered by a continental army. Sparsely settled Georgia—beset by Indian raids from Spanish-held

Florida—also needed help from a strong federal force. In Pennsylvania and Massachusetts, powerful trading interests in Philadelphia and Boston had controlled the majorities of convention delegates—despite popular opposition to the Constitution in both states. To eke out their victory, Massachusetts Federalists pledged to "recommend" a bill of rights to the First Congress, while Pennsylvania Federalists simply stole their victory. Benjamin Franklin, of all people, ignored all principles of self-government by leading the delegation out of the Constitutional Convention and marching into the Pennsylvania Assembly hall in the same building. Interrupting the Assembly's proceedings, he all but promised that Philadelphia would be the new federal capital if Pennsylvania was first to ratify the Constitution. He urged state legislators to call a state ratification convention immediately, without debate. Like other major property owners in the city—along with merchants and business owners—Franklin stood to reap enormous profits if the new government established the capital in Philadelphia.

Angry backcountry Antifederalists, however, refused to appear in the Assembly and left it two members short of a quorum. Speaker Thomas Mifflin, the wealthy Philadelphia merchant, ordered a sergeant at arms and a clerk to find at least two absent members and order them to the hall. A mob of Federalists followed the two to the boarding house where many Antifederalists lodged and physically dragged two assemblymen back to their seats in the State House, where, despite their shouts of protest, sentries physically restrained them while Federalists voted to hold the ratification convention on November 20. In the days and weeks that followed, Antifederalists in the backcountry protested the Assembly's actions, attacking Federalists and burning effigies of Federalist leaders and copies of the Constitution.

"The whole county is alive with wrath," a reporter wrote from Cumberland County to Philadelphia's *Independent Gazetteer*, "and it is spreading from one county to another so rapidly that it is impossible to say where it will end or how far it will reach."[20]

French chargé d'affaires Louis-Guillaume Otto was appalled, writing to his foreign minister in Versailles that

> the legislative Assembly of Pennsylvania imprudently . . . revived the jealousy and anxiety of democrats. In a blunder that is difficult to explain,

Pennsylvania limited its delegation to the Constitutional Convention to Philadelphians; the other counties, whose interest have always been different from those of the capital, were hardly satisfied. . . . In forcing the minority to ratify the new government without debate, the legislature has acted so harshly and precipitously as to render any new government suspect. . . . It could strike a fatal blow . . . the alarm is sounded, the public is on guard and they are now examining in detail what they would have adopted almost blindly.[21]

Henry was equally appalled, saying that Pennsylvania had been "tricked" into ratifying the Constitution. "Only ten thousand were represented in Pennsylvania," he charged, "although seventy thousand had a right to be represented."[22]

Ironically, the Pennsylvania ratification convention did not meet until November 20, and, while it was still debating two and a half weeks later, Delaware became the first state to ratify the Constitution—on December 7, 1787.

Although elections to the Virginia ratification convention were not to be held until April, Henry began campaigning in February. By April he had written to leaders in Kentucky and other parts of western Virginia and spoken to crowds outside every courthouse he visited on his legal rounds. "Mr. Henry is supposed to aim at disunion," Madison wrote to Jefferson. "Colonel Mason is growing every day more bitter, and outrageous in his effort to carry his point, and will probably in the end be thrown by the violence of his passions into the politics of Mr. Henry. . . . I think the Constitution and the Union will both be endangered."[23]

A few weeks later, Jefferson received a letter from his friend Edward Carrington: "Mr. H. does not openly declare for a dismemberment of the Union, but his arguments in support of his opposition to the Constitution go directly to that issue. He says that three confederacies would be practicable and better suited to the good of commerce than one."[24]

By the time Virginians elected delegates to their state ratification convention, Maryland had ratified, and with the Federalist-dominated convention in South Carolina preparing to ratify in May, only one more state—either Virginia, New Hampshire, New York, North Carolina, or Rhode Island—

would have to ratify to implement the new government. Rhode Island, however, had refused even to consider the Constitution. Convinced that the state's minuscule proportions would leave it impotent in the new union, its legislature refused to call a convention, and the people confirmed their legislature's decision in a popular referendum in March 1788. Although New Hampshire's legislature had called a ratification convention in February, the convention was so divided about ratification that it adjourned without a decision and agreed to reconvene in June. North Carolina's ratification convention would not meet until July, leaving Virginia, New Hampshire, and New York as the only candidates to become the ninth and definitive member of the new nation.

New York's Governor George Clinton, however, seemed prepared to secede rather than allow his state to ratify the Constitution and cede its sovereignty to a national government. He believed he would find an ally in Patrick Henry. A commander of the New York militia during the Revolution, Clinton won Washington's friendship by sending supplies to Valley Forge and inviting him to participate in a successful land investment in upstate New York. Indeed, Clinton rode in his full brigadier general's regalia alongside Washington to take command of New York City on "Evacuation Day," when the British quit the city after Britain recognized U.S. independence. Elected governor *and* lieutenant governor, he won the unfailing support of state farmers by reducing property taxes. He added to that support by transferring the state capital from New York City to Poughkeepsie for half the year—to make it easier for farmers to influence legislative and judicial matters. Eighty-five miles up the Hudson River north of New York, the little rural town lay in the heart of the richest agricultural area of the Northeast, stretching from the Berkshire hills on the Massachusetts border, westward to the Pennsylvania border on the Delaware River. A farmer himself, Clinton lived just across the Hudson River from Poughkeepsie and, like Patrick Henry, he espoused individual liberty—including the liberty to own eight slaves to harvest his wealth.

When the British left New York, the state began earning as much as $250,000 a year (about $5 million in today's dollars) from port duties— about half the state's annual income and enough to keep property taxes low enough to ensure Clinton's reelection every year. Embraced by farmers and other property owners, Clinton had more power in his state than any other governor in America. The state constitution vested him with "supreme executive power and authority," including the powers of former royal governors to call the legislature into special session or to prorogue it for as long as sixty days. It gave him the longest term in office—three years—and set no limit on the number of consecutive terms he could remain in his chair. Far more powerful in New York than Henry was in Virginia, Clinton dispensed hundreds of jobs and local judgeships across the farm belt and built America's first great political machine. He became America's wealthiest governor after seizing his share of about $4 million in confiscated Tory properties. Faced with a federal constitution that would cost the state control of international trade and the flow of import duties into the state treasury, Clinton joined Antifederalists as a bitter foe of ratification.

Washington's friend Gouverneur Morris, who had written the final draft of the Constitution and its Preamble, condemned Clinton as part of a "wicked industry of those who have long habituated themselves to live on the public and cannot bear the idea of being removed from power and profit of state government, which has been and still is the means of supporting themselves, their families, and dependents."[25]

When Congress sent the Constitution to the states in the fall of 1787, the New York State legislature was not in session and not scheduled to reconvene until the new year. Like Patrick Henry, Clinton planned to block the call for a ratification convention as long as he could, but, when that became impossible, his Antifederalist allies in the New York Senate set about undermining the convention by requiring all state officeholders to take an oath "never to consent to any act or thing which has a tendency to destroy or alter the present constitution of the state."[26] The oath did not preclude calling a ratification convention—or attending it. It simply made it illegal to vote for ratification. The concept of the oath, however, so violated the principles of antifederalism and individual liberty that even Clinton's staunchest allies voted against it. They nonetheless agreed to postpone elections for the ratification convention until April 29, a month after the Virginia convention elections.

Calling themselves "Federal Republicans," Clinton and his Antifederalist allies in New York's farm belt set out to defeat ratification in the remaining states and provoke rescindment in Pennsylvania, where controversy continued raging over the elections to the ratification convention. Rumors swirled that he was attempting to form a "middle confederacy" tying New York and Virginia and the states in between them—Maryland, Delaware, and New Jersey—in an economic union that would isolate New England from the deep South.

Henry responded enthusiastically. "It is a matter of great consolation to find that the sentiments of a vast majority of Virginians are in unison with those of our northern friends," Henry wrote from Richmond.

> I am satisfied that four-fifths of our inhabitants are opposed to the new scheme of government. Indeed, in the part of this country lying south of the James River, I am confidant that nine-tenths are opposed to it. . . . I can assure you that North Carolina is more decidedly opposed to the new government than Virginia. The people there seem rife for hazarding all before they submit. Perhaps the organization of our system may be so contrived as to include lesser associations throughout the state.[27]

Henry conceded that "the numbers" at the Virginia ratification convention were "equal on both sides" and that "the majority, which way soever it goes, will be small. . . . Colonel George Mason has agreed to act as chairman of our republican society . . . and we have concluded to send you . . . a copy of the Bill of Rights and of the particular amendments we intend to propose. . . ."[28]

Henry arrived in Richmond brimming with confidence, certain that his four overriding objections to the Constitution would defeat its ratification. First and foremost was the lack of a bill of rights. His second objection was the unlimited power of the new national government to tax the people without the consent of their state legislatures—one of the issues that provoked the Revolutionary War. A third objection was the federal government's power over the military and the right to send it into any state to enforce federal laws——again, an issue that provoked the Revolutionary War. His fourth major objection—and he was adamant on this point—was the right of the smallest possible majority in Congress to legislate against the interests of Virginia (or any other state, for that matter)—as it almost did with the Jay-Gardoqui negotiations to cede Mississippi River navigation rights of western farmers to Spain.

Henry went to Richmond with a tactical advantage: The state legislature was to reconvene in only four weeks, on June 30. Most of the delegates at the convention were also members of the legislature and would, by law, have to leave the convention to take their seats as lawmakers. The Federalists led by the diminutive James Madison would have but four weeks to win ratification in the face of Henry's oratorical blasts and the arguments of his formidable allies: the sitting governor Edmund Randolph, former governor Benjamin Harrison, and both of Virginia's popular delegates to Congress, James Monroe and William Grayson, who had helped put an end to the Jay-Gardoqui negotiations with Spain. Henry hoped that among the five of them—and planter George Mason—they could talk the convention to death. Indeed, Henry would come close to doing the job by himself, speaking on seventeen of the convention's twenty-two days, often three times a day and five times on one day. On another, he was the only speaker, standing seven hours to deliver his address.

After a day devoted to organization, the convention opened, with Henry, of course, shooting to his feet. Well-wishers had surrounded his gig when he rode into town, and wherever he went, they surrounded him, walked with him, joked with him, even sang with him—always addressing him with adoring familiarity. Kentucky's fourteen delegates and their followers let loose a chorus of raucous whoops when they came to town and hailed their hero. Nearly half the 100,000 settlers in Kentucky were Virginia transplants who relied on Henry to protect their interests. In tasseled buckskins, bucktailed hats, rifles slung over their shoulders, and knives in their belts, they drew nervous stares from Tidewater aristocrats in powdered wigs, velvet jackets, ruffled silk shirts, knee breeches, silk hose, and buckle-top shoes.

Fifty-two-year-old Henry stood apart from both the eastern dandies and rough-hewn frontiersmen. Still frail from his recurring illnesses, his coarse black homespun, white neck wrap, and sunken cheeks gave him a Christ-like look to some—although other, less charitable onlookers compared him to "a scarecrow with a wig." It was no surprise that he was first to rise after the convention had fixed the rules of order and heard the contents of the Constitution.[29]

"Mr. Chairman," he began,

> I consider myself as the servant of the people of this commonwealth, as a sentinel over their rights, liberty, and happiness. I represent their feelings when I say that they are exceedingly uneasy . . . Before the meeting of the late Federal Convention at Philadelphia, a general peace and a universal tranquility prevailed in this country. But since that period . . . I conceive the republic to be in extreme danger. . . . Whence has arisen this fearful jeopardy? It arises from this fatal system—it arises from a proposal to change our government. A proposal that goes to the utter annihilation of the most solemn engagement of the states. . . . That this is a consolidated government . . . instead of a confederation . . . is demonstrably clear, and the danger of such a government is, to my mind very striking.[30]

Henry went on to accuse the authors of the Constitution of having usurped powers and staged a coup d'état by violating the mandate of Congress. Congress had called the Constitutional Convention, he reminded Virginians, "for the sole and express purpose of revising the Articles of Confederation and reporting to Congress and the several legislatures such alterations and provisions therein." Instead, he charged, they effectively set out to overthrow the Confederation and replace it with a national government.

> I have the greatest veneration for . . . those worthy characters who composed a part of the late federal convention . . . but, sir, give me leave to demand what right they had to say, *We, the People*? My political curiosity . . . leads me to ask who authorized them to speak the language of *We, the People* . . . The people gave them no power to use their name. That they exceeded their power is perfectly clear . . . The federal convention ought to have amended the old system—for this purpose they were solely delegated. The object of their mission extended to no other consideration.[31]

Henry questioned the motives of delegates at the Constitutional Convention: "I would demand the cause of their conduct . . . even from that illustrious man who saved us by his valor." His unmistakable reference to Washington drew gasps of outrage from Federalists.

I would demand . . . a faithful historical detail of the . . . reasons that ac-
tuated its members in proposing an entire alteration of government—and
to demonstrate the dangers that awaited us. . . . Disorders have arisen in
other parts of America, but here, Sir, no dangers, no insurrection or tumult has happened—everything has been calm and tranquil. . . . What
are the causes of this proposal to change our government?[32]

Henry's ally, Governor Edmund Randolph, then took the floor for
what Henry expected would be the coup de grace for ratification. Henry
and Mason gave Randolph a warm nod of approval, but the governor
fixed his eyes on the president, reminding him that, as a member of the
Constitutional Convention,

I refused to sign, and if the same were to return, again would I refuse . . .
but I never will assent to any scheme that will operate a dissolution of the
Union or any measure which may lead to it. . . . The Union is the anchor
of our political salvation, and I will assent to the lopping of this limb [he
raised his right arm] before I assent to the dissolution of the Union.

George Mason's face turned red with anger at Randolph's evident mockery of Mason's dramatic refusal to sign the Constitution in Philadelphia.

Randolph then looked at Henry: "I shall now follow the honorable
gentleman in his enquiry," he continued in mocking tones. "The honorable gentleman . . . inquires why we assumed the language of "We, the
People." I ask why not? The government is for the people. . . . Is it unfair?
Is it unjust? I take this to be one of the least and most trivial objections
that will be made to the Constitution. . . ." As Henry's eyes bulged red
with rage, Randolph shocked the convention by abruptly switching political allegiance: "In the whole of this business, I have acted in the strictest
obedience to my conscience, in discharging what I conceive to be my
duty to my country. I refused my signature . . . I would still refuse; but as
I think that those eight states which have adopted the Constitution will
not recede, I am a friend to the Union."[33]

Randolph's speech left the entire hall in stunned silence—Federalists as
well as Antifederalists. It left Henry and Mason irate—and Henry deeply

hurt. No one had ever mocked him before in private, let alone in public. To be mocked by a member of the Tidewater aristocracy was doubly painful. For years, Henry had believed that his service in the Assembly and as governor, along with his marriage to Dolly and his ties to her family, had bridged the social divide between the old Virginia aristocracy and backcountry folk like himself. With Randolph's sudden espousal of the Constitution, Henry now believed that Tidewater aristocrats intended to use the new national government to recapture powers they had held under the British monarchy in the House of Burgesses. In recalling Randolph's betrayal a few years later, Jefferson would characterize the governor as "the poorest chameleon I ever saw, having no color of his own and reflecting that nearest him."[34] As Henry seethed with anger, however, the lion in him bared his oratorical claws, ready to spring at his prey.

Chapter 14

A Bane of Sedition

Randolph's attack proved the beginning of a concerted Federalist plan to discredit Henry by mocking him with excessive praise: "I feel every power of my mind moved by the language of the honorable gentleman yesterday," declared General Henry ("Lighthorse Harry") Lee, a hero at the battle of Guilford Courthouse and a close friend and confidant of Washington.

> The éclat and brilliancy which have distinguished that gentleman, the honors with which he has often been dignified, and the brilliant talents which he has so often displayed have attracted my respect and attention. On so important an occasion . . . I expected a new display of his powers of oratory, but instead of proceeding to investigate the merits of the new plan of government, the worthy character informed us of the horrors which . . . made him tremblingly fearful of the fate of the commonwealth.[1]

Accusing Henry of failing to examine the Constitution objectively, Lee sneered, "The gentleman sat down as he began, leaving us to ruminate on the horrors which he opened with . . . but, sir, this system is to be examined on its own merit. . . . Mr. Chairman, was it proper to appeal to the fear of this house? . . . I trust he is come here to judge and not to alarm."

A night's sleep left Henry ready to repel the Federalists, however, and he sprang to his feet the next day to punish Randolph and Lee. He glanced up at the coagulum of adoring buckskins in the gallery and, like the young backcountry lawyer in nearby Saint John's Church two decades earlier, he felt the same rush of "unearthly fire." As then, "the tendons of his neck stood out white and rigid like whipcords."[2] As then, he began softly, this time with a snide grin: "I am much obliged to the very worthy gentleman for his encomium," he mocked Lee. "I wish I was possessed of talents, or possessed of any thing that might enable me to elucidate on this great subject. . . ." He paused to send an understanding wink to buckskins in the gallery. "I rose yesterday to ask a question," he explained. "I thought the meaning . . . was obvious. . . ." His voice rose:

> Here is a revolution as radical as that which separated us from Great Britain . . . if in this transition, our rights and privileges are endangered, and the sovereignty of the states be relinquished. And cannot we plainly see that this is actually the case? The rights of conscience, trial by jury, liberty of the press, all your immunities and franchises, all pretensions to human rights and privileges are rendered insecure, if not lost.

'Is this tame relinquishment of rights worthy of freeman?' he cried out.

'*No!*' came the cry from gallery buckskins. Presiding officer George Wythe gaveled the hall to order.

'Is the relinquishment of the trial by jury necessary and the liberty of the press necessary for your liberty?'

'*No!*' And again, the rap of Wythe's gavel.

'Will the abandonment of your most sacred rights tend to the security of your liberty?'

'*No!*'

'The new form of government . . . will oppress and ruin the people!'

The gallery erupted in angry noes until Wythe's gavel restored order.

'It is said eight states have adopted this plan. I declare that if twelve and one half had adopted it, I would with manly firmness . . . reject it!'

The gallery cheered.

'But I am fearful I have lived long enough to become an old-fashioned fellow. . . .' His voice softened, and he smiled at the gallery. 'If so, I am contented to be so. . . . Twenty-three years ago I was supposed a traitor to my country.'

'*No-o-o-o-o!*' the gallery protested.

'I was then said to be a bane of sedition, because I supported the rights of my country. . . . I say now our privileges and rights are in danger. . . .' He paused, then appealed to the gallery buckskins again. 'Is not the ancient trial by jury preserved in the Virginia Bill of Rights?'

'*Yes!*' they answered.

'And is that the case in the new plan?'

'*No!*' the gallery responded angrily.

'No, sir!' he echoed their response.

Why do we love this trial by jury? Because it prevents the hand of oppression from cutting yours off. They may call anything rebellion and deprive you of a fair trial by an impartial jury of your neighbors. . . . Shall Americans give up that which nothing could induce the English people to relinquish? The idea is abhorrent to my mind . . . It gives me comfort that as long as I have existence my neighbors will protect me. . . .[3] Guard with jealous attention the public liberty. Suspect every one who approaches that jewel. Unfortunately nothing will preserve it but downright force; whenever you give up that force you are inevitably ruined. . . . Something must be done to preserve your liberty and mine.[4]

Henry insisted that the existing Confederation of American States deserved "the highest encomium: It carried us through a long and dangerous war: It rendered us victorious in that bloody conflict with a powerful nation: It has secured us territory greater than any European monarch possesses.

"Consider what you are about to do before you part with this Government," he thundered.[5]

In arguing for perpetuation of the Confederation, Henry cited Switzerland as proof that we might be in amicable alliance with those states without adopting this Constitution. Switzerland is a confederacy . . . of dissimilar governments . . . that has stood upwards of four hundred years. . . . They have braved all the power of France and Germany . . . In this vicinity of powerful and ambitious monarchs, they have retained their independence, republican simplicity, and valor.[6]

With Federalists shifting uncomfortably in their seats, Henry went on and on, hour after hour, haranguing the delegates and spectators, turning from one delegate to another, staring one down, then another, then pointing to the heavens and opening his arms wide to appeal to the galleries—to the heavens—to God himself, as he had at Richmond's St. John's Church twenty-three years earlier.

"There was a perfect stillness throughout the House and in the galleries," Henry's cousin Judge Edmund Winston recalled. "One spectator in the gallery was so stirred by Henry's vivid description of federal enslavement that he involuntarily felt his wrists to assure himself that the fetters were not already pressing his flesh."[7]

"The Constitution is said to have beautiful features," Henry turned to Federalist chairman Wythe.

But when I come to examine these features, Sir, they appear to me horribly frightful. Among other deformities, it has an awful squinting; it squints towards monarchy. And does not this raise indignation in the breast of every American? Your President may easily become King. . . . Where are your checks in this government? . . . There will be no checks, no real balances in this government. It is on a supposition that your American governors shall be honest that all the good qualities of this government are founded; but its defective and imperfect construction puts it in their power to perpetrate the worst of mischiefs, should they be bad men.

Henry stopped suddenly.

A murmur spread through the hall as Henry's eyes focused on the crowd at the door, then bent over to whisper to the delegate seated beside him, "I see my son in the hall."

Henry had left his oldest son, William, at home as guardian of his wife and family and the plantation. Fearing some emergency had brought the young man to Richmond, he asked his colleague to find out. While Henry remained standing and pretended to search his notes so as not to lose the floor, his friend marched up the aisle, found William Henry, then trotted back to Henry's side—beaming: Dolly had given birth to another son, he whispered. Alexander Henry was her sixth—and Henry's twelfth. Henry broke into a grin, but, in the charged atmosphere of the convention hall, he decided against an announcement and simply contorted his face. The grinning Belgian hare turned back into an avenging American lion:

> Show me that age and country where the rights and liberties of the people were placed on the sole chance of their rulers being good men, without a consequent loss of liberty. . . . If your American chief be a man of ambition and abilities, how easy is it for him to render himself absolute! The army is in his hands . . . the president, in the field, at the head of his army, can pre- scribe the terms on which he shall reign master, so far that it will puzzle any American ever to get his neck from under the galling yoke. . . . and what have you to oppose this force? What will then become of you and your rights? My great objection to this government is that it does not leave us the means of defending our rights or of waging war against tyrants.

Edmund Pendleton had claimed that the Constitution provided ample means to prevent tyranny and abuses in government: "We will assemble in convention, recall our delegated powers, and punish those servants who have perverted powers . . . to their own emolument."[8]

Henry repeated Pendleton's claim, then stared at the old man for sev- eral moments, his head cocked to one side in evident disbelief.

"O, Sir," he replied. "We should have fine times indeed, if, to punish tyrants, it were only sufficient to assemble the people."

After the roars of laughter subsided, he asked the embarrassed Pendleton,

> Did you ever read of any revolution in any nation, brought about by the punishment of those in power, inflicted by those who had no power at all? . . . If Congress in the execution of their unbounded powers shall have

done wrong, how will you come at them to punish them, if they are at the distance of five hundred miles. At such a great distance they will evade responsibility altogether. . . . A standing army we shall have . . . to execute the execrable demands of tyranny, and how are you to punish them?[9]

Henry scoffed at Washington's claim that anarchy would ensue without the new Constitution. "I am not well versed in history," Henry argued, "but I will submit to your recollection whether liberty has been destroyed most often by the licentiousness of the people or by the tyranny of rulers? I imagine, sir, you will find the balance on the side of tyranny." Henry predicted that the Constitution would create "a great and mighty president with . . . the powers of a king" and give Congress the power of "unlimited . . . direct taxation" and powers "to counteract and suspend" state laws. Like the British government's Intolerable Acts, the proposed American government would have powers to send troops into any state to enforce federal laws. Those powers in the hands of Parliament, he reminded the convention, had provoked the Revolutionary War.

But, he added, the most insidious power given to Congress was the right under Article 1, Section 8, "to make all laws necessary for carrying their powers into execution."

"Will you be safe," he all but shouted, "when you trust men at Philadelphia with power to make any law that will enable them to carry their acts into execution? By this, they have a right to pass any law that may facilitate the execution of their acts." He warned that the "necessary and proper" clause gave Congress the right to hang men "who shall act contrary to their commands" and order the army "to aid the execution of their laws?"

"One of our first complaints under the former government," he reminded the convention,

was the quartering of troops upon us. This was the one of the principal reasons for dissolving the connection with Great Britain. Here we may have troops in time of peace. They may be billeted in any manner—to tyrannize, oppress, and crush us. We are told . . . to trust ourselves. That our own representatives, Congress, will not exercise their powers oppressively. That we will not enslave ourselves. . . . Who have enslaved France, Spain, Germany, Turkey, and other countries which groan under tyranny? They have been enslaved by the hands of their own people! . . . Is there any act, however atrocious, which Congress cannot do by virtue of this clause? Congress will become the supreme power.

A wonderful and unheard of experiment it will be, to give unlimited powers unnecessarily. . . . This is dishonorable and disgraceful. It will be as oppressive in practice as it is absurd in theory.[10]

Henry then demanded amendments to the Constitution securing to the states and the people every right which was not conceded to the general government.

I trust that gentlemen . . . will see the great objects of religion, liberty of the press, trial by jury, interdiction of cruel punishments, and every other sacred right secured before they agree to that paper. . . . You have a bill of rights to defend you against the state government . . . and yet you have none against Congress . . . If you intend to reserve your unalienable rights, you must have the most express stipulation. . . . It was expressly declared in our [Articles of] Confederation that every right was retained by the states . . . which was not given up to the government of the United States. But there is no such thing here. You therefore by a natural and unavoidable implication give up your rights to the general government. . . .[11]

Henry paused, then startled the hall with a roar:
"Why not give us our rights!
"In express terms!
"In language that could not admit of evasions or subterfuges?
"We are giving power," he boomed.
"They are getting power!"
Henry went on to condemn Federalists for rigging earlier convention elections. He insisted that the majority of Americans opposed the Constitution, but were "egregiously misled." Pennsylvania, he charged, has "perhaps" been tricked into it.

If the other States who have adopted it have not been tricked, still they were too much hurried into its adoption . . . a clear majority of the people are averse to it. . . . If you will . . . stipulate that there are rights which no man under heaven can take from you, you shall have me going along with you. Not otherwise. . . . I speak as one poor individual—but when I speak, I speak the language of thousands![12]

With that, the gallery erupted into whoops and cheers. Antifederalist delegates rose to their feet to join the mass acclaim. "And," Henry tried shouting over the crowd: "And, Sir . . . And, Sir." As the audience grew quiet, Henry smiled, "But Sir, I mean not to breathe the spirit nor utter the language of secession."

Again the gallery erupted, and after the chair restored order, Henry stood silent in a dramatic pose, looking down at his feet before whispering apologetically, "I have trespassed so long on your patience." Henry had held the floor for seven hours.

I have, I fear, fatigued the Committee, yet I have not said the one hundred thousandth part of what I have on my mind, and wish to impart. . . . Having lived so long—been so much honored—my efforts, though small, are due my country. . . . I trust you will indulge me. . . . Old as I am, it is probable that I may yet have the appellation of rebel. . . . As this government stands, I despise and abhor it.

After a long silence, Governor Randolph tried to regain the initiative, protesting Henry's refusal to yield the floor. "Mr. Chairman! If we go on in this irregular manner . . . instead of three or six weeks, it will take us six months to decide this question"—which, of course, was exactly what Henry had in mind. With the dinner hour long past, Randolph wanted to convince the convention of "the necessity of establishing a national government," but he conceded, "it is too late to enter into the subject now."[13] Henry had won the day.

Aware now of Henry's intention of dragging out the proceedings to a stalemate, Federalists returned the next day intent on seizing the floor to prevent another interminable Henry oration. One after another, they spoke, each attacking one of Henry's objections before yielding to his colleague. Governor Randolph dealt with Henry's objection to national government control over the military, asking, "Can Virginia send her navy . . . to bid defiance to foreign nations? . . . We must have a navy, sir . . . a navy will require money . . . how shall we raise it?."[14]

Randolph ceded the floor to Madison, "but he spoke so low that his exordium could not be heard distinctly," according to David Robertson, the reporter of the convention. His head all but invisible to most of the delegates, Madison stood barely taller than a dwarf, reading in short feeble bursts from notes inside his hat, which he held like a bucket of water into which he was about to dip his head for apples. His voice was that of cold, albeit dull, reason and logic, arguing simply that the Constitution did not grant the new national government any powers beyond those spelled out in the document.

"The powers of the federal government are enumerated," he explained. "It has . . . defined and limited objects, beyond which it cannot extend its jurisdiction." In reasoned, measured tones, he pointed out the contradiction between Henry's demands for American navigation rights on the Mississippi and his opposition to a standing federal army to obtain and ensure those rights.

"Congress ought to have the power to provide for the execution of the laws, suppress insurrections, and repel invasions," he said simply. "Without a general controlling power to call forth the strength of the Union, to repel invasions, the country might be overrun and conquered by foreign enemies." He then cited Washington's own argument that Article V gave opponents of the Constitution the right to amend it, and, in a stunning reversal of his previous position, he pledged to work to amend the Constitution with a bill of rights if he won election to the First Congress.[15]

After Madison had spoken, the Federalists decided to gamble by ceding the floor to the brilliant young attorney Francis Corbin, who had fled to London with his loyalist parents at the beginning of the Revolution. Corbin spent the war years studying at Cambridge University and reading law at London's Inner Temple. He then returned to America to reclaim his vast family properties, claiming he had been but a boy—unable to prevent his family's flight to England and too young to remain behind. His distinct

English accent, regal dress, and aristocratic airs—and his failure to fight in the war—clearly annoyed backcountry delegates, who listened impatiently as he demolished Henry's argument that the government of the Confederation had been adequate to meet the nation's needs.

"The honorable gentleman must be well acquainted with the debts due by the United States and how much is due to foreign nations," Corbin asked in the same mocking tones that Randolph and Lee had used. "Have not the payment of these been shamefully withheld? . . . No part of the principal is paid to those nations—nor has even the interest been paid as honorably and punctually as it ought. . . . What is to be done? Compel the delinquent states to pay requisitions to Congress? How are they to be compelled?"

Corbin's relentless delineation of the specific deficiencies of the government of the Confederation left Henry uncharacteristically speechless—so much so that he allowed Edmund Randolph to take the floor again—and then Madison—while he let the opposition display all its arguments as he tried to collect his thoughts. Randolph expanded his demonstration of Virginia's inability to survive as an independent state. Her inability to raise an army would leave citizens unprotected from internal seditions and external attacks, and her inability to raise a navy would leave her trade and coastline constantly open to attack.

> In case of a conflict between us and Maryland or Pennsylvania, they would be aided by the whole strength of all . . . the adopting states. . . . The other states have upwards of 330,000 men capable of bearing arms. . . . Our militia amounts to 50,000. . . . Till France joined us, our troops were not able to withstand the enemy. Yet the fate of many other nations ought to convince us that the assistance of foreigners is the most dangerous and the last experiment that ought to be recurred to.[16]

And before Henry could take a breath, Madison had taken the floor, asking,

> How have we dealt with our benevolent ally [France]? Have we complied with our most sacred obligations to that nation? Have we paid the interest punctually from year to year? Is not the interest accumulating, while not a

shilling is discharged? . . . The honorable member told us we might rely on the punctuality and friendship of the states and that they will discharge their quotas for the future. The contributions of the states have been found inadequate from the beginning and are diminishing instead of increasing.[17]

The relentless Federalist attack caught Henry unprepared. Isolated in the Piedmont for so many years, with only periodic trips to Richmond to deal with mostly local issues, he had not set foot out of state for more than thirteen years and was less aware than Madison of the national and international problems facing all thirteen states. Even as governor, he tended to ignore the lengthy reports from Virginia's delegates at the Confederation Congress, which was the only mechanism for dealing with collective state problems. Henry now realized that his failure to participate in the Constitutional Convention had cost him the opportunity to contribute to—or even contemplate—a solution. Still a backcountry man at heart, he believed that states could endure like farmers on self-sufficient properties in the Piedmont, independent of their neighbors and united with them for only a handful of collective actions such as barter, defense against intruders, and mutual aid after natural disasters. Still embracing the specious concept of "natural rights," he had no reasoned answers to Madison's or Randolph's or Corbin's arguments other than an emotional—albeit accurate—argument that ratification of the Constitution would strip states of their sovereignty and inevitably reduce individual liberties.

On June 9, a week after the convention had started, Henry "Light-Horse Harry" Lee continued the Federalist attack. Using Henry's opposition to a standing federal army, he questioned Henry's character and failure to fight in the Revolutionary War, then mocked Henry's "rage for democracy and zeal for the rights of the people. . . . He tells us that he is a staunch republican, and that he adores liberty," Lee said of Henry. "I believe him, and when I do so, I wonder that he should say . . . that militia alone ought to be depended upon for the defense of every free country. . . .

I have had a different experience of their service from the Honorable Gentleman. It was my fortune to be a soldier of my country. In the discharge of my duty . . . I saw what the Honorable Gentleman did not see: Our men fighting with the troops of the King. . . . I have seen incontrovertible evidence that militia cannot always be relied upon. . . . Let the Gentleman recollect the action of Guilford [North Carolina]. The American regular troops behaved there with the most gallant intrepidity. What did the militia do? The greatest numbers of them fled. . . . But says the Honorable Gentleman, we are in peace. Does he forget the insurrection in Massachusetts? . . . Had Shays been possessed of abilities . . . nothing was wanting to bring about a revolution.[18]

Henry ignored Lee's jab at his failure to fight in the Revolution, but when Randolph resumed the attack, he could no longer contain his bitterness at the governor's betrayal. Henry suspected that Washington had offered the governor an enticement for switching political camps and all but called Randolph a turncoat. "It seems to be very strange and unaccountable," Henry said of Randolph, "that that which was the object of his execration should now receive his encomium." Although he stopped short of suggesting bribery, Henry did not stop short enough. He went on to tell the convention that "something extraordinary must have operated so great a change in his opinions."[19]

Insulted by Henry's charges, Randolph retorted, "I find myself attacked, in the most illiberal manner by the Honorable Gentleman. I disdain his aspersions and his insinuations. His asperity is warranted by no principle of parliamentary decency, nor compatible with the least shadow of friendship, and if our friendship must fall, *Let it fall like Lucifer, never to rise again.*

Let him remember that it is not to answer him, but to satisfy this respectable audience that I now get up. He has accused me of inconsistency in this very respectable assembly. Sir, if I do not stand on the bottom of integrity and pure love for Virginia, as much as those who can be most clamorous, I wish to resign my existence. Consistency consists in actions, and not in empty specious words. . . . I understand not him who wishes to give a full scope to licentiousness and dissipation, who would advise me to reject the proposed plan and plunge us into anarchy.[20]

Randolph's reference to Lucifer's fall set all the delegates—indeed all of Richmond abuzz—with its meaning. Most interpreted the phrase as a challenge to a duel—an interpretation that left the forty-eight-year-old Henry visibly shaken by the prospects of facing the thirty-five-year-old governor with drawn pistols. At the first opportunity, Henry told the convention he had had "no intention of offending anyone"—that he "did not mean to wound the feelings of any Gentleman." He said he was "sorry if I offended the Honorable Gentleman without intending it." But Randolph grew only more enraged, saying that "were it not for the concession of the Gentleman, I would have made some men's hair stand on end by the disclosure of certain facts."[21]

Now it was Henry's turn to anger, telling Randolph that if he had something to say against him to disclose it. Randolph responded calmly, "I beg the Honorable Gentleman to pardon me for reminding him that his historical references and quotations are not accurate. If he errs so much with respect to his facts, as he has done in history, we cannot depend on his information or assertions."[22]

That evening, Henry and his second called on Randolph, and all Richmond jabbered about the prospects of a duel between the two great Virginia governors, with many tavern habitués suggesting small wagers. Although no record exists of their discussion, Henry did not press his challenge and left without provoking violence.

Talk of the duel, however, drew a clear line between Tidewater aristocrats and backcountry delegates—especially Kentuckians and other frontier buckskins—and Henry saw a chance to reply to Madison's attack on his opposition to a standing federal army. He turned the floor over to the young war hero James Monroe, who had served in the Continental Congress when it narrowly rejected John Jay's instructions to forfeit Mississippi River navigation rights to Spain. Monroe described how seven northeastern states had voted to further the interests of their own merchants and shipping companies by sacrificing the interests of the rest of the nation—especially those of westerners and southerners in states like Virginia, whose boundaries lay on the Mississippi River.

"We are told," Henry smiled, pointing at Madison,

that in order to secure the navigation of that river, it was necessary to give it up for twenty-five years to the Spaniards and that thereafter we should enjoy it forever . . . Is it imagined that Spain will . . . give it up to you again? Can credulity itself hope that the Spaniards wish to have it for that period, wish to clear the river for you? . . . America saw the time when she had the reputation of common sense at least. Do you suppose they will restore it to you?

If you do,[he wagged his finger at Madison], you depart from that rule. Common observation tells you that it must be the policy of Spain to get it first and then retain it forever.[23]

Madison had little choice but to concede the north's treachery, and Henry exploded with rage:

"No constitution under heaven, founded on the principles of justice, can warrant the relinquishment of the most sacred rights of the society to promote the interest of one part of it. . . . Are not the rivers and waters that wash the shores of the country appendages, inseparable from our right of sovereignty? . . . The people of Kentucky, though weak now, will not let the President and Senate take away this right."[24] It was Henry at his best again, and the gallery loved him for it. Madison's dry reasoning had been lost on them; it was Henry they had come to hear, and he used the advantage he had in the gallery to lash out at Madison's—and, indeed, George Washington's—recurring ripostes to opponents of the Constitution—that the document contained "a constitutional door . . . for amendment."[25]

"I am constrained to make a few remarks on the absurdity of . . . relying on the chance of getting it amended afterwards," Henry sneered.

When it is confessed to be replete with defects, is it not offering to insult your understandings to attempt to reason you out of the propriety of rejecting it till it be amended? Does it not insult your judgments to tell you—adopt first, and then amend? Is your rage for novelty so great that you are first to sign and seal, and then to retract? . . . You agree to bind yourselves hand and foot—for the sake of what? Of being unbound? You go into a dungeon—for what? To get out? Is there no danger when you go in that the bolts of federal authority shall shut you in?[26]

"Human nature," he roared, "never will part from power!" He noted that nothing in any law forbad the offering of amendments to other states before ratification. "Have we not a right to say, 'Hear our propositions,'" he asked. "If this moment goes away, we shall never see its return."[27]

Henry's evident rhetorical recovery—and Madison's own failure to foresee and head off the Jay-Gardoqui Treaty controversy—left Federalists discouraged. "Appearances are at present less favorable," Madison wrote to Washington.

> Our progress is slow and every advantage is taken of delay, to work on the local prejudices of particular sets of members. . . . There is reason to believe that the event may depend on the Kentucky members; who seem to lean more against than in favor of the Constitution. . . . The majority will certainly be very small on whatever side it may finally lie; and I dare not encourage much expectation that it will be on the favorable side.[28]

Madison discovered that the publisher of Philadelphia's Antifederalist *Independent Gazetteer* had arrived in Richmond "with letters for the antifederal leaders from New York and probably Philadelphia" and spent time "closeted" with Henry, Mason, and other Antifederalists. Although Madison had no knowledge of it, New York Governor Clinton was in the first stages of uniting New York and Virginia to thwart ratification of the Constitution by linking New York, Pennsylvania, and Virginia in a new "middle confederacy." Henry, meanwhile, had taken a more significant step with an approach to the French minister plenipotentiary to determine how France might react to a declaration of independence by Virginia.

In a letter to his foreign minister in Paris, the Comte de Moustier reported the plan by "Monsieur Patrick Henri . . . to detach his state from the confederation. If he carries the votes from North Carolina . . . he would be able to form a body strong enough to sustain itself against the efforts of the party opposed to his plan."[29]

On June 24, with only five days left for delegates to vote the Constitution up or down—or adjourn without a decision—Henry came to the hall elated by the support he had built with the Mississippi River issue. He was certain he could now crush Federalist chances for ratification over an explosive issue no one had yet dared address: the power of the new federal government to decree that "every black man must fight . . . that every black man who would go into the army should be free." As looks of horror spread across the hall, Henry stared directly at Madison and demanded to know, "May they not pronounce all slaves free?" Without giving the shaken little Federalist leader a chance to respond, Henry roared his own answer, in words that would echo across the South for the next seventy-five years to justify secession:

> They have the power in clear unequivocal terms and will clearly and certainly exercise it! As much as I deplore slavery, I see that prudence forbids abolition. I deny that the general government ought to set them free, because a decided majority of the States have not the ties of sympathy and fellow-feeling for those whose interests would be affected by their emancipation. The majority of Congress is in the North, and the slaves are to the South. In this situation, I see a great deal of the property of Virginia in jeopardy. . . . I repeat it again, that it would rejoice my very soul that everyone of my fellow beings was emancipated . . . but is it practicable by any human means to liberate them, without producing the most dreadful and ruinous consequences? We ought to possess them, in the manner we inherited them from our ancestors, as their manumission is incompatible with the felicity of our country. . . . This is a local matter and I can see no propriety in subjecting it to Congress.[30]

As shouts of anger spewed from the gallery, Madison stood to try to refute Henry, but Henry would not be silenced. After proposing a rapid-fire series of amendments, including a bill of rights, his voice rose to a crescendo as he called on God's wrath to punish the authors of the Constitution.

"He [Madison] tells you of important blessings, which he imagines will result to us and mankind in general from the adoption of this system," Henry thundered. "I see the awful immensity of the dangers with which it is pregnant.

"I see it!

"I feel it!"

*Patrick Henry as Governor of Virginia by
unknown artist.* (LIBRARY OF CONGRESS)

He spread wide his arms and quaking hands and looked to the heavens, playing the scene like the veteran actor he was. Outside the skies blackened suddenly and turned day into night.

> I see *beings* of a higher order—anxious concerning our decision. When I see beyond the horizon . . . those intelligent beings which inhabit the ethereal mansions, reviewing the political decisions and revolutions which in the progress of time will happen in America . . . Our own happiness alone is not affected by the event. All nations are interested in the determination. We have it in our power to secure the happiness of one half of the human race. Its adoption may involve the misery of the other hemispheres.[31]

Lightning struck the ground outside, then an explosion of thunder shook the entire hall. Henry closed his eyes and lifted his face to the heavens, as his ghostly words continued echoing through the chamber:

"I see it!

"I feel it!"

And the heavens responded with another bolt of lightning and jolt of thunder. Terrified delegates fell to their knees or raced to the door. "The spirits he had called seemed to come at his bidding," cried Federalist delegate Judge Archibald Stuart, "and, rising on the wings of the tempest, he seized upon the artillery of heaven, and directed its fiercest thunders against the heads of his adversaries. The scene became insupportable, and . . . without the formality of adjournment, the members rushed from their seats with precipitation and confusion."[32]

The lion of liberty had summoned the very heavens to set men free of government tyranny.

Chapter 15

Beef! Beef! Beef!

When the convention resumed the following morning, some spectators in the gallery returned convinced that Henry had summoned the "black arts" and called down lightning bolts on his antagonists. Black arts or not, he nonetheless failed to win enough votes to block ratification. James Madison had summoned a few black arts of his own by approaching moderate Antifederalists with a pledge to fight for passage of a bill of rights in the First Congress if they switched their votes in favor of ratification. He succeeded in organizing an eighty-nine to seventy-nine vote in favor of ratification, allowing Virginia to become what delegates believed was the decisive ninth state to ratify the Constitution.

Henry won just three of fourteen Kentucky votes, with eleven of the buckskins deciding that a federal army would give them greater protection against Indian attacks and a better chance to seize control of the Mississippi River from Spain. Most delegates agreed that Madison's pledge to champion a bill of rights was the decisive factor in the Federalist victory. Henry had no faith in Madison's pledge, but he learned about it too late to mitigate its effects. Before the convention adjourned, Madison urged Federalists to try to heal the wounds of discord by supporting Antifederalist proposals to recommend forty amendments to the Constitution, including a bill of rights, "to the consideration of the Congress which should first assemble under the Constitution."[1]

Although Washington never set foot in the convention hall, Federalists and Antifederalists agreed that he, rather than Henry, had dominated the exhausting drama. Indeed, Henry seemed at times to be debating Washington rather than Madison, Randolph and the other Federalists in the convention hall. Delegates sensed Washington's presence in every utterance, and, knowing he was the nation's all but unanimous choice for president, he exerted his political power behind the scenes by neutralizing two of Virginia's most influential political leaders: former governor Thomas Jefferson and the state's sitting governor Edmund Randolph. A year after the critical Virginia convention, Washington, by then the nation's chief executive, would confirm Henry's suspicions by appointing Jefferson the nation's first secretary of state and Randolph the first attorney general.

"Be assured," James Monroe declared, "General Washington's influence carried this government."[2] Antifederalist William Grayson concurred. "I think that, were it not for one great character in America," he growled in his closing argument, "so many men would not be for this Government. . . . We have one ray of hope. We do not fear while he lives, but we can only expect his *fame* to be immortal. We wish to know, who besides him can concentrate the confidence and affections of all America."[3]

After the vote, all eyes turned to Henry. Many feared he would rise from his seat and cry for vengeance as in 1775: "We must fight!" Some buckskins in the gallery were ready to cock their rifles. Seeing the looks of fear on the faces of some delegates, Henry acted to calm the situation and forestall civil disobedience, but he nonetheless vowed to continue his struggle for a bill of rights.

If I shall be in the minority, I shall have those painful sensations which arise from a conviction of being overpowered in a good cause. Yet I will be a peaceable citizen! My head, my hand, my heart shall be at liberty to retrieve the loss of liberty and remove the defects of that system—in a constitutional way. I wish not to go to violence, but will wait with hopes that the spirit which predominated in the revolution is not yet gone, nor the cause of those who are attached to the revolution yet lost. I shall therefore patiently wait in expectation of seeing that Government changed so as to be compatible with the safety, liberty and happiness of the people.[4]

By the time transcripts of his address reached the nation's newspapers, enough words and phrases, such as "in a constitutional way," had been smudged or omitted to produce a revolutionary manifesto—especially when paired with the statements of Henry's confederates. Mason, Monroe, and their "Federal Republicans" had been far less conciliatory than Henry after the ratification convention. They had stormed out of the hall, intent on continuing the fight, gathering at a nearby tavern, and sending for Henry to propose ways to reverse the convention result. Although Henry had suffered a humiliating defeat at the convention, Virginia's farmers and frontiersmen still looked to him to defend their rights.

After calming the angry gathering, he proposed various schemes for reversing the effects of ratification "in a constitutional way." First and foremost, he would try to prevent the remaining four states from ratifying. At the same time, he would call on state legislatures that had ratified to call a second constitutional convention to undo the work of the first convention and prevent a new government from taking office. If, however, the states rejected the idea of another convention and the new Constitution took effect, Antifederalists had other weapons at their disposal to undo the Constitution: They could use their popular majority to elect an Antifederalist majority to the new congress and, once installed, they could propose constitutional amendments to guarantee individual rights and states' rights and to dilute the powers of the new government.

When Madison learned of the meeting, he reported to Washington that "although Henry and Mason will give no countenance to popular violence, it is not to be inferred that they are reconciled to the event." He warned that Henry planned to work for the election of a Congress "that will commit suicide on their own authority."[5]

After Virginia's ratification convention, jubilant Federalists spent two days of raucous, self-congratulatory celebrations before learning that theirs had not been the decisive ninth state to ratify. New Hampshire had reconvened its convention and ratified four days before Virginia, on June 21.

With Virginia's ratification, however, New York's Antifederalist Governor George Clinton recognized the futility of continuing his own struggle. Although an independent and sovereign New York might have presented physical obstacles to overland trade between New England and the rest of the Union, traders could easily bypass New York harbor over a sea link between Philadelphia and Boston—via a canal then under consideration across the base of Cape Cod at Buzzard's Bay. On July 26, 1788, New York ratified and became the eleventh state in the Union.

In the end, Patrick Henry and his Antifederalists scored their only success in North Carolina, where an overwhelming majority of delegates at the ratification convention voted against ratification. Like Henry's own Piedmont area, North Carolina was almost entirely rural, sparsely populated by relatively poor, but fiercely independent, farmers and frontiersmen who resented government intrusions in their lives and had been unrepresented at the Constitutional Convention. Desperate to secure at least one political base, Henry's acolytes warned that wealthy big-city merchants and bankers were plotting to control the country. Willie Jones, the state's political boss, pleaded with the ratification convention to keep North Carolina out of the Union until it could negotiate more advantageous terms for joining. Jones read the letter from Thomas Jefferson, declaring, "Were I in America, I would advocate it warmly till nine should have adopted it and then as warmly take the other side to convince the other four that they ought not to come into it till the declaration of rights is annexed to it."[6] On August 2, North Carolina voted to defer ratification 184 to 84.

After a brief rest at his Prince Edward County plantation, Henry returned to the Virginia legislature on October 20, determined to oppose every measure to organize the new government without prior passage of a bill of rights. He then moved that the Virginia Assembly issue a formal request to the new Congress "to call a convention for proposing amendments . . . as soon as practicable."[7]

Of all people, young Corbin stood to oppose Henry's motion, arguing in aristocratically coated words, with gestures learned at Cambridge, that "the gentleman tells us that he bows to the majesty of the people."

With that, according to William Wirt, Corbin bowed deeply "in so exaggerated a way as to elicit laughs." Henry sat stone-faced, staring at Corbin in disbelief and rage.

"Yet," Corbin continued unperturbed,

> he has set himself in opposition to the people throughout the whole course of this transaction. The people approved of the Constitution; the suffrage of their constituents in the last convention proved it. The people wished, most anxiously wished, the adoption of the Constitution as the only means of saving the credit and honor of the country and producing the stability of the Union. The gentleman, on the contrary, had placed himself at the head of those who opposed its adoption—yet the gentleman is ever ready and willing at all times and on all occasions to bow to the majesty of the people.

According to Wirt, "He made another deep bow, sweeping one arm gracefully out to the side."

Corbin added a bit of arrogance to his irritatingly haughty English accent: "It is of little importance whether a country was ruled by a despot with a tiara on his head or by a demagogue in a red cloak and a caul-bare wig, although he should profess on all occasions to bow to the majesty of the people."[8]

And still another bow . . . thirteen in all—"graceful and deep as those before a magisterial throne," according to Wirt. Although Corbin finally took his seat "with the gayest of triumph," Henry was not amused. Indeed, Corbin's performance left Henry deeply hurt and delegates all but gasping. "The friends of Mr. Henry," his grandson commented, "considered such an attack on a man of his years and high character as . . . sacrilege."[9]

The old patriot rose slowly, "heavily . . . awkwardly," according to his grandson, who was familiar with his grandfather's huge repertoire of acting tricks. After a long silence, Henry spoke, contorting his face in apparent pain.

> Mr. Speaker, I am a plain man and have been educated altogether in Virginia. My whole life has been spent among . . . other plain men of similar

education, who have never had the advantage of that polish which a court alone can give and which the gentleman . . . has so happily acquired. Indeed, sir, the gentleman's employments and mine, in common with the great mass of his countrymen, have been as widely different as our fortunes. For while that gentleman was availing himself of the opportunity which a splendid fortune afforded him, of acquiring a foreign education, mixing among the great, attending levees and courts, basking in the beams of royal favor at St. James's, and exchanging curtsies with crown heads . . .

Now it was Henry's turn, and he made "one elegant, but most obsequious and sycophantic bow," according to Mecklenberg delegate William L. Tabb.

. . . I was engaged in the arduous toils of the revolution and was probably as far from thinking of acquiring those polite accomplishments which the gentleman has so successfully cultivated, as that gentleman then was from sharing in the toils and dangers in which his unpolished countrymen were engaged. I will not therefore presume to vie with the gentleman in those courtly accomplishments, of which he has just given the house so agreeable a specimen. Yet such a bow as I can make shall ever be at the service of the people.[10]

Henry then caricatured Corbin by making a bow "so ludicrously awkward and clownish" that the house exploded with laughter.

"The gentleman, I hope," Henry croaked in a voice he used to feign the helplessness of old age, "will commiserate the disadvantages of education under which I have labored and will be pleased to remember that I have never been a favorite with that monarch, whose gracious smile he has had the happiness to enjoy."

Another roar from the members who remembered George III's death sentence on Henry, among others. "I believe there was not a person," William Tabb recalled, "who did not feel every risible [laughter-inducing] nerve affected. His adversary meantime hung down his head, and sinking lower and lower until he was almost concealed behind the interposing forms."[11]

Henry's son-in-law Judge Spencer Roane confirmed that "it exceeded anything of the kind I ever heard. He spoke and acted his reply, and Corbin sank at least a foot in his seat."[12]

Having underestimated the reverence of friends and foes alike for Patrick Henry, Corbin could only watch in embarrassment as his crude—and cruel—assault produced the opposite of its intended effect. Virginia's House of Delegates—Federalists and Antifederalists—voted overwhelmingly to endorse Henry's proposals and send them to Congress. In acknowledging Virginia's ratification of the Constitution, the message of the House of Delegates to Congress asserted that

> the good people of this commonwealth . . . gave their most unequivocal proofs that they dreaded its operation under the present form. . . . The cause of amendments we consider as a common cause . . . We do therefore . . . make this application to Congress, that a convention be immediately called of deputies from the several states, with full power to take into their consideration the defects of this constitution.[13]

With that, Henry proposed a series of amendments that drew wild cheers from Antifederalists—among them the requirement that three-fourths of the members of *both* houses (instead of two-thirds of the senators) approve a treaty before it can take effect. He demanded that the passage of *any* federal law require a two-thirds majority instead of a simple majority—and that a similar two-thirds majority be required for Congress to raise a standing army in peacetime. Most significantly, however, was an amendment that would force Congress to requisition funds from each state before it could tax the people of that state directly. Henry would thus have denied Congress and the federal government the power of direct taxation unless a state government failed to meet its financial obligations to the federal government.

"We are told the sword and purse are necessary for the national defense," he said thoughtfully, then answered his own postulate. "The junction of these without limitations in the same hands is . . . the description of despotism. . . . It is easier to supply deficiencies of power than to take back excess of power. This no man can deny!"[14]

Rather than appear to endorse young Corbin's attack on Henry, Madison and other Federalists ceded the battleground over what were nothing more than suggestions to the First Congress—if indeed it decided to amend the Constitution. Madison then set about thwarting the second part of Henry's plan to undermine ratification by stacking Congress with Antifederalists pledged to amend or undo the Constitution. Madison declared himself a candidate for the first U.S. Senate. Henry was too savvy a politician, however, and enlisted two of the state's most beloved Antifederalists to run against Madison—Richard Henry Lee, a "father" of independence, and William Grayson, a prominent attorney and devoted Patrick Henry supporter, who had fought gallantly in the Revolution, served as a Washington aide-de-camp, and helped defeat the Jay-Gardoqui negotiations in the Confederation Congress. Comparing the patriotism of Lee and Grayson to Madison's failure even to lift a rifle in the Revolution, Henry's Antifederalists warned the House of Delegates that Madison was untrustworthy. Having betrayed his own Federalist friends, including Washington, by pledging to support a bill of rights, he would almost certainly betray Antifederalists in the Senate, where a six-year tenure would immunize him from retaliation by his constituents. A Madison victory, Henry warned, would ensure a Federalist victory, and a Federalist victory would ensure civil war and send "rivulets of blood" flowing across the country.

Henry's Antifederalists crushed Madison's bid and sent Richard Henry Lee and William Grayson to the first U.S. Senate with substantial pluralities. Antifederalists even gave Henry twenty-six unsolicited votes rather than seat Madison in the national capitol.

Pleased by Madison's defeat—and his own role in contributing to it—Henry was eager to go home to rest, embrace his wife, and romp with his children, but, as he wrote to his daughter Elizabeth Aylett, he realized that "I have not a moment to spare" to ensure Antifederalist control of the new Congress. Indeed, he did not even have time to see his own latest newborn.

I have a son . . . four months old. The dear little family were all well a few days ago, when your mama wrote me a letter and desired her love to Annie and you. We hope to have the pleasure to see you . . . I hope my dear child . . . that Providence may dispense its favors to you and yours is the prayer of, my dear Betsey,

Your affectionate Father,

P. Henry [15]

Henry wrote to congratulate his old friend and ally Richard Henry Lee on the latter's election to the Senate and told him he had cast aside all ambitions for public office under the new Constitution. "I mean not to take any part in deliberations held out of this state, unless in Carolina, from which I am not very distant and to whose politics I wish to be attentive." He told Lee that parts of Virginia, North Carolina and Kentucky might secede if the new Congress "do not give us substantial amendments" to the Constitution—and that he might then move to North Carolina. Although he did not say he would encourage secession, he conceded that he had invested in large tracts of land in the Carolina and Kentucky frontier areas contiguous to western Virginia and that he was in close contact with western leaders.

> I will turn my eyes to that country. I am indeed happy where I now live in the unanimity that prevails on this subject, for in near twenty adjoining counties, I think at least nineteen-twentieths are antifederal, and this great extent of country in Virginia lays adjoining to North Carolina and with her forms a great mass of opposition not easy to surmount. . . . I firmly believe the American union depends on the success of amendments. God grant I may never see the day when it shall be the duty of . . . Americans to seek shelter under any other government than that of the United States.[16]

Undeterred by his defeat in the Senate election, James Madison declared for the House of Representatives—only to have Henry direct the Assembly to redraw boundaries of Madison's congressional district to include counties with large enough Antifederalist majorities to offset the Federalist majority in Madison's home county.

"In plain English," Washington's private secretary Tobias Lear wrote from Mount Vernon to his friend the governor of New Hampshire, "he

[Henry] ruled a majority of the Assembly, and his edicts were registered by that body with less opposition than those the Grand Monarch has met from his parliaments. . . . And after he settled everything relative to the government . . . to his satisfaction, he mounted his horse and rode home, leaving the little business of the state to be done by anybody who chose to give themselves the trouble of attending to it."[17]

Madison countered Henry's political tactic by repeating his earlier pledge to champion a bill of rights in Congress. Hoping to woo moderate Antifederalists, the coauthor of *The Federalist* essays pledged to fight for religious freedom, a major issue among Virginia's Baptists and other dissenters. He stopped short, however, of espousing Henry's call for another constitutional convention and the structural amendments that Henry favored to change the form of government under the Constitution.

Before leaving Richmond for home, Henry made the political misjudgment of coaxing James Monroe to run against Madison for the House of Representatives. Monroe and Madison were not only close friends, they shared close political and personal ties to the same political mentor—Thomas Jefferson. Monroe expressed his reluctance to Henry, but Henry "pressed me to come forward in this government on its commencement . . . and that I might not lose an opportunity of . . . forwarding an amendment of its defects . . . I yielded."[18] The result of the Monroe-Madison matchup was a less than vigorous campaign, with Monroe refusing to attack Madison personally and even traveling with Madison on the campaign trail, sharing the same room at inns and private homes—and echoing his pledges to champion a bill of rights.

On February 2, 1789, Madison easily defeated Monroe and joined nine other Virginians—six other Federalists and three Antifederalists—as the largest delegation in the House. Irate Federalists called Madison a turncoat for pledging to work for passage of a bill of rights, and even some moderates thought him disingenuous. But Jefferson and Monroe called Madison's shift a courageous political gesture aimed at reconciling legitimate differences between Americans. By supporting the most important Antifederalist demands for a bill of rights, Madison extended a hand of compromise that separated moderates from Patrick Henry's radicals, who sought to emasculate the new national government. Madison was not unmindful that a strong central authority might infringe on individual liberties, but the years of the Continental Congress and Confederation Congress had persuaded him—as it had once persuaded Henry—of the need for a stronger national government to organize a collective military response by the states to attacks by foreign enemies.

In a separate election, Patrick Henry won a seat in the Electoral College and cast his vote for George Washington as president. Allowed to cast two votes, he cast his other vote for Antifederalist George Clinton as vice president. Washington won by a unanimous vote, while Federalist John Adams received the second largest vote total and defeated Clinton for the vice presidency.

With Washington's approval, Madison fulfilled his campaign pledge to champion Henry's bill of rights. After taking his seat in the House of Representatives, he moved for "Amendments . . . that may serve the double purpose of satisfying the minds of well-meaning opponents, and of providing additional guards in favor of liberty."[19] Madison failed to address the issue of states' rights, however, and Antifederalist Senator Grayson expressed his outrage to Henry:

> Some gentlemen here . . . have it in contemplation to effect amendments which shall affect personal liberty alone, leaving the great points of the judiciary, direct taxation, etc., to stand as they are. Their object is . . . unquestionably to break the spirit of the Antifederalist party . . . After this I presume many of the most sanguine expect to go on cooly in sapping the independence of the state legislatures.[20]

The seeds of civil war were taking root.

Four months later, Madison resolved that the Constitution be amended with "a declaration of the rights of the people" to ensure "the tranquility of the public mind, and the stability of the government."[21] Although members proposed seventy-five amendments, the House approved only seventeen, and the Senate reduced the number to twelve. The states ratified ten, which became known collectively as the Bill of Rights. After reading them,

Henry exploded with rage over the failure of the amendments to restrict national government powers over the states. "I wrote the first of those amendments in these words," he exploded in front of his sons. "'Each state in the Union *shall respectively retain* every power, jurisdiction and right which is not by this Constitution delegated to the Congress of the United States or to the departments of the Federal Government.' But they have omitted it . . . and changed it into this *equivocal* thing . . . 'or to the people.' My sons, this Constitution cannot last. It will not last a century. We can only get rid of it by a most violent and bloody struggle."[22]

The South would long remember his words.

Despite Henry's objections to the amendments, Americans of all political persuasions hailed him as father of the Bill of Rights and champion of individual liberties, although it was Madison who had proposed them in Congress and fought for their adoption.

The overwhelming Federalist victory in the congressional and presidential elections swept Federalists to power in most state legislatures, and, when the Virginia legislature reconvened in October 1789, the Federalist majority all but emasculated Henry as a major political force. "In the business of the lately proposed amendments," he wrote despondently to his old friend and political ally, Richard Henry Lee, "I see no ground to hope for good, but the contrary."[23] After a few weeks, he left for home—a certain indication that Dorothea would bear him another child nine months later.

Knowing nothing of the joys that awaited Henry at home, Edmund Randolph told Washington that "Mr. Henry has quitted rather in discontent that the present assembly is not so pleasant as the last."[24]

With Henry's departure, Antifederalists lost heart. Even in North Carolina, they realized that Henry's struggle to limit federal government powers had come to an end. On November 21, 1789, North Carolina ratified the Constitution and became the twelfth state to join the Union. Rhode Island followed suit the following spring. In March 1790, Henry's staunch ally Senator William Grayson died. Virginia's moderate Federalist governor, General Henry ("Lighthorse Harry") Lee, believed that appointing Henry to fill Grayson's seat would reconcile some of the political differences between Federalists and Antifederalists and the personal differences between America's two most revered patriots. Lee wrote to Washington, saying that Henry believed that "you consider him a factious and seditious character. . . . He seems to be deeply and sorely affected. It is very much to be regretted; for he is a man of positive virtue . . . and, were it not for his feelings above expressed, I verily believe he would be found among the most active supporters of your administration."[25]

Unaware, apparently, of the rumors of his enmity for Henry, Washington replied immediately, charging that "these reports are propagated with evil intentions to create personal differences. . . . With solemn truth . . . I can declare that I never expressed such sentiments of that gentleman . . . " Though born in the Tidewater region of Virginia, Washington had chopped his way through the wilderness as a surveyor and soldier and knew western thinking better than most. His differences with Henry were purely philosophical: Washington believed that only strict law enforcement by a strong federal government could protect individual liberties from the ravages of anarchy; he believed the patchwork of independent sovereign states that Henry favored would provoke incessant European-style wars. Their political differences, however, had never eroded their mutual respect—nor had either ever questioned the other's patriotism or love of country.

"On the question of the Constitution," Washington acknowledged to Lee, "Mr. Henry and myself, it is well known, have been of different opinions; but personally, I have always respected and esteemed him; nay, more, I have conceived myself under obligation to him for the friendly manner in which he transmitted to me some insidious writings that were sent to him in . . . 1777, with a view to embark him in the opposition that was forming against me."[26]

After showing Henry the Washington letter, Lee offered Henry Virginia's Senate seat. Deeply moved by the president's words, Henry waxed eloquent, saying he was "grateful . . . to know that some portion of regard remains for me amongst my countrymen; especially those . . . whose opinions I most value." Calling Washington's words "most flattering," he said the fear that he had "forfeited the good-will of that personage" had pained him, and the knowledge that "there was no ground to believe I had incurred his censure gives very great pleasure." Henry nonetheless declined

Lee's offer of a Senate seat, saying that "my present views are to spend my days in privacy."[27]

Henry went on to serve out his term in the legislature, but refused to stand for reelection in the fall of 1791 and would never again serve in public office. He had lost his battle against big government, and he knew it. He also needed to earn some money.

"I am obliged to be very industrious and to take on me great fatigue to clear myself of debt," he explained to daughter Betsey. "I hope to be able to accomplish this in a year or two if it pleases God to continue me in health and strength."[28]

Not surprisingly, with Henry at home full time, Dolly gave birth to her seventh and his thirteenth child—Nathaniel West, born on April 7, 1790. To his great distress, however, his sister Anne died, and Henry, in effect, adopted her son, his nephew, twelve-year-old John Henry Christian ("Johnny"), raising him as his own, sending him to Hampden-Sydney College at sixteen and then training him for the law. Other relatives took in Anne's six orphaned daughters. Johnny had no sooner entered the Henry household, however, when death claimed grandson Edward Fontaine, one of Martha's four children. Weeks later, Martha's husband, John Fontaine, succumbed to malaria. All but broken emotionally, Martha and her three surviving children came to live with the Henrys. By late summer of 1792, the Henrys were harboring fifteen children, along with his grown daughter Martha.

"What a weight of worldly concerns rest upon this old man's shoulders," his neighbor Richard Venable said in disbelief as he arrived at the Henrys' home for dinner. "He supports it with strength, but nature must sink under the load ere long."[29] Within weeks, Henry received another crushing blow: his twenty-one-year-old son Edward—never robust—had fallen ill. Although he made a partial recovery and went to stay with his aunt and uncle, he relapsed within a few months and died at the age of twenty-three.

At the time, Henry was doing his best to supervise his farms and rebuild his law practice—not an easy task for a man of fifty-six suffering the debilitating aftereffects of repeated bouts with malaria and intestinal infections. To reduce the amount of time away from home, he built an office on his property on "an avenue of fine black locusts—a walk in front of it . . . at some distance from his dwelling," according to one of his grandsons.

> He spent one hour every day in this office in private devotion. His hour of prayer was the close of the day including sunset. He usually walked and meditated, when the weather permitted, in this shaded avenue. He rose early in the mornings of the spring, summer, and fall, before sunrise, while the air was cool and calm, reflecting clearly and distinctly the sounds of the lowing herds and singing birds.[30]

After years away from home, his new office allowed him to spend more time treasuring his children, grandchildren and, of course, his wife. Although clients often came to see him at Pleasant Grove, his practice nonetheless required hours, and sometimes days, of travel in his bumpy gig, mile after mile, on unimproved roads across vast spaces of farmland and through dark forests, where brigands, runaway slaves, and renegade Indians often lurked to prey on passersby. His account books often showed little pecuniary return for his efforts—the ubiquitous "barrel of rum" from one client, £2.10 (about $100 today) from another, three shillings (£0.15, or about $15 today) from a third, and nothing from many others. His practice led him on a 200-mile circuit across five counties into the Blue Ridge Mountains and back, and, little by little, case by case, he restored his pre-Revolution reputation and climbed back to the pinnacle of his profession as America's finest defense attorney.

In rebuilding his practice, Henry naturally took on high-profile cases where possible, but he never disdained cases of lesser importance and almost always managed to turn them into causes célèbres that received regional, and sometimes national, attention—often for their humor as much as their legal significance. After a wagon driver ran over and killed a turkey, then drove away with the dead bird, the turkey's owner sued both driver and passenger. Rather than serve time in jail, the wagon driver submitted to a whipping, but the passenger refused, saying he was innocent.

"Gentleman of the jury," Henry pleaded on behalf of the turkey farmer, "this man tells you he had nothing to do with the turkey. I dare say he didn't . . .

" . . . until it was roasted!"

Judge Roane said Henry had pronounced the word *roasted* "with such rotundity of voice and comicalness of manner and gesture that it threw everyone into a fit of laughter. . . . I have likened this faculty of Mr. Henry of operating upon the feelings, whether tragic or comic, by the mere tone of his voice . . . "

> Yet he ranted not . . . He had a perfect command of a strong and musical voice, which he raised or lowered at pleasure and modulated so as to fall in with any given chord of the human heart. . . . Although his language was plain, and free from unusual or high-flown words, his ideas were remarkably bold, strong, and striking. By the joint effect of these two faculties . . . the power of his tone or voice and the grandness of his conceptions, he had a wonderful effect upon the feelings of his audience.[31]

In one of Henry's first cases after the Virginia ratification convention, John Hook, a wealthy Scottish storekeeper with Tory sympathies, sued a former Continental Army procurement officer for confiscating two of Hook's steers to feed the troops during the 1781 Cornwallis invasion of Virginia. After the plaintiff's lawyer had clearly proved his client's case, Henry stood and stared at the floor, motionless, in prayer-like silence. He turned to the jury and, according to Judge Archibald Stuart, "painted the distresses of the American army, exposed almost naked to the rigor of a winter's sky, marking the frozen ground over which they marched with the blood from their unshod feet."[32]

"Where was the man," Henry asked, "who had an American heart in his bosom who would not have thrown open his fields, his barns, his cellars, the doors of his house, the portals of his breast to have received with open arms, the meanest soldier in the little band of famished patriots? Where is the man?"

Henry turned to the defendant with an accusing finger and roared:

"There he stands!"

After a pause, Henry turned back to the jury: "But whether the heart of an American beats in his bosom, you, gentlemen, are to judge."[33]

Judge Stuart described the rest of Henry's presentation:

Henry then carried the jury, by the powers of his imagination, to the plains around Yorktown, the surrender of which had followed shortly after the act complained of. He depicted the surrender in the most noble and glowing colors of his eloquence. The audience saw before their eyes the humiliation and dejection of the British as they marched out of their trenches. They saw the triumph which lighted up every patriot face, and heard the shouts of victory and the cry of Washington and liberty, as it rang and echoed through the American ranks and reverberated from the hills and shores of the neighboring river.

"But hark!" Henry sang out. "What notes of discord are these which disturb the general joy and silence the acclamations of victory? They are the notes of *John Hook,* hoarsely bawling through the American camp: *'Beef! Beef! Beef!'*"

"The whole audience convulsed," according to Judge Stuart. "The clerk of the court, unable to command himself and unwilling to commit any breach of decorum . . . rushed out of the courthouse and threw himself on the grass, in the most violent paroxysm of laughter." Stuart said that Hook's lawyer was "not able to make an intelligible or audible remark." When the jury sought to decide the case by acclamation, the judge ordered them to retire "for form's sake," but they returned almost instantly with a verdict for the defendant. The court overruled the verdict and awarded Hook one penny in damages and another penny for court costs. As the crowd poured out of the courthouse, "Hook began to hear around him a cry more terrible than that of *beef.* It was the cry of *tar and feathers.*" All that saved the Scotsman was "a precipitate flight and the speed of his horse."[34]

Henry's most important case—a civil suit—came two years later and helped rebuild his fortune. In a precedent-setting "British Debts Case"— the first of many similar cases—he joined three other lawyers, including

Sketches of Patrick Henry at the British Debts Case of 1791. Drawn by the famed American architect and artist Benjamin Henry Latrobe (1764–1820) when Henry was 55, they are among the few sketches of Henry drawn from life—probably in the mid-1780s. (FROM A NINETEENTH-CENTURY PHOTOGRAPH).

future Chief Justice John Marshall, in defending a Virginian whom British creditors had sued for nonpayment of debts incurred before the Revolutionary War. Hundreds of British merchants were attempting to collect about £5 million in unpaid pre-Revolutionary War debts, *plus* £2 million in interest. Among the 30,000 debtors, half were Virginians—about 10 percent of the adult white male population. On the list of American debtors were President George Washington, who owed British merchants £3,999 plus £1,600 interest, Edmund Randolph, £210 plus interest, and Patrick Henry himself, who owed £972 plus interest. Although most American debtors had hoped the war would wipe out their debts to British creditors, the Treaty of Paris of 1783 that ended the Revolutionary War specifically required American subjects to repay all such debts, and it gave British merchants the right to sue in American courts.

"British debts have served to kindle a wide-spreading flame," Attorney General Edmund Randolph reported to President Washington. "The debts are associated with the antifederalists and the discontented federalists, and they range themselves under the standard of Mr. Henry, whose ascension had risen to immeasurable height."[35]

Complicating the issue, however, were two laws that Virginia (and a few other states) had passed during the Revolution. The first one had ordered Americans to deposit the moneys they owed British creditors into the state treasury. The second law—a ruse to subsidize state war efforts—allowed the state to seize all moneys in British accounts, including the funds that American debtors had deposited in the Virginia treasury. With the British Debts Cases, Virginia debtors faced having to pay their debts a second time if the court ruled in favor of the British plaintiffs—a financial burden few could afford after the deprivations of war. Because it involved foreigners and sums exceeding $100 (the cutoff value for hearings in district court), two U.S. Supreme Court justices riding the circuit and one district court judge agreed to hear the case in federal circuit court and rule on it.

"Next fall the great question will come on as to their right to recover from our citizens," one of his co-counsels wrote to Henry. "Your countrymen look up to you on that occasion."[36]

According to William Wirt, "The deep interest . . . from a national point of view and the manner in which it involved . . . the honor of the state of Virginia and the fortunes of its citizens had excited Mr. Henry to a degree of preparation which he had never made before." Indeed, his grandson Patrick Henry Fontaine, who was then studying law with his grandfather, said that Henry "shut himself up in his office for three days, during which he did not see his family. His food was handed to him by a servant through the office door." In the middle of the first day, he sent his grandson galloping sixty miles and back to fetch a copy of Swiss jurist Emmerich von Vattel's *Le Droit des gens* (translated as *The Law of Nations*). He went into court with "a manuscript volume more than an inch thick with closely written notes and heads of arguments. . . . He came forth a perfect master of every principle of law, national and municipal, which touched the subject . . . in the most distant point."[37]

With thousands of Americans—and many Britons—anxiously awaiting the outcome of the trial, Henry rode off to Richmond in late October, and lodged at the home of his co-counsel, John Marshall. "Together," argues one historian, "they would provide their client with the most formidable combination of legal talent ever assembled" in America. The two not only worked well together, they enjoyed each other and "became warm friends."[38]

On November 23, 1791, plaintiff's lawyers presented what seemed to be clear-cut, irrefutable arguments. When Henry went to begin his rebuttal two days later, he found the way into the capitol all but blocked. The legislature was in session, but when members learned that Henry was to appear, they poured out of their chamber, filling every courtroom seat "to hear this great man on this truly great . . . problem" and leaving an enormous throng of would-be spectators jamming the halls and doorways of the capitol.

"The portico and the area in which the statue of Washington stands were filled with a disappointed crowd," recalled William Wirt. "In the courtroom itself, the judges . . . relaxed the rigor of respect which they were in the habit of exacting, and permitted the vacant seats of the bench and even the windows behind it to be occupied by the impatient multitude. The noise and the tumult . . . were at length hushed, and the profound silence which reigned . . . gave notice to those without that the orator had risen."[39]

Rising slowly from his seat, his body wrapped in his customary drab, black clothes, he wore his practiced facial expression of a suffering martyr. One spectator commented, "You might readily have taken him for a common planter who cared very little about his personal appearance."[40]

Henry apologized to the court for his infirmities, then swayed a bit as if losing his balance, but caught himself: "I stand here, may it please your honors, to support, according to my power, that side of the question which respects the American debtor. I beg leave to beseech the patience of this honorable court; because the subject is very great and important."

He went on for three consecutive days, arguing that even if his client's failure to pay his alleged debts had inadvertently violated the Treaty of Paris, Britain had made such a violation moot by its own gross violations of the treaty—seizing American cargo ships, impressing American seamen, and failing to evacuate forts in American territory along the northern and western frontiers. With his voice growing in strength and intensity, he charged Britain with having plundered Americans of assets with far greater value than the debts that British merchants were trying to collect.

How would the British have treated Americans had they won the war, he asked, as spectators rose to shout at the plaintiff's lawyers. "In the wars of the revolution which have taken place in that island, life, fortune, goods, debts, and everything were confiscated. . . . Every possible punishment has been inflicted on suffering humanity that it could endure."

"Gracious God! He is an orator indeed," one of the Supreme Court justices recalled saying to himself. He had never heard Henry before.[41]

In contrast to many of his cases, Henry relied on more than oratory in his presentation. He quoted renowned legal authorities who claimed that creditors risked forfeiture of debts incurred in revolutions, and he cited revolutions in Britain in 1715 and 1745 to demonstrate that if the British government had defeated the Americans, "the most horrid forfeitures, confiscations, and attainders would have been pronounced against us." Indeed, had the British caught Henry, they would have hung him as a traitor, then drawn and quartered him.

"Would not our men have shared the fate of the people of Ireland?" he boomed.

"What confiscations and punishments were inflicted in Scotland? The plains of Culloden and the neighboring gibbets would show you.

I thank heaven that the spirit of liberty, under the protection of the Almighty, saved us from experiencing so hard a destiny. But had we been subdued, would not every right have been wrested from us? What right would have been saved? . . . Would it not be absurd for us to save their debts, while they should burn, hang, and destroy? . . . Had our subjugation been effected and we pleaded for pardon . . . would our petition have availed? . . . I would not wish to have lived to see the sad scenes we should have experienced. Needy avarice and savage cruelty would have had full scope. Hungry Germans, blood-thirsty Indians, and nations of another color would have been let loose upon us. Sir, if you had seen . . . the simple but tranquil felicity of helpless unoffending women and children, in little log huts on the frontiers . . . the objects of the most shocking barbarity . . . by British warfare and Indian butchery.[42]

Just before Christmas 1791, the court reserved decision and adjourned for the holidays, allowing Henry to return home to his wife and family after an absence of two months. On arrival, he shocked them all by announcing plans to move them all to a new home that Governor Henry "Light-Horse Harry" Lee, his wife's cousin, had sold him about forty miles to the west in Campbell County.

"He regarded as nothing the trouble of moving," brother-in-law Samuel Meredith remarked. "He would change his dwelling with as little concern as a common man would change a coat of which he was tired."[43] Indeed, by the time he died, Henry had lived in more than a dozen different homes in five counties—all of them within a radius of 200 miles in Virginia. His inexplicable propensity for moving, however, was curious for a man who despised traveling out of state and was so loathe to distance himself from his family that he refused to participate in what was the nation's most important gathering in history at the Constitutional Convention in Philadelphia.

Henry's new home was a 2,500-acre plantation overlooking Long Island—a picturesque island in the Staunton River. Long Island proved a profitable property, with 35 slaves producing about 17,500 pounds of tobacco a year, along with corn, wheat, oats, and rye. Livestock included 93 head of cattle, 48 sheep, 240 hogs, 14 horses, and 4 yoke of oxen.[44] Its quiet isolation inspired Henry to write poetry and "little sonnets he adapted to old Scotch songs," then played on his fiddle. The solitude he enjoyed, however, quickly drove Dolly and the lively—and unmarried—Henry girls to distraction.

The court did not issue a ruling on the British Debts Case until June 7, 1793, when it rejected Henry's argument that a breach of a treaty by either side automatically nullifies the entire treaty. Henry's other arguments, however, won as much of a victory for his client as he might have hoped for: The court awarded his client full credit for the amount he had paid into the Virginia state treasury and left him owing his British creditors only the difference between that amount and the original debt. Legal scholars in America and Britain—along with creditors and debtors—hailed the decision as just and equitable and a legal triumph for Henry that rescued some 30,000 American debtors from financial disaster. An Anglo-American commission appointed to determine the exact amounts Americans owed British merchants was unable to reach agreement on the sum owed. After a series of discussions in 1802, the U.S. government agreed to pay the British Government £600,000 to settle the issue—a mere 12 percent of the £4,930,000 owed to British creditors. In the end, individual American debtors escaped without paying an extra penny.

"As long as I live," Supreme Court Justice James Iredell commented, "I shall remember with pleasure and respect the arguments which I have heard in this case. They have discovered an ingenuity, a depth of investigation, and a power of reasoning fully equal to anything I have ever witnessed, and some of them have been adorned with a splendor of eloquence surpassing what I ever felt before."[45]

Clergyman Archibald Alexander of Princeton explained Henry's uncanny skills this way:

> The power of Henry's eloquence was due, first, to the greatness of his emotion and passion, accompanied with a versatility which enabled him to assume at once any emotion or passion which was suited to his ends. Not less indispensible . . . was a matchless perfection of the organs of expression, including the entire apparatus of voice, intonation, pause, gesture, attitude, and indescribable play of countenances.[46]

Another witness to the proceedings put it in simpler terms. "The spell of the magician was upon us."[47]

Chapter 16

The Sun Has Set in All Its Glory

Patrick Henry's legal triumphs restored his fame and yielded unprecedented wealth as he accumulated moneyed clients from across the state. Some paid him in choice acreage and afforded him opportunities to acquire vast tracts of rich farmland. By the mid-1790s, he ranked with George Washington and the Lees as one of Virginia's greatest landowners, with direct ownership in more than 100,000 acres and indirect ownership of 15 million more. Among his properties under cultivation, he could count three productive plantations with nearly 25,000 acres in Virginia, 10,000 acres that he leased out in Kentucky, and 23,000 acres in western North Carolina. He also received rents from farms and plantations that he owned in twelve counties, stretching from Chesapeake Bay to the Blue Ridge Mountains. He owned at least 100 slaves, close to 300 cattle producing milk and meat, flocks of sheep for wool, hogs for more meat, and horses to work the fields, pull wagons, or ride to hunt.

"I believe . . . he was better pleased to be flattered as to his wealth than as to his great talents," Spencer Roane recalled. "He seemed proud of the goodness of his lands and, I believe, wished to be thought wealthy. I have thought indeed that he was too much attached to property. This I have accounted for by reflecting that he had long been under narrow and difficult circumstances from which he was at length happily relieved."[1]

In addition to his lands under cultivation, Henry was a successful speculator, buying thousands of acres in the western and northwestern parts of Virginia, North Carolina, Kentucky, and other parts of the frontier, then reselling them in small parcels to would-be settlers. With ratification of the Constitution, however, the character of some of his land speculations began to change. As he warned Richard Henry Lee, ratification had provoked North Carolina and large sections of the west to entertain secession. Although he now opposed all talk of secession, he nonetheless hedged against the possibility by snapping up lands in secession-prone areas—at the bend of the Tennessee River in northern Georgia, just south of the North Carolina line, for example, and, much later, 6,000 acres in North Carolina proper. Henry also joined other investors in forming the Virginia Yazoo Land Company, one of three Yazoo Land Companies in South Carolina, Tennessee, and Virginia, to which the governor sold an astonishing 35 million acres in the western Yazoo River area of Georgia for an even more astonishing price of $500,000, or one and a half cents an acre. Yazoo Company lands stretched across almost all of present-day Alabama and Mississippi to the Mississippi River where the city of Memphis now stands—and where Henry's partners hoped to secede from the United States and found a new and independent sovereign state.[2] Henry and his partners actually cut a better deal than investors in the other Yazoo companies.

"I congratulate you on the purchase you have made in Georgia," wrote Theodore Bland, one of Virginia's Antifederalists in the House of Representatives. "I hope [it] will turn out to your most sanguine expectations and be not only a provision for your family, but an asylum from tyranny whenever it may arise or become oppressive to that freedom which I know you so highly prize, and for which you have been so long a firm and unshaken advocate."[3] The seeds of secession and civil war were now firmly rooted in much of the South.

From the first, however, Henry's investments in North Carolina and Georgia turned against him. As it turned out, members of the Georgia legislature sought out their own investors and secretly sold them nearly 9 million acres of the same lands the governor had sold to Henry and the Yazoo Land Companies. As the scandal unfolded and threatened to provoke bloodshed, President Washington stepped into the picture and proclaimed that all the Yazoo Land Company lands belonged to the Creek Indians under an earlier treaty, and, in 1791, he signed a new treaty reconfirming their title to almost all Yazoo lands, including the lands Henry had purchased. Henry was furious, but helpless.

"I need not . . . point out to you the danger consequent to all landed property in the Union from an acquiescence in such assumption of power," he raged at Georgia's governor. Citing his preratification prophecy that the Constitution gave Congress tyrannical powers, he warned that "if Congress may of right forbid purchases from the Indians of territory included in the charter limits of your state . . . it is not easy to prove that any individual citizen has an indefeasible right to any land claimed under a state patent."[4]

In the months that followed, southern newspapers charged that the Virginia Yazoo Companies had bribed Georgia's governor and many of its legislators to acquire their lands. Georgia voters responded by ousting the governor and most of the legislature. A new, reform-minded legislature repudiated the Yazoo deal and burned all records relating to it in hopes of destroying evidence that could be used in subsequent legal proceedings by Yazoo shareholders to recoup their holdings. Henry lost his entire investment.[5]

The loss of his Yazoo Land Company holdings climaxed a year of financial reverses for Henry and many other southern investors at the hands of the new Federal Government—reverses that Henry had predicted in his angry outbursts at the Virginia ratification convention two years earlier. The first and costliest came in January 1790, when Federalist Treasury Secretary Alexander Hamilton reported that federal government debts had ballooned to almost $60 million—$44 million in domestic debts and $12 million foreign. With no specie to pay the debts, market values of outstanding government debt certificates plunged so low that the government could no longer borrow to meet current expenses. To restore government credit, Hamilton asked Congress to recall all outstanding debt certificates at par—at their face value—and pay for them with a combination of new government bonds and certificates of title to government wilderness lands in the West. The government would, in other words, back the new bonds with "real" estate of unquestioned value.

Hamilton's plan provoked outrage across the nation. Throughout the Revolutionary War and Confederation years, the government had paid soldiers, merchants, farmers, craftsmen, and other citizens with government certificates, which they, in turn, had to resell to bankers and speculators for whatever they could get—never more than 75 percent of face value and sometimes less than 15 percent.

Hamilton's proposal to recall certificates at face value promised untold riches for the bankers and speculators who had exploited American veterans when they were struggling to survive. Adding to the outrage was a second Hamilton scheme for the federal government to assume $25 million in state war debts—and pay those debts with proceeds from a federal tax on whiskey—the most popular beverage in America. Americans consumed whiskey for both pleasure and medicinal purposes, and, in a barter society, they used various sized jugs to buy staples and other dry goods at market. In the West, the tax threatened every farmer's earnings. With no wagon roads across the rugged Appalachians, farmers could only market their grain by converting it to whiskey, which they could carry in jugs by mule or packhorse along the narrow mountain trails. A whiskey tax was as abhorrent to Americans in 1790 as Britain's tea tax had been to Bostonians in 1773, when they staged the Boston Tea Party.

Southern states were irate—especially Virginia, which had already repaid most of its own war debts and felt no obligation to help repay debts accumulated by profligate states such as Massachusetts. Even Federalists, including Virginia Governor Henry Lee, reviled Hamilton and the northern Federalists. Recalling Patrick Henry's words at the Virginia ratification convention, Lee raged at Madison, who was still a member of the House, that disunion would be preferable to domination and economic exploitation by "an insolent northern majority.

"Henry is considered a prophet," Lee growled. "His predictions are daily verified. His declarations with respect to the divisions of interests which would exist under the Constitution and predominate on all the doings of government already have been undeniably proved. But we are committed and we cannot be relieved, I fear, only by disunion."[6]

Despite higher taxes and losses from his Yazoo Land Company investment, Patrick Henry's profits from other land speculations, from his lands under cultivation, and from his law practice left him with abundant wealth in his last years. Nor did the Yazoo scandal diminish the adulation of his countrymen, for whom he remained a legendary patriot whom they flocked to see and hear whenever he tried a case. More often than not, he gave them a show to remember—as in the case of a young man on trial for abduction of a minor after eloping with his underaged girlfriend. The young man had had the foresight to consult Henry before the "kidnapping." Henry told him to ask the young lady to ride to their rendezvous on her father's horse and let her husband-to-be mount behind her for the ride to the marriage ceremony. When the case came to trial, Henry put her on the witness stand and asked whether her husband had abducted her. She answered truthfully: "No, sir. I ran away with him." After the roars of laughter died down, the judge dismissed the case.

In 1794, the isolation of Long Island proved "so much as to disgust" Dolly that Henry bought another estate about twenty miles to the east—still on the Staunton River, but just across the Campbell County line in Charlotte County, where the Henrys could lead a richer social life. Named Red Hill for the color of its soil, their new home—his twelfth over the course of his life—had four rooms, with magnificent views of the valley. Before they moved, Dorothea gave birth to their eighth surviving child and fourth son, whom they named Edward, after Henry's late son "Neddy."

Only fifty-eight, but ailing, Henry finally retired from the law to live at home full time and "see after my little flock and the management of my plantations." Despite the move to Red Hill, he kept the profitable Long Island plantation and, indeed, moved the family back to its healthier climate each year during the "sickly season" when mosquitoes swarmed across most of the bottom land at Red Hill. Red Hill nonetheless proved to be his most profitable property, with nearly 3,000 acres, on which 69 slaves produced more than 20,000 pounds of tobacco annually and tended nearly 130 head of cattle, 186 hogs, 38 sheep, 5 yoke of oxen, and 19 horses.[7] Near the kitchen garden stood an apple and a peach orchard, along with fig trees. Like his Long Island farm, Red Hill was on the Staunton River, where flat-bottomed "bateaux" could carry his tobacco and grains to market. As he had done at his previous homes, he built a separate, freestanding law office from which he not only practiced law but trained his son, Patrick Jr., his

Patrick Henry's home at "Red Hill," near Brookneal, in Charlotte County, Virginia, where he spent his retirement years and died on June 6, 1799. He is buried on the property alongside his second wife, Dorothea. (FROM A NINETEENTH-CENTURY PRINT)

two nephews Johnny Christian and Nathaniel West Dandridge II, and his grandson Patrick Henry Fontaine for the law.

As Henry had predicted at the Virginia ratification convention, Federalist Treasury Secretary Alexander Hamilton lured the Federalist-dominated Congress into using its unrestricted powers under the "necessary and proper" clause of the Constitution to expand the scope of the whiskey tax to include stills. The tax proved a disproportionately heavy burden on farmers west of the Appalachian Mountains after the Spanish closure of the Mississippi River to American navigation left them unable to ship their grain to market in New Orleans. Farmers could only market their grain by converting it to whiskey. The tax on stills, therefore, threatened every western farmer's earnings.

For the first two years of the tax, Hamilton's collectors resisted making the arduous trip across the Appalachians, where farmers greeted them with tar and feathers and other forms of brutalization. As armed federal agents appeared to protect tax collectors, farmers responded violently and, on August 1, 1794, they declared "a state of revolution,"[8] gathering by the thousands outside Pittsburgh and threatening to burn the city and march to Philadelphia to overthrow the federal government. A week later, President Washington issued a proclamation ordering rebels to return to their homes or face arrest. His words echoed those of British governors to stamp tax protestors thirty-five years earlier and further raised Henry's status as a prophet. Dismissing comparisons to the British, Washington ordered 13,000 state militiamen drafted into a federal force to march against the rebels. It was Patrick Henry's worst nightmare come true. As he had predicted at the Virginia ratification convention, the Constitution had replaced the tyranny of Parliament and the British king with the tyranny of Congress and the American president. Congress had indeed taxed the people without the consent of their state legislatures—as Parliament had done—and the president was sending troops to enforce tax collections—as King George III had done.

As Washington's troops neared Pittsburgh, however, the rebels vanished, realizing that rifles and pitchforks were no match for army field artillery. Although federal troops captured twenty laggard "Whiskey Boys," as they were called, all the others had either returned to their homes or fled into the wilderness. The troops carted their prisoners back to Philadelphia expecting cheers as they paraded them down Market Street, but the thousands who watched stood in silence—mourning the powers they had ceded to the federal government by ignoring Patrick Henry's warnings against granting unrestricted powers "over the sword and the purse" to a national government. Although the courts convicted only two of the Whiskey Boys—and Washington pardoned them both—the president became the target of ferocious criticism for suppressing the very type of citizen protest he had led before the Revolutionary War. Although Washington shrugged off the comparisons, his aura of infallibility evanesced in a ceaseless rain of press criticism that left the old warrior bitter about having remained in office as long as he had. "I can religiously aver," Washington complained, "that no man was ever more tired of public life or more devoutly wished for retirement than I do."[9]

Although furious at Washington's response to the Whiskey Rebellion, Henry no longer wielded the regional or national political power of his days in the Virginia capital. In any case, there was little he or anyone else could do. Richard Henry Lee and George Mason had both died in 1792, and most of the other Antifederalist leaders had drifted off the national political scene—as, indeed, he had done. "It is time for me to retire," he admitted to his daughter Betsey. "I shall never more appear in a public character . . . My wish is to pass the rest of my days as much as may be unobserved by the critics of the world, who show but little sympathy for the deficiencies to which old age is so liable. May God bless you, my dear Betsey, and your children."[10]

The sun that had set on Henry's political life, however, did not cease to shine over his home life. Still the "Belgian hare," prolific Patrick fathered yet another son. In 1795, Dorothea gave birth to John, her ninth surviving child and Patrick's fifteenth. Patrick's son John, by his first marriage, had died four years earlier.

To try to calm the furor associated with the Whiskey Rebellion, Washington asked Virginia Governor Lee to renew his offer of a Senate seat to Henry. Senator Grayson's old seat, which Antifederalist James Monroe had filled, was vacant again after Washington appointed Monroe minister to Paris. Attorney General Edmund Randolph, the former Virginia governor, told Washington he believed that Henry had embraced the Constitution and the concept of a strong national government. "He grows rich every hour," Randolph explained, "and thus his motives to tranquility must be multiplying every day."[11]

Henry quickly disavowed Randolph's assertions. "The reports you have heard of my changing sides in politics," he told his daughter Betsey, "are not true. I am too old to exchange my former opinions, which have grown up into fixed habits of thinking." Calling Federalist policies "quite void of wisdom and foresight," he accused them of twisting his most casual words "to answer party views. Who can have been so meanly employed, I know not—nor do I care; for I no longer consider myself as an actor on the stage of public life."[12]

Henry again declined Lee's offer of a Senate seat in a simple note that avoided political controversy: "It gives me great pain to declare that existing circumstances compel me to decline this appointment . . . arising from my time of life—combined with the great distance to Philadelphia."[13]

Randolph and other Federalist leaders, however, remained convinced that the wily old Antifederalist simply wanted a higher-profile post than the Senate, where he would have to compete with and continually compromise his beliefs with more than two dozen other senators. Washington countered Henry's refusal to enter the Senate with the offer of a mission as "envoy extraordinary" to Spain to wrest a treaty guaranteeing American navigation rights on the Mississippi—an almost sacred quest for Henry and his constituents in the West. Success might have propelled him to the presidency or, certainly, the vice presidency. But again, Henry confounded the political world by declining. "The importance of the negotiation and its probable length in a country so distant," he explained, "are difficulties not easy to reconcile to one at my time of life."[14]

When in 1795, Edmund Randolph resigned as secretary of state after being accused of soliciting a bribe from the French government, Henry's earlier rejections of federal appointments convinced Washington to turn to other candidates to replace Randolph. But after they refused the post, he again approached Henry, warning that "a crisis is approaching that must . . . soon decide whether order and good government shall be preserved, or anarchy and confusion ensue. . . .

My ardent desire is . . . to keep the United States free from political connections with every other country, to see them independent of all and under the influence of none. In a word, I want an *American* character, that the powers of Europe may be convinced we act for *ourselves*, and not for others. . . . I am satisfied these sentiments cannot be otherwise than congenial to your own. Your aid therefore in carrying them into effect would be flattering and pleasing to, dear Sir,

Go. Washington[15]

Henry again declined, acknowledging that

to disobey the call of my country into service when her venerable chief makes the demand of it must be a crime unless the most substantial reasons justify declining it . . .

My domestic situation pleads strongly against a removal to Philadelphia, having no less than eight children by my present marriage, and Mrs. Henry's situation [she was pregnant again!] now forbidding her approach to the small pox, which neither herself nor any of our family have ever had. To this may be added other considerations arising from loss of crops and consequent derangement of my finances—and what is of decisive weight with me, my own health and strength I believe are unequal to the duties of the station you are pleased to offer me.

Aware of the political suspicions that most Federalists harbored toward him, Henry pledged Washington his full support: "Believe me, Sir, I have bid adieu to the distinctions of federal and antifederal ever since the commencement of the present government, and . . . have often expressed my fears of disunion amongst the states from collision of interests, but especially from the baneful effects of faction. . . . If my country is destined to encounter the horrors of anarchy, every power of mind or body which I possess will be exerted in support of the government."[16]

Convinced of Henry's loyalty to the new government, Washington offered to appoint him Chief Justice of the United States in 1795, but by then Henry's health was indeed failing. The long-term effects of his many bouts with malarial fever and intestinal infections had taken their toll; he had lost interest in political affairs and, when he wasn't doting over his children, he read the Bible incessantly—at dawn and again by candlelight in the evening. "This book is worth all the books that ever were printed," he concluded, "and it has been my misfortune that I have never found time to read it with the proper attention and feeling till lately. I trust in the mercy of heaven that it is not yet too late."[17]

Henry hired a tutor for his children and, when they weren't at their studies, he spent as much time with them as possible to compensate for the time he had lost while traveling the legal circuits. As with his new-found attention to the Bible, he put his trust "in the mercy of heaven that it was not yet too late" to show his family how much he loved them. According to his brother-in-law Samuel Meredith, "His visitors have not unfrequently caught him lying on the floor with a group of these little ones climbing over him in every direction, or dancing around him with obstreperous mirth to the tune of his violin, while the only contest seemed to be who could make the most noise." In retirement, Henry again grew "fond of entertaining himself and his family with his violin and flute and often improvising the music."[18]

The Federalists, though, refused to believe that so political an animal as Patrick Henry would reject an offer of political power. "Most assiduous court is paid to Patrick Henry," Thomas Jefferson growled to James Monroe. "If they thought they could count on him, they would run him for their vice president."[19]

In fact, Henry's successful defense of so many American debtors in the British Debts Case had restored his status as the most popular figure in the nation after George Washington. Like no one else among the Founding Fathers, he consistently defended the interests of the ordinary citizen. Federalist leader Alexander Hamilton had harbored ambitions to succeed Washington to the presidency, but he knew that the taxes he had imposed as secretary of the treasury had left him too unpopular to do so. Rather than see his party fall from power, he decided to offer the nomination of his party to Patrick Henry, whom he believed to be a convert to federalism. Hamilton knew that Henry would automatically win the support of the Antifederalist South and West, while Hamilton and other Federalist leaders would rally support for Henry in the largely Federalist Northeast.

At Hamilton's behest, Massachusetts Federalist Rufus King wrote to John Marshall, who went to see Henry with Governor Henry Lee, but found him "unwilling to embark in the business. His unwillingness I think proceeds from an apprehension of the difficulties to be encountered by those who shall fill high executive offices."[20] Henry explained to his daughter Elizabeth that he had watched "with concern our old Commander in Chief [Washington] abusively treated. If he whose character as our leader during the whole war was above all praise is so roughly handled in his old age, what may be expected by men of the common standard of character?"[21]

Despite his refusal to run, a groundswell of popular support for his candidacy developed across the nation among moderate Antifederalists, Federalists, and independents who shunned radical politics. "A strong reason for the appointment of Mr. Henry is that it may have a tendency to unite all parties," wrote Virginia's Leven Powell, who was campaigning to be a presidential elector. He predicted that Henry's election would "do away with the spirit of contention which . . . threatens the destruction of the Union."[22]

Elated by the prospects of Henry's elevation to the presidency, the Virginia legislature elected him to a sixth term as governor in November—without his knowledge. Henry decided the efforts to draw him back into public office had gone too far. After rejecting the governorship, he wrote to the *Virginia Gazette and General Advertiser*:

> I am informed that some citizens wish to vote for me . . . to be president of the United States. I give them thanks for their goodwill and favorable opinion of me. I think it is incumbent upon me thus publicly to declare my fixed intention to decline accepting that office if it would be offered to me, because of my inability to discharge the duties of it in a proper manner. . . .
>
> I am consoled for the regret I feel on account of my own insufficiency by a conviction that within the United States a large number of citizens may be found, whose talents and exemplary virtues deserve public confidence, much more than anything I can boast of.
>
> That wisdom and virtue may mark the choice about to be made of a president is the earnest desire of your fellow citizen and well wisher,
>
> Patrick Henry[23]

In the ensuing election, Henry finished fourth in the electoral balloting, with Adams elected president and Thomas Jefferson vice president. South Carolina Federalist Thomas Pinckney, a Revolutionary War hero and successful diplomat in the Washington administration, finished third.

In 1798, increased threats of war with France and other European powers provoked a "spy scare" and consequent passage by President John Adams's Federalist majority in Congress of the Alien and Sedition Acts, effectively stripping Americans of their First Amendment rights to free speech and freedom of the press. The Alien Enemies Act gave the president powers "to arrest, imprison, or banish alien subjects of an enemy power" in time of war, while the Sedition Act made it illegal for citizens or aliens to incite "insurrection, riot, unlawful assembly, or combination" or prevent a federal officer from enforcing federal laws. It also made it illegal to publish "any false, scandalous and malicious writing" about the U.S. government, Congress, or the president. The acts outraged Antifederalists, who called them unconstitutional. Vice president Jefferson went a step farther, setting the stage for a confrontation with the federal government over state sovereignty. Jefferson declared the Constitution only "a compact" among sovereign states in which the states retained the authority to restrain federal government actions that exceeded its constitutional mandate. Jefferson rode to the new state of Kentucky and convinced the Antifederalist majority of former Virginians in the legislature to approve a resolution that any federal government exercise of powers not specifically delegated to it by the Constitution was, by definition, unconstitutional and, therefore, subject to nullification by state government.

Meanwhile, James Madison, a staunch Jeffersonian republican, won a similar resolution in the Virginia legislature, which added a clause asserting a state's right "to interpose" its authority to prevent "the exercise of . . . powers" by the federal government not granted by the Constitution.[24] Federalist legislatures in other states, however, declared the Virginia and Kentucky Resolutions "mad and rebellious" and rejected them with declarations that U.S. courts were the sole judges of constitutionality.

Early in 1799, Virginia's legislature issued orders for the construction of an armory in Richmond and for its militia to take up arms to resist any federal government attempts to enforce the Alien and Sedition Laws.[25] As

Richmond lawmakers talked of secession, George Washington stepped out of retirement to recruit Federalists to run for Congress and the Richmond Assembly. In addition to the staunch Federalist John Marshall, he wrote to Patrick Henry, reminding him of his recent pledge to exert "every power of mind or body which I possess . . . in support of the government."[26] Recognizing Henry's reluctance to distance himself from his home and family, he pleaded with him to stand for the state legislature, asserting his "fears that the tranquility of the Union . . . is hastening to an awful crisis." He warned Henry of the "endeavors of a certain party . . . to set the people at variance with their government. . . . Your weight of character and influence would be a bulwark against such dangerous sentiments . . . I conceive it to be of immense importance at this crisis that you should be there."[27]

Frail as he was, Henry agreed. Although a bitter opponent of the Constitution, it was the law of the land, and he was, above all, a law-abiding citizen. He had preferred a loose confederation of states to federation under a national government, but he preferred the latter to disunion and the inevitable European-style interstate wars that would follow. In March 1799, he rode the twenty difficult miles to the Charlotte County courthouse, where a crowd gathered to hear the legendary patriot—a figure from the past, stepping out of the pages of history to inspire the nation as he had more than two decades earlier. The entire faculty and student body of Hampden-Sydney College journeyed nearly twenty miles from Prince Edward County to witness the event.

"He was very infirm," one of the Hampden-Sydney students recalled.

> Immense multitudes . . . were pouring in from all the surrounding country to hear him. At length he arose with difficulty and stood somewhat bowed with age and weakness. His face was almost colorless. His countenance was careworn, and when he commenced his exordium, his voice was slightly cracked and tremulous. But in a few moments a wonderful transformation of the whole man occurred as he warmed with his theme. He stood erect; his eye beamed with a light that was almost supernatural; his features glowed with the hue and fire of youth; and his voice rang

clear and melodious, with the intonations of some grand musical instruments whose notes filled the area and fell distinctly and delightfully upon the ears of the most distant of thousands gathered before him. He told the people that . . .

the late proceedings of the Virginia Assembly have filled me with apprehension and alarm . . . they have drawn me from that happy retirement which it hath pleased a bountiful Providence to bestow and in which I had hoped to pass, in quiet, the remainder of my days . . . The state has quitted the sphere in which she has been placed by the Constitution! In daring to pronounce upon the validity of federal laws, Virginia has gone out of her jurisdiction in a manner not warranted by any authority and in the highest degree alarming to every considerate man.

After a pause, the man who himself had flirted with secession a few years earlier, expressed what had now become his worse fear: "Such opposition to the acts of the general government must beget their enforcement by military power and probably produce civil war; civil war, foreign alliances; and foreign alliances must necessarily end in subjugation to the powers called in." Henry lashed out at the hypocrisy of Jefferson and Madison for having supported ratification of a Constitution that they then proceeded to undermine with the Kentucky and Virginia Resolutions. "Whatever the merits or demerits . . . of the Alien and Sedition Acts," he stormed, "they were passed by Congress . . . and it belongs to the people who hold the reins over the head of Congress—and to them alone—to say whether they were acceptable or otherwise—not the Virginia state government. . . ."

If I am asked what is to be done when a people feel themselves intolerably oppressed, my answer is . . . overturn the government. But do not, I beseech you, carry matters to this length without provocation. Wait at least until some infringement is made upon your rights which cannot be otherwise redressed; for if ever you recur to another change, you may bid adieu forever to representative government. . . . We should use all peaceable remedies first before we resort to the last argument of the oppressed—revolution—and avoid as long as we can the unspeakable horrors of civil war. . . . Let us not split into factions which must destroy the union upon which our existence hangs. Let us preserve our strength for the French, the English, the Germans or whoever else shall dare invade our territory and not exhaust it in civil commotions and intestine wars.[28]

Henry's speech was his last. The trip to Charlotte left him exhausted. He managed to make it back to Charlotte to vote in the election the following month, but returned home so weak that his servants had to carry him to his bed. He would never again appear in public.

In the days that followed, Henry learned that he had won election by a sizable majority. To add to his triumph, Secretary of State Timothy Pickering wrote to tell him that the Senate had confirmed his selection by the president as one of three ministers plenipotentiary to negotiate growing differences with France. The letter—like the election results—found him "so sick as scarcely able to write." He replied to Washington on April 16. "I have been confined for several weeks by a severe indisposition . . . My advanced age and increasing debility compel me to abandon every idea of serving my country."[29]

Early in June, he barely managed to scribble an appeal to his oldest daughter Martha: "I am very unwell, and Dr. Cabell is with me." She immediately knew the meaning of his words and roused as many other family members as she could before rushing to Red Hill, where Henry was dying of what the doctor described as "intussusception," involving the slippage of the small intestine into the opening of the large intestine and a consequent blockage of the digestive tract.

"All other remedies having failed, Dr. Cabell proceeded to administer to him a dose of liquid mercury . . . on June 6," according to Henry's grandson Patrick Henry Fontaine. By then, Henry had indeed tried every available remedy except mercury, which had been used to treat syphilis and other diseases for more than two centuries with mixed successes. It now fell it in the category of that era's kill-or-cure "miracle" drugs that doctors prescribed after exhausting all other possible remedies. "Taking the vial in his hand . . . the dying man said, 'I suppose, doctor, this is your last resort.' The doctor replied, 'I am sorry to say, Governor, that it is.'"

Henry drew his nightcap over his eyes and began to pray "in clear words, a simple child-like prayer for his family, for his country, and for his own soul then in the presence of death. Afterward, in perfect calmness, he swallowed the medicine. . . . He continued to breathe very softly for some moments, after which, they who were looking upon him, saw that his life had departed."[30]

Of his many eulogies, the most eloquent said simply, "The sun has set in all his glory."[31]

Afterword

Patrick Henry had just turned sixty-three when he died. His family buried him without ceremony at Red Hill in a simple grave. His children would later mark the site with a plain marble slab bearing his name, the dates of his birth and death, and the words, "His fame is his best epitaph." In 1796, his wife, Dorothea, had given birth to her tenth child—his seventeenth—a daughter Jane Robertson, who died after only four days. One more child— his eighteenth—would be born eighteen months before Henry's death.

George Washington died at his home in Mount Vernon, in December, six months after Henry, thus ending the century of the American Revolution with the deaths of the two beloved patriots who had fathered that revolution. Each had sought different outcomes, however. Washington had envisioned freedom from Britain as a return to life as it was before the Seven Years' War in 1763, but under an American rather than British national government. Henry envisioned independence leaving each colony a self-governing sovereign state within a loose confederation of states, united only for common defense against foreign attack and mutual commercial advantages. Washington believed Henry's confederation would produce anarchy, while Henry predicted that the strong central government created by the constitution that Washington endorsed would inevitably restore the tyranny Americans had endured under the British imperial government.

Henry's prophesies quickly proved all too true.

As noted earlier, Congress imposed a national whiskey tax without the consent of state legislatures—much as the British had done with the stamp tax—and President Washington sent troops to crush tax protests in western Pennsylvania, much as the British had in Boston. In 1798, President John Adams and Congress "colluded" to pass the Alien and Sedition Acts, suppressing free speech, freedom of the press, and freedom of assembly—much as the British king and Parliament had done in 1774.

In the last year of Henry's life, his political foes Jefferson and Madison—once champions of the Constitution—conceded Henry's prescience and, with the Constitution in place as the law of the land, they scurried to mitigate its effects. Jefferson drafted resolutions adopted by the Kentucky state legislature giving any state the right "to judge for itself" whether the national government has acted unconstitutionally and to determine "the mode and measure of redress." Virginia's state legislature adopted an even stronger set of resolutions drafted by Madison that gave states "the right and . . . duty to interpose for arresting the evil" of federal government acts that exceed its rights under the Constitution.

Other states, however, rejected the resolutions, and since then, almost every president, Congress, and Supreme Court has fulfilled Henry's prophesies by usurping powers not delegated by the Constitution. Presidents have routinely failed to enforce many laws that do exist and exercised powers that do not; Congress has just as routinely enacted laws in areas the Constitution originally reserved to the states; and the U.S. Supreme Court has routinely issued decisions tantamount to legislation and exercised powers the Constitution reserves to the executive. Whether for better, worse, good, or evil—whether to protect the public or restrict it—the all-pervasive reach of the federal government and its laws is not what even the most ardent Federalists among the Founding Fathers had in mind when they wrote and signed the Constitution. Laws, by definition, are either proscriptive or enabling, but in both cases, they all necessarily restrict individual liberty and, to one degree or another, they fulfill Patrick Henry's definition and prophecy of tyranny under big government. While Washington subscribed to John Locke's contention that "Wherever laws end, tyranny begins," Henry held just as strongly to Plutarch's argument (and Jonathan Swift's) that laws were like "spiders' webs [which] could catch . . . the weak and poor, but easily be broken by the mighty and rich."[1]

The nation has yet to resolve the differences between the political visions of Washington and Henry. At various times in the early nineteenth-century, ten states—Pennsylvania, Kentucky, South Carolina, Virginia, Wisconsin, and the five New England States—attempted individually or collectively to promulgate the concept of "nullification"—always without success, despite the Tenth Amendment. As General Henry "Lighthorse Harry" Lee, then Virginia governor, predicted they would, the southern states seceded from the Union in 1860 and 1861 at an ultimate cost of one million dead or wounded. Even the Civil War, however, failed to resolve the conflict: Almost a century later, President Dwight D. Eisenhower fulfilled a Henry prophesy by sending troops into Little Rock, Arkansas, in 1957, to enforce federal law. And, in June 1963, Alabama Governor George Wallace invoked the Jefferson-Madison doctrine of nullification and stood "in the schoolhouse door" in Tuscaloosa to try to prevent desegregation of the all-white University of Alabama. Citing the Tenth Amendment, which relegates to the states all powers not assigned to the federal government by the Constitution, Wallace argued that the federal government had usurped state authority over public-school education—a subject not mentioned in the Constitution. Federal officers physically removed the governor to enforce what was then a relatively new federal law passed in response to a Supreme Court decision.

Although individual states persist in trying to nullify federal laws and restrict federal activities to constitutionally designated limits, federal courts serve as inevitable arbiters, and they seldom rule against the federal government, whose officials appoint them to the bench and of which they then become an integral part.

Henry's cry for "liberty or death" continues to provoke profound emotions in the hearts of most patriotic Americans, but they—like their forefathers at the Constitutional Convention—seem unable to reach a consensus on the meaning of liberty. Their passive acquiescence to ever-increasing government intrusions into their lives, however, indicates that few would define it as Patrick Henry did when he cried out to his countrymen, "We must Fight!"

Appendix A: The Speech

On March 23, 1775, Patrick Henry stood before the Second Revolutionary Convention of Virginia in Richmond and proposed three resolutions to organize and arm a militia. After some members of the Assembly expressed their opposition, Henry presented his arguments in the most inspiring oratory in American history until Abraham Lincoln's Gettysburg Address. *Henry's speech was a declaration of war against the British government that set her American colonies on the road to independence. The following is what remains of Henry's original text. Ellipses represent missing or obscured elements in the original text. Some of the original punctuation (but no spellings) have been changed for greater clarity and consistency.[1]*

Resolved, That a well-regulated militia, composed of gentlemen and yeomen is the natural strength and only security of a free government; that such a militia in this colony would forever render it unnecessary for the mother country to keep among us for the purpose of our defence any standing army of mercenary forces, always subversive of the quiet and dangerous to the liberties of the people, and would obviate the pretext of taxing us for their support.

Resolved, That the establishment of such a militia is at this time particularly necessary, by the state of our laws for the protection and defence of the country, some of which have already expired, and others will shortly do so; and that the known remissness of government in calling us together in a legislative capacity, renders it too insecure, in this time of danger and distress, to rely that opportunity will be given of renewing them in general assembly, or making any provision to secure our inestimable rights and liberties from those further violations with which they are threatened.

Resolved, therefore, That this colony be immediately put into a posture of defence; and that . . . be a committee to prepare a plan for embodying, arming, and disciplining such a number of men as may be sufficient for that purpose.

No man, Mr. President, thinks more highly than I do of the patriotism, as well as the abilities, of the very honorable gentlemen who have just addressed the House. But different men often see the same subject in different lights; and, therefore, I hope it will not be thought disrespectful to those gentlemen if, entertaining as I do, opinions of a character very opposite to theirs, I should speak forth my sentiments freely and without reserve. This is no time for ceremony. The question before the house is one of awful moment to this country. For my own part, I consider it as nothing less than a question of freedom or slavery. And in proportion to the magnitude of the subject ought to be the freedom of the debate. It is only in this way that we can hope to arrive at truth and fulfill the great responsibility which we hold to God and our country. Should I keep back my opinions at such a time, through fear of giving offence, I should consider myself guilty of treason towards my country and of an act of disloyalty towards the majority of Heaven, which I revere above all earthly kings.

Mr. President, it is natural for man to indulge in the illusions of hope. We are apt to shut our eyes against a painful truth and listen to the song of that siren till she transforms us into beasts. Is this the part of wise men engaged in a great and arduous struggle for liberty? Are we disposed to be of the number of those who, having eyes, see not, and having ears, hear not the things which so nearly concern their temporal salvation? For my part, whatever anguish of spirit it may cost, I am willing to know the whole truth; to know the worst and to provide for it.

I have but one lamp by which my feet are guided, and that is the lamp of experience. I know of no way of judging the future but by the past. And judging by the past, I wish to know what there has been in the conduct of the British ministry for the last ten years to justify the hopes with which gentlemen have been pleased to solace themselves and the House. Is it that insidious smile with which our petition has been lately received [by King George III]? Trust it not, Sir; it will prove a snare to your feet. Suffer not yourselves to be betrayed with a kiss. Ask yourselves how this gracious reception of our petition comports with those warlike preparations which cover our waters and darken our land. Are fleets and armies necessary to a work of love and reconciliation? Have we shown ourselves so unwilling to be reconciled that force must be called in to win back our love? Let us not deceive ourselves, Sir. These are the implements of war and subjugation—the last arguments to which kings resort.

I ask gentlemen, Sir, what means this martial array, if its purpose be not to force us to submission? Can gentlemen assign any other possible motive for it? Has Great Britain any enemy in this quarter of the world to call for all this accumulation of navies and armies? No, Sir, she has none. They are meant for us; they can be meant for no other. They are sent over to bind and rivet upon us those chains which the British ministry have been so long forging.

And what have we to oppose them? Shall we try argument? Sir, we have been trying that for the last ten years. Have we anything new to offer upon the subject? Nothing. We have held the subject up in every light of which it is capable, but it has been all in vain. Shall we resort to entreaty and humble supplication? What terms shall we find which have not already been exhausted?

Let us not, I beseech you, Sir, deceive ourselves longer. Sir, we have done everything that could be done to avert the storm which is now coming on. We have petitioned; we have remonstrated; we have supplicated; we have prostrated ourselves before the throne and have implored its interposition to arrest the tyrannical hands of the ministry and Parliament. Our petitions have been slighted; our remonstrances have produced additional violence and insult; our supplications have been disregarded; and we have been spurned with contempt from the foot of the throne.

In vain after these things may we indulge the fond hope of peace and reconciliation. There is no longer any room for hope. If we wish to be free; if we mean to preserve inviolate those inestimable privileges for which we have been so long contending; if we mean not basely to abandon the noble struggle in which we have been so long engaged and which we have pledged ourselves never to abandon until the glorious object of our contest shall be obtained—we must fight! I repeat it, Sir—we must fight! An appeal to arms and to the God of hosts is all that is left us.

They tell us, Sir, that we are weak—unable to cope with so formidable an adversary. But when shall we be stronger? Will it be the next week or the next year? Will it be when we are totally disarmed and when a British guard shall be stationed in every house? Shall we gather strength by irresolution and inaction? Shall we acquire the means of effectual resistance by lying supinely on our backs and hugging the delusive phantom of hope, until our enemies shall have bound us hand and foot?

Sir, we are not weak if we make a proper use of those means which the God of nature hath placed in our power. Three millions of people armed in the holy cause of liberty, and in such a country as that which we possess, are invincible by any force which our enemy can send against us.

Besides, Sir, we shall not fight our battles alone. There is a just God who presides over the destinies of nations and who will raise up friends to fight our battles for us. The battle, Sir, is not to the strong alone; it is to the vigilant, the active, the brave. Besides, Sir, we have no election. If we were base enough to desire it, it is now too late to retire from the contest. There is no retreat but in submission and slavery. Our chains are forged. Their clanking may be heard on the plains of Boston. The war is inevitable. And let it come! I repeat it, Sir, let it come!

It is in vain, Sir, to extenuate the matter. Gentlemen may cry peace, peace, but there is no peace. The war is actually begun. The next gale that sweeps from the north will bring to our ears the clash of resounding arms. Our brethren are already in the field. Why stand we here idle? What is it the gentlemen wish? What would they have? Is life so dear or peace so sweet as to be purchased at the price of chains and slavery? Forbid it, Almighty God! I know not what course others may take, but as for me, give me liberty, or give me death![2]

Appendix B: Henry on Slavery

Patrick Henry's letter to Quaker leader Robert Pleasants, January 1773.

It is not a little surprising that the professors of Christianity, whose chief excellence consists in softening the human heart and in cherishing and improving its finer feelings, should encourage a practice so totally repugnant to the first impressions of right and wrong. What adds to the wonder is that this abominable practice has been introduced in the most enlightened ages. Times, that seem to have pretensions to boast of high improvements in the arts and sciences and refined morality, have brought into general use and guarded by many laws, a species of violence and tyranny which our more rude and barbarous, but more honest, ancestors detested. Is it not amazing that, at a time when the rights of humanity are defined and understood with precision in a country, above all others, fond of liberty, that in such an age and in such a country, we find men professing a religion the most humane, mild, gentle, and generous, adopting a principle as repugnant to humanity as it is inconsistent with the Bible and destructive to liberty? Every thinking, honest man rejects it in speculation; how few in conscientious motives!

Would anyone believe I am master of slaves of my own purchase? I am drawn along by the general inconvenience of living here without them. I will not, I cannot justify it. However culpable my conduct, I will so far pay my devoir to virtue as to own the excellence and rectitude of her precepts and lament my want of conformity to them.

I believe a time will come when an opportunity will be offered to abolish this lamentable evil. Everything we can do is to improve it, if it happens in our day; if not, let us transmit to our descendants, together with our slaves, a pity for their unhappy lot and an abhorrence of slavery. If we cannot reduce this wished-for reformation to practice, let us treat the unhappy victims with lenity. It is the furthest advance we can make toward justice. It is a debt we owe to the purity of our religion, to show that it is at variance with that law which warrants slavery.

I know not when to stop. I should say many things on the subject, a serious view of which gives a gloomy perspective to future times.[1]

Appendix C: Henry's Heirs

Dorothea Henry married Judge Edmund Winston a few years after Patrick Henry's death—a common and often essential practice in early America for widows and widowers with children to raise. A cOceived their proper shares of Henry's estate. Dorothea died in 1831 and chose to be buried beside Henry at Red Hill, with the "Henry" surname inscribed on her slab. Henry's house at Red Hill burned to the ground in 1919, although the property remained in the Henry family until 1944, when the Patrick Henry Foundation was formed to purchase the property and reconstruct its original buildings—the house, law office, and outbuildings. Now a national memorial, Red Hill, in Brookneal, Virginia, is open to visitors the year around.

Few of Patrick Henry's children and grandchildren achieved national eminence or renown. "For the most part," says historian Edith C. Poindexter, former curator of the Patrick Henry National Memorial at Red Hill, "they became solid citizens, but were more often than not remembered as being children of Patrick Henry." Of his ten surviving sons by his two marriages, six attended Hampden-Sydney College in Prince Edward County, although one—Nathaniel—was expelled. Three of Henry's sons became sheriffs: William, Edward, and John. Three others—Edward ("Neddy"), Fayette, and Patrick, Jr.—became lawyers, but all died young, at twenty-three, twenty-seven, and twenty-one, respectively. All three sons by his first marriage died in the 1790s before Henry himself. John the older, who went "raving mad" after the Battle of Saratoga, recovered his health and became a farmer on the 1,000-acre parcel his father gave him at Leatherwood, in Henry County. John married, but, in 1791, only months after the birth of his only child (a son), he died at the age of thirty-four. William, the next oldest, was a sheriff and died in 1798 at thirty-five, and Edward ("Neddy") died in 1794 at the age of twenty-three.

Of his seven sons by his second marriage, Patrick Jr. and Fayette, as mentioned, were lawyers who died in their twenties. Alexander and Nathaniel married into wealthy families, became land speculators and died penniless, Alexander at age sixty-five and Nathaniel at age sixty-one. Edward Winston, a successful farmer, died at seventy-eight, and John the younger inherited half of Red Hill and spent his life there, running the plantation, raising a family, following "the gentle pursuits of literature," and dying at seventy-one after "a peaceful and honorable life." All of Henry's daughters married well and lived normal lives for their era as housewives and mothers.

Most of Patrick Henry's seventy-seven grandchildren simply blended into the rest of the American population, assuming the same range of skills and occupations as their countrymen as doctors, lawyers, teachers, ministers, legislators, judges, farmers, craftsmen, salesmen, and so forth. Quite a few served in the Confederate Army in the Civil War. One grandson became a U.S. Senator. A second—attorney William Wirt Henry, the younger John Henry's son—became a leader in the Virginia House of Delegates and a renowned historian. His remarkable effort to collect his grandfather's papers produced an epic, three-volume work published in 1891: *Patrick Henry: Life, Correspondence and Speeches.* A graduate of the University of Virginia, William Wirt Henry also wrote a critically acclaimed book on the trials of Aaron Burr and Jefferson Davis, and he became president of the American Historical Association and of the Virginia Historical Society.

Patrick Henry bequeathed Red Hill to his wife, Dorothea, for the duration of her life, along with twenty slaves. He owned at least six plantations when he died, totaling more than 26,000 acres: his Red Hill plantation (2,920 acres) in Charlotte County; two farms in Campbell County (1,000 acres and 2,500 acres); the 1,400-acre Seven Islands plantation in Halifax County; his 10,000-acre Leatherwood plantation; and 8,500 acres in North Carolina. He also owned 8,000 acres in the Dismal Swamp, south of Norfolk. In 1794, he transferred 1,000 acres each to his sons by his first wife—all of them adults by then, of course, and, because John the older had died, Henry gave the land to John's son. As for his children by his second wife, Dorothea, Henry gave Dorothea the right to divide each of three properties in Campbell and Charlotte counties and his North Carolina lands as she determined between the six boys: Patrick, Fayette, Alexander, Nathaniel, Edward and John. Henry left each of his daughters from both marriages amounts varying from £500 to £2,000, along with some slaves.

"This is all the inheritance I can give to my dear family," he wrote at the end of his will. "The religion of Christ can give them one which will make them rich indeed."[1]

Notes

Introduction

1. Bernard Mayo, *Myths and Men: Patrick Henry, George Washington, Thomas Jefferson* (Athens: University of Georgia Press, 1959), 1.

2. Merrill Jensen, John P. Kaminski, Gaspare Saladino, Richard Leffler, and Charles H. Schoenleber, eds., *The Documentary History of the Ratification of the Constitution*, (Madison, WI: State Historical Society of Wisconsin, 1976–[in progress], 22 vols. to date), IX:951–968 [Hereafter, DHRC].

3. Mayo, *Myths and Men*, 2, 17.

4. George Mason to Martin Cockburn, May 26, 1773, George Morgan, *The True Patrick Henry* (Philadelphia: J. B. Lippincott Company, 1907), 140.

Chapter 1. Tongue-tied . . .

1. William Wirt Henry, *Patrick Henry: Life, Correspondence and Speeches* (New York: Charles Scribner's Sons, 1891, 3 vols.), I:3.

2. Moses Coit Tyler, *Patrick Henry* (Boston: Houghton, Mifflin and Company, 2nd ed., 1898), 5, citing William Wirt, *Sketches of the Life and Character of Patrick Henry* (Philadelphia: 1818).

3. Richard R. Beeman, *Patrick Henry: A Biography* (New York: McGraw-Hill Book Company, 1974), 4.

4. Henry, I:10.

5. Ibid., I:8–9.

6. Ibid., I:10, citing Nathaniel Pope.

7. Judge Spencer Roane's memorandum, Appendix B, in George Morgan, *The True Patrick Henry* (Philadelphia: J. B. Lippincott Company, 1907), 435–454.

8. Edmund Randolph, *History of Virginia* (Charlottesville: The University Press of Virginia, 1970), 179.

9. Henry, I:17.

10. Ibid., I:18–19.

11. William Iverton Winston to Nathaniel Pope Jr., in Robert Douthat Meade, *Patrick Henry: Patriot in the Making* (Philadelphia: J. B. Lippincott Company, 1957), 91.

12. *Pretty Polly*, old Appalachian Mountain ballad, derived from a number of similar eighteenth-century English ballads. Carl Sandburg, *The American Songbag* (New York: Harcourt Brace Jovanovich, 1927), 60–61.

13. Sir Edward Coke (1552–1634) was, successively, a British member of parliament, speaker of the House of Commons, British attorney general, and chief justice of the Court of Common Pleas. Apart from his many important legal decisions, he gained renown for his epochal history of British law and court decisions relating thereto (*Reports*–1600–1615) and his four in-depth analyses of British laws entitled *Institutes of the Lawes of England, or, A Commentarie upon Littleton* (1628–1644). Littleton was Sir Thomas Littleton (1422–1481). Also spelled Lyttleton and Luttelton, Littleton was an English jurist and legal author who produced the earliest compilation of English land laws, which became a basic element of British legal education for more than three centuries. (*Merriam-Webster's Biographical Dictionary* [Springfield, MA: Merriam-Webster, Inc., 1995].)

14. The wildly popular eighteenth-century concept of "natural rights" sprang from Jean-Jacques Rousseau's *Le Contrat Social* (1762), which begins, "Man is born free, and everywhere he is in chains."

15. William Wirt, *The Life of Patrick Henry* (New York: Derby & Jackson, 1860), 35–36, citing Judge (later Virginia Governor) John Tyler, who assured him that Henry himself had related the anecdote.

Chapter 2. Tongue Untied

1. Manuscript of Colonel Samuel Meredith memorandum made for William Wirt, in Henry I:57.

2. Maury letter of December 12, 1763, in Ann Maury, *Memories of a Huguenot Family* (New York, 1872), 419–420.

3. Wirt, 43.

4. Ibid., 41.

5. Henry, I:39.

6. Wirt, 23–27.

7. Henry, I:39–40.

8. Ibid., I:40.

Chapter 3. The Flame Is Spread

1. Henry, I:44, citing *Memoirs of a Huguenot Family*, 423.

2. Ibid., I:48.

3. Tyler to Wirt, Henry, I:47.

4. Morgan, 433.

5. Harlow Giles Unger, *John Hancock: Merchant King and American Patriot* (New York: John Wiley & Sons, 2000), 78.

6. Robert Douthat Meade, *Patrick Henry, Patriot in the Making* (Philadelphia: J. B. Lippincott Company, 1957), 155, citing G. E. Howard, *Preliminaries of the American Revolution*, 138.

7. Beeman, 33, citing Jack P. Greene, "Foundations of Political Power in the Virginia House of Burgesses," *William and Mary Quarterly*, ser. 3, X (1959), 485–506.

8. Randolph, 167–168.

9. Henry I:76–77, citing Paul Leicester Ford, *The Writings of Thomas Jefferson* (New York, G. P. Putnam's Sons, 1892–1899, 10 vols.), IX, 339, 465–466, and *Journal of House of Burgesses*, 1761–1765 (Richmond, VA: Colonial Press), 350–351 [hereafter, JHB].

10. Henry, I:77.

11. Ibid., I:78.

12. Randolph, 178.

13. From Patrick Henry's notes, in Henry, I:80–81.

14. Ibid.

15. Ibid.

16. Ibid., I:86. Edmund Randolph recalled the speech differently, saying Henry actually retreated at the end of his attack. Here is how Randolph recalled this part of the speech: "'Caesar,' cried he, 'had his Brutus; Charles the first his Cromwell, and George the third . . . ' 'Treason, sir,' exclaimed the Speaker, to which Henry instantly replied, 'and George the third, may he never have either.'" (Randolph, 169). But another burgess who heard Henry's speech rebuts Randolph: "If Henry did speak any apologetic words, they were doubtless uttered almost tongue in cheek to give him some legal protection" (Randolph, 169 38n–170n).

17. From Henry manuscript, in Tyler, 85.

18. Henry I:87.

19. Randolph, 168–169.

20. Reverend William Robinson to the Bishop of London, August 12, 1765, Tyler, 87.

21. Tyler, 85.

22. *Maryland Gazette*, July 4, 1765.

23. Letter from Fauquier, November 3, 1765, in Meade, *Patrick Henry, Patriot . . .* , 184.

24. Tyler, 82.

25. Henry, II:305–309.

26. Henry Lawrence Gipson, *The Coming of the Revolution, 1763–1775* (New York: Harper & Brothers, 1954), 100.

27. Unger, *John Hancock*, 31.

28. Henry, I:100.

Chapter 4. We Are Slaves!

1. John Hancock to Jonathan Bernard, October 14, 1765, in Unger, *John Hancock*, 98.

2. George Washington to Francis Dandridge, September 20, 1765, W. W. Abbott and Dorothy Twohig, eds., *The Papers of George Washington, Colonial Series, 1748–August 1755* (Charlottesville: University Press of Virginia, 1983–1995, 10 vols.), 7:395–396.

3. Unger, *John Hancock*, 106.

4. From the original Henry manuscript, quoted in Henry, I:116.

5. George Washington to Robert Morris, April 12, 1786, W. W. Abbott, ed., *The Papers of George Washington, Confederation Series* (Charlottesville: University Press of Virginia, 1992–1997, 6 vols.), 4:15–17.

6. Patrick Henry to Robert Pleasants, January 18, 1773, in Meade, *Patriot . . .* , 299–300.

7. Ibid.

8. Ibid.

9. Henry, I:117–118, citing Robert B. Semple's "History of Baptists in Virginia."

10. Ibid., I:119, citing Spencer Roane.

11. Ibid., I:125–127.

12. Morgan, 116, citing Nathaniel Pope, Henry's intimate.

13. Henry, I:123–124.

14. William Wirt, *The Life of Patrick Henry* (New York: Derby & Jackson, 1860), 94.

15. John Hancock to William Reeve, September 3, 1767, in Unger, *John Hancock*, 113.

16. George Washington to Bryan Fairfax, July 20, 1774, PGW Colonial, 10:128–131.

17. For the complete text of Dickinson's *Letters from a Farmer in Pennsylvania*, see Paul Leicester Ford, ed., *The Writings of John Dickinson* (1895), 307–406.

18. *JHB, 1766–1769*, 170.

19. Unger, *John Hancock*, 121.

20. William Nelson, York, to John Norton, London, November 14, 1768, in Meade, *Patrick Henry, Patriot . . .* , 266.

21. Ford, *Jefferson*, X:340–341.

22. Thomas Jefferson in conversation with Daniel Webster, 1824, ibid., IX:327–328

23. JHB, *1766–1769*, 218, as cited in Meade, *Patrick Henry, Patriot . . .* , 270.

24. Donald Jackson and Dorothy Twohig, eds., *The Diaries of George Washington* (Charlottesville: University Press of Virginia, 1976–1979, 6 vols.), 3:xiii–xiv.

25. James Curtis Ballagh, *The Letters of Richard Henry Lee* (New York, 1911–1914, 2 vols.), I:37.

Chapter 5. To Recover Our Just Rights

1. *Virginia Gazette*, March 8, 1770, reprinted from the *London Public Ledger*. See also *Letters of Junius* (Boston, 1827).

2. *Boston Gazette*, cited in Unger, *John Hancock*, 140.

3. Charles F. Adams, ed., *The Works of John Adams, Second President of the United States: With a Life of the Author* (Boston: Little, Brown & Company, 1850–1856, 10 vols.), I:349–350.

4. Ibid., II:229–230.

5. Unger, *John Hancock*, 144.

6. Morgan, 245–246.

7. Ibid., 242.

8. Ibid.

9. Dr. Thomas Hinde, as reported, written, and published by his son in 1843, in Meade, *Patrick Henry, Patriot . . .* , 281.

10. Nelly C. Preston, *Paths of Glory* (pamphlet, Richmond, VA, 1961), 101–103, cited in Robert Douthat Meade, *Patrick Henry: Practical Revolutionary* (Philadelphia: J. B. Lippincott Company, 1969), 15–16.

11. Henry, I:151.

12. *William and Mary Quarterly*, ser. 2, 1921, 107–109, cited in Meade, *Patrick Henry, Patriot . . .* , 297–298.

13. Boston Town Records, 93, cited in William M. Fowler, Jr., *The Baron of Beacon Hill: A Biography of John Hancock* (Boston: Houghton, Mifflin Company, 1980), 148.

14. Boston Town Records, 95–108, in Fowler, 149.

15. *Boston Gazette*, January 11, 1773.

16. Adams, *Works . . .* , II:310–314.

17. Henry I:160–161.

18. Tryon to Lord Dartmouth, January 3, 1774, in Unger, *John Hancock*, 172. A British colonial administrator of North Carolina from 1765 to 1771, where he crushed the Regulators' revolt of 1771, Tryon was governor of New York from 1771 to 1778.

19. Edmund Burke, *First Speech on the Conciliation with America and American Taxation* before Parliament, April 19, 1774, as cited in John Bartlett, Justin Kaplan, eds., *Familiar Quotations* (Boston: Little, Brown and Company, 16th ed., 1992), 331.

20. Ford, *Writings*, I:9–10.

21. Samuel Adams to Richard Henry Lee, April 10, 1773, and New Hampshire *Gazette*, June 18, 1773, in Henry, I:167–168.

Chapter 6. We Must Fight!

1. Henry, I:164.
2. George Mason to Martin Cockburn, May 26, 1773, in Morgan, 140.
3. *Virginia Gazette*, July 28, 1774.
4. Henry, I:193.
5. Ibid., I:198.
6. Ibid., I:213.
7. Douglas Southall Freeman, *George Washington*. Completed by John Alexander Carroll and Mary Wells Ashworth (New York: Charles Scribner's Sons, 1957, 7 vols.), III:383.
8. Benjamin Franklin to James Parker, March 20, 1750, Leonard W. Labaree, et al., *Papers of Benjamin Franklin* (New Haven: Yale University Press, 1959–[in progress], 38 vols. to date), IV:117–121.
9. Henry, I:219.
10. Ibid., I:221.
11. Ibid., I:223.
12. Adams, *Works*, IX:347.
13. Charles-Louis de Secondat, Baron de la Brède et de Montesquieu (1689–1755) was born to and married into wealth. An attorney and later a justice on the court in Bordeaux called *le Parlement*, he began writing in his early thirties, publishing the popular *Lettres persanes*, a satire of Parisian life and mockery of the reign of Louis XIV, as seen through the eyes of two Persian travelers. After selling his government post, he traveled extensively from court to court and emerged as a renowned political philosopher and historian, publishing his *De la monarchie universelle en Europe* (1734, "On the Universal Monarchies in Europe"), Considerations sur les causes de la grandeur des Romains et de leur decadence (1734, Consideration of the causes of the greatness and decadence of the Romans), and the landmark French work of political science of the Enlightenment, *De l'esprit des lois, ou du rapport que les lois doivent avoir avec la constitution de chaque gouvernement, les moeurs, le climat, la religion, le commerce, etc.* (1748, *The Spirit of Laws,* translated by Thomas Nugent, 2 vols., 1750).
14. Henry, I:234.
15. Ibid.
16. Roger Atkinson to Samuel Pleasants, in Henry, I:197.
17. Henry, I:236.
18. Meade, *Patrick Henry, Patriot . . .* , 333–334.
19. Patrick Henry to Samuel Overton (no date), Wirt, *Henry*, 111.

Chapter 7. "Give Me Liberty . . . "

1. Letter from Charles Dabney, in Henry, I:180.
2. Edmund Burke, *Second Speech on Conciliation with America, The Thirteen Resolutions*, March 12, 1775, in *Bartlett's Familiar Quotations*, 331.

3. Robert Douthat Meade, *Patrick Henry, Practical Revolutionary* (Philadelphia: J. B. Lippincott Company, 1969), 3.

4. Randolph, *History* . . . , 212.

5. Henry, I:257–258.

6. Ibid.

7. Randolph, *History* . . . , 260.

8. Henry, I:267–268, citing the description of "an old Baptist clergyman who was one of the auditory."

9. Ibid., I:262–264.

10. Ibid., 266. (Author's note: No actual transcript of Henry's speech exists, and the words shown here represent a reconstruction by Henry's first biographer William Wirt, who extrapolated its contents from recollections—forty years after the event—by those present at St. Paul's, including Judge John Tyler, an intimate of Henry's, Thomas Jefferson, Edmund Randolph, and Judge St. George Tucker, among others. Hardly a friend of Henry, Jefferson did not alter a word in Wirt's reconstruction of the speech and reiterated his appraisal of Henry as the greatest orator in history. As I stated previously, I believe that word for word accuracy is less important than an accurate presentation of Henry's meaning, his passion, and his eloquence.)

11. Tyler, 146–149, citing manuscript of John Roane, who heard the speech.

12. Unger, *John Hancock*, 191.

13. G. R. Barnes and J. H. Owens, eds., *The Private Papers of John, Earl of Sandwich, First Lord of the Admiralty, 1771–1782* (Naval Records Society Publications, 1932–1938), I:61, cited in Unger, *John Hancock*, 195.

14. Percy to Edward Harvey, April 20, 1775, in Charles K. Bolton, ed., *Letters of Hugh Earl Percy . . . 1774–1776*, cited in Knollenberg, *Growth*, 195.

15. *Essex Gazette*, April 25, 1775, Boston Public Library.

16. Henry, I:200.

17. Ibid., I:202.

18. Ibid., I:280.

19. Ibid., I:280.

20. Hayes, 79.

21. Tyler, 167.

Chapter 8. *"Don't Tread on Me"*

1. Tyler, 185.

2. Ibid.

3. George Washington to Lieutenant Colonel Joseph Reed, February 26–March 9, 1776, W. W. Abbott, ed., *The Papers of George Washington, Revolutionary War Series* (Charlottesville: University Press of Virginia, 1985–in progress, 19 vols. to date) [hereafter PGW Rev.], 3:369–379.

4. *Virginia Gazette*, March 1, 1776.

5. Ibid.

6. Ibid.

7. Henry, I:349–350.

8. Charles Louis de Secondat, Baron de Montesquieu, *The Spirit of Laws* (2 vols., Geneva, 1748), as cited in John P. Kaminski and Richard Leffler, eds., *Federalists and Antifederalists: The Debate Over the Ratification of the Constitution* (Lanham, MD: Rowan & Littlefield Publishers, 1989, 1998), 9–10.

9. John Adams, *Thoughts on Government* (Philadelphia: John Dunlop, 1776).

10. Patrick Henry to John Adams, May 20, 1776, in Henry, I:410–412.

11. John Adams to Patrick Henry, June 8, 1776, ibid., I:414–416.

12. Randolph, 255–256.

13. Max Farrand, *The Fathers of the Constitution: A Chronicle of the Establishment of the Union* (New Haven, CT: Yale University Press, 1921), 45.

14. Henry, I:349–350.

15. Richard D. Morris, *Encyclopedia of American History* (New York: Harper & Brothers, 1953), 91, 98.

16. Tyler, 271.

17. Henry, I:453–454.

18. Meade, *Patrick Henry, Practical Revolutionary*, 168.

19. Kips Bay is near present-day 34th Street on the east side of Manhattan Island; Harlem Heights stretched from present day 110th Street to 125th Street, on the west side of Manhattan, where Columbia University now stands.

20. Freeman, *George Washington*, IV: 198.

22. George Washington to Patrick Henry, October 5, 1776, PGW Rev., 6:479–482.

23. Patrick Henry to the Governor of Cuba, October 18, 1777, Henry, III:103–104.

24. Patrick Henry to Richard Peters at the War Office, December 6, 1776, ibid., III:32.

25. Patrick Henry to the Virginia Delegates in Congress, October 11, 1776, ibid., III:19.

26. Patrick Henry to John Hancock, March 28, 1777, ibid., III:48.

27. Patrick Henry to the Speaker of the House of Delegates, May 27, 1777, ibid., III:78.

28. Patrick Henry to William Preston, February 19, 1778, ibid., III:144–148.

29. Patrick Henry to the Virginia Delegates in Congress, June 20, 1777, ibid., III:83.

Chapter 9. Hastening to Ruin

1. Henry, I:505.

2. Ibid., II:148.

3. Thomas Jefferson to James Brown, October 27, 1808, in John P. Kaminski, *The Quotable Jefferson* (Princeton, NJ: Princeton University Press, 2006), 164.

4. Henry, II:118.

5. Patrick Henry to George Washington, March 29, 1777, PGW Rev., 9:12–13.

6. Patrick Henry to Richard Henry Lee, January 9, 1777, Henry, II:511–513.

7. Patrick Henry to Richard Henry Lee, March 29, 1777, ibid., II:515–516.

8. Morgan, 319.

9. Meade, *Patrick Henry, Practical Revolutionary*, 167.

10. George Washington to Patrick Henry, November 13, 1777, PGW Rev., 12:242–247.

11. George Washington to Horatio Gates, January 4, 1778, ibid., 13:138–140.

12. English-born General Horatio Gates; English-born General Charles Lee, and Irish-born soldier of fortune General Thomas Conway.

13. Unknown to Patrick Henry, January 12, 1778, PGW Rev., 13:610n–611n.

14. Patrick Henry to George Washington, February 20, 1778, ibid., 13:609

15. George Washington to Patrick Henry, March 27, 1778, ibid., 13:328–329.

16. Ibid., March 28, 1778, 13:336–337.

17. Marquis de Lafayette to George Washington, February 19, 1778, ibid., 13:594–597.

18. George-Washington Lafayette [Gilbert Motier, Marquis de Lafayette], *Mémoires, Correspondence et Manuscrits du Général Lafayette, publiés par sa famille* (Bruxelles: Société Belge de Librairie, Etc., Hauman, Cattoir et Compagnie, 2 vols., 1837), I:36–37.

19. George Washington to Patrick Henry, December 27, 1777, PGW Rev., 13:17–18.

20. Ibid., 9:12–13.

21. Patrick Henry to Committee of Congress, January 20, 1778, Henry, II:554–557.

22. George Washington to Patrick Henry, February 19, 1778, PGW Rev., 13:591–592.

23. Patrick Henry to Richard Henry Lee, April 7, 1778, Henry, II:559–560.

24. Henry, II:562.

25. Harlow Giles Unger, *Lafayette* (Hoboken, NJ: John Wiley & Sons, 2002), 72.

26. Henry, II:564.

Chapter 10. Obliged to Fly

1. Henry, II:565–566.

2. Ibid.

3. George Washington to Patrick Henry, September 13, 1778, PGW Rev., 16:600–601.

4. George Washington to Patrick Henry, November 3, 1778, ibid., 18:30–31.

5. Patrick Henry to Richard Henry Lee, June 18, 1778, in Henry, II:564–565.

6. Captain John Wilson to Patrick Henry, May 20, 1778, Henry, III:169–170.

7. Benson Bobrick, *Angel in the Whirlwind: The Triumph of the American Revolution* (New York: Simon & Schuster, 1997), 345.

8. George Washington Parke Custis, *Recollections and Private Memoirs of Washington* (New York: Derby & Jackson, 1860), 220.

9. Mémoires . . . *Lafayette,* I:26.

10. George Washington to John Augustine Washington, July 4, 1778, PGW Rev., 16:25–26.

11. George Washington to Patrick Henry, July 4, 1778, ibid., 16:21–25.

12. Patrick Henry to George Rogers Clark, December 12, 1778, Henry, III:209–212.

13. Patrick Henry to Virginia delegation in Congress, Tyler, 258.

14. Patrick Henry to John Todd, December 12, 1778, Henry, III:212–216.

15. Patrick Henry to George Washington, March 13, 1779, ibid., III:229–231.

16. Henri Doniol, *Histoire de la Participation de la France à l'Établissement des États-Unis d'Amérique* (Paris: Imprimerie Nationale, 1886, 5 vols.), III:243.

17. Ibid., III:266.

18. Ibid., III:43.

19. Ibid., III:67–68.

20. Two of Henry's seventeen children died at an early age: Richard, born to Dolly in 1792, died at eighteen months, and Jane Robertson, the last born of Henry and Dolly's children, lived only four days after her birth in 1798.

21. Doniol, *Histoire,* III:67–68.

22. Ibid., III:324.

23. Tyler, 282–283.

24. Boyd, *Jefferson Papers*, VI:204–205 (Meade, II:250)

25. Henry, II:143.

26. Randolph, 295–296.

27. "Yorktown Day" remains an official state holiday in Virginia.

28. Henry, II:151.

29. Boyd, *Jefferson Papers*, VI, 204–205.

30. Morgan, 311.

Chapter 11. A Belgian Hare

1. Johann David Schoepf, *Travels in the Confederation*, translated and edited by Alfred J. Morrison (Philadelphia, 1911), cited in W. P. Cresson, *James Monroe* (Chapel Hill: University of North Carolina Press, 1946), 66.

2. William Short [citing Henry] to Thomas Jefferson, May 15, 1784, in Meade, *Patrick Henry, Practical Revolutionary*, 273.

3. Henry, II:226–227.

4. Ibid., II:191.

5. Ibid., II:193.

6. Ibid., II:193–196.

7. Ibid., II:219.

8. Ibid., II:214.

9. John P. Kaminski, *James Madison, Champion of Liberty and Justice* (Madison, WI: Parallel Press, 2006), 17–18.

10. Thomas Jefferson to James Madison, February 17, 1826, ibid., 387.

11. Henry wrote to Thomas Jefferson, then American minister in Paris, for help in finding a sculptor. Jefferson enlisted the renowned French sculptor Jean Houdon, who traveled to Mount Vernon, made sketches and a clay bust of Washington, along with a life mask. He returned to France with the sketches and life mask, from which he then sculpted the full statue, which stands in the capitol at Richmond. His original of Lafayette stood in Paris until its destruction during the French Revolution. The Lafayette statue in Richmond is a copy of the original. Houdon's original clay bust of Washington remains at Mount Vernon and is the most valuable artwork there.

12. George Washington to James Madison, November 17, 1788, W. W. Abbott, ed., *The Papers of George Washington, Presidential Series* (Charlottesville: University Press of Virginia, 1987–present [in progress], 15 vols.), 1:112–116.

13. Meade, *Patrick Henry, Practical Revolutionary*, 319, citing Henry Aylett Sampson, *Sonnets and Other Poems*, 122.

14. Patrick Henry to the Mayor of Richmond, January 13, 1785, Henry, III:267–268.

15. Patrick Henry to the Governor of Georgia, February 28, 1786, ibid., III:248.

16. Richard Henry Lee to Patrick Henry, December 18, 1784, ibid., III:247–248.

17. Tyler, 300.

18. Edward Fontaine, "Patrick Henry," published as "A Patrick Henry Essay (No. 3–07)" by the Patrick Henry Memorial Foundation, 2008.

19. Henry, II:286–287.

20. George Washington to William Gordon, July 8, 1783, Fitzpatrick, *Writings*, 26:483–496.

21. Henry Knox to George Washington, January 31, 1785, in PGW Confed., 2:301–306.

22. DHRC, XIII:25.

23. James Monroe, *The Autobiography of James Monroe* (Syracuse, NY: G. P. Putnam's Sons, 1926), 45.

24. Morris, *Encyclopedia of American History*, 114.

25. John Marshall to Arthur Lee, in Beeman, 140.

26. James Monroe to Patrick Henry, August 12, 1786, Daniel Preston, ed., *The Papers of James Monroe* (Westport, CT: Greenwood Press, 2003–2006, 2 vols. [in progress]), II:331–334.

27. DHRC, XIII:154–155.

28. Ibid., II:57.

29. Morris, *Encyclopedia of American History*, 115.

Chapter 12. Seeds of Discontent

1. Henry, II:305–309. An article by Thomas E. Buckley, S.J., in *The Virginia Magazine of History and Biography* 91 (January, 1983), 98–104, presents an identical letter as having been written by Bishop James Madison (1749–1812) to his daughter in 1811, twenty-five years after the date of Henry's letter. There is at present no way

to authenticate the origins of the letter. A cousin of President James Madison, Bishop Madison was president of the College of William and Mary at the time and may well have had access to some of Patrick Henry's letters and papers, then in the hands of Henry's many heirs. On the other hand, Henry took the unusual step for his era of designating his daughter as administrator of the estate of one of his late sons and attorney-in-fact for her late husband's estate—a show of confidence in a woman so rare in his day that it seems incongruous with the tone of his letter of advice to his other daughters. Regardless of its origins and author, however, the letter is of interest as a reflection of the times.

2. Patrick Henry to Mrs. Annie Christian, October 20, 1786, Henry, III:379–380.

3. Morris, *Encyclopedia of American History*, 115.

4. Edmund Randolph to Patrick Henry, December 6, 1786, Henry, II:310–311.

5. James Madison to George Washington, December 7, 1786, in Tyler, 310.

6. James Madison to George Washington, March 18, 1787, PGW Confed., 5:92–95.

7. James Madison to Edmund Randolph, March 25, 1786, Henry, II:313.

8. James Madison, *Notes of Debates in the Federal Convention of 1787 Reported by James Madison* (New York: W. W. Norton, 1987), 19. [Author's note: Madison's *Notes of Debates in the Federal Convention of 1787* detail only part of the proceedings of the Constitutional Convention. A more complete compilation may be found in the four-volume work, *The Records of the Federal Convention of 1787*, edited by Max Farrand (New Haven: Yale University Press, 1966).]

9. Harlow Giles Unger, *America's Second Revolution* (Hoboken, NJ: John Wiley & Sons, Inc., 2007).

10. Madison, *Notes*, 28.

11. Ibid., 31.

12. PGW Confed., 5:239–241.

13. Madison, *Notes*, 42–43.

14. Ibid., 39–40.

15. Carl Van Doren, *The Great Rehearsal: The Story of the Making and Ratifying of the Constitution of the United States* (New York: The Viking Press, 1948), 189–190.

16. Madison, *Notes*, 652–654.

17. Ibid., 385.

18. Ibid., 502–503.

19. George Washington to the Marquis de Lafayette, August 17, 1787, Freeman, 6:105.

20. Madison, *Notes*, 651.

Chapter 13. On the Wings of the Tempest

1. DHRC, VII:337–339.

2. Richard Henry Lee to Patrick Henry, September 14, 1789, Henry, III:399–400.

3. George Washington to Patrick Henry, September 24, 1787, PGW Confed., 5:339–340.

4. Patrick Henry to George Washington, October 1787, ibid., 5:384.

5. Ibid.

6. Meade, *Patrick Henry, Practical Revolutionary*, quoting "Journal of William Loughton Smith, 1790–1791," in *Massachusetts Historical Society Publication*, October, 1917.

7. Spencer Roane's memorandum to William Wirt, in Morgan, 445.

8. Ibid.

9. DHRC, VIII:65–67.

10. Ibid.

11. George Washington to Benjamin Lincoln, April 2, 1788, PGW Confed., 6:187–188.

12. Thomas Jefferson to John Adams, November 13, 1787, in Lester J. Cappon, ed., *The Adams-Jefferson Letters: The Complete Correspondence between Thomas Jefferson and Abigail and John Adams* (Chapel Hill: University of North Carolina Press, 1959), 211–212.

13. Thomas Jefferson to George Washington, May 2, 1788, PGW Confed., 6:251–257.

14. Max Farrand, *The Records of the Federal Convention of 1787* (New Haven, CT: Yale University Press, 1911, 4 vols.), III:123–127.

15. George Washington to Charles Carter, December 14, 1787, PGW Confed., 5:489–492.

16. George Washington to Henry Knox, October 15, 1787, PGW Confed., 5:288–290.

17. *Massachusetts Centinel*, November 17, 1787, DHRC, IV:259–262.

18. Centinel I, Philadelphia *Independent Gazetteer*, October 5, 1787, ibid., XIII:326–337.

19. Philadelphia *Freeman's Journal*, September 26, 1787, ibid., XIII:243–245.

20. Philadelphia *Independent Gazetteer*, January 12, 1788, DHRC, V:817.

21. Louis-Guillaume Otto to French minister of foreign affairs, comte de Montmorin, October 10, 1787, Correspondence politique, États-Unis 32, 368 ff., Archives du Ministre des Affaires Étrangères, Paris.

22. Henry, III:579.

23. Meade, *Patrick Henry, Practical Revolutionary*, 339.

24. Tyler, 317.

25. Gouverneur Morris to George Washington, October 30, 1787, PGW Confed., 5:398–401.

26. DHRC, XX:688.

27. Henry, II:342–343.

28. Ibid.

29. Author's note: The most complete text of Henry's speeches to the Virginia Ratification Convention can be found in two sources. Volume III, pp. 431–600 of *Patrick Henry, Life Correspondence and Speeches*, by his grandson William Wirt Henry (New York: Charles Scribner's Sons, 1891, reprinted by Sprinkle Publications, Harrisonburg, VA, 1993) contains his speeches with brief summaries of responses by

other delegates. The complete proceedings of the Virginia Ratification Convention, including Henry's speeches, may be found in volumes VIII–XI, of DHRC.

30. Morris, *Encyclopedia of American History*, 115.

31. DHRC, IX:929–931.

32. Ibid.

33. Ibid., IX:931–936.

34. Richard B. Morris, *Witnesses at the Creation: Hamilton, Madison, Jay, and the Constitution* (New York: Holt, Rinehart and Winston, 1985), 197.

Chapter 14. A Bane of Sedition

1. DHRC, IX:949–951.

2. Henry, II:267–268, citing the description of "an old Baptist clergyman who was one of the auditory."

3. Henry, III:568.

4. DHRC, IX:951–968.

5. Ibid.

6. Ibid.

7. Henry, II:359.

8. Ibid., II:381.

9. Ibid., II:382.

10. Ibid., II:536–537; Henry, III:471–472.

11. Henry, II:544–545.

12. DHRC, IX:951–968.

13. Ibid., IX:968.

14. Ibid., IX:971–989.

15. Ibid., IX:689–998.

16. Ibid., IX:1016–1028.

17. Ibid., IX:1028–1035.

18. Ibid., IX:1072–1080.

19. Ibid., IX:1036.

20. Ibid., IX:1082.

21. Ibid.

22. Ibid., IX:1082–1083.

23. Henry, III:518–519.

24. DHRC, IX:1246.

25. George Washington to Patrick Henry, September 24, 1787, PGW Confed., 5:339–340.

26. Henry, III:501.

27. Ibid., III:582–583.

28. James Madison to George Washington, June 13, 1788, PGW Confed., 6:329.

29. Comte de Moustier to Comte de Montmorin, June 23, 1788, DHRC, XXI: 1227–1228.

30. DHRC, X:1476–1477.

31. Henry, III:586; Morgan, 354.

32. Wirt, 313; Henry II:371.

Chapter 15. Beef! Beef! Beef!

1. Henry, II:364.

2. James Monroe to Thomas Jefferson, July 12, 1788, Dumas Malone, *Jefferson and His Time, Volume Two: Jefferson and the Rights of Man* (Boston: Little, Brown and Company, 1951), 175.

3. DHRC X:1498.

4. Ibid., X:1537.

5. James Madison to George Washington, June 27, 1788, PGW Confed., 6: 356–357.

6. Thomas Jefferson to William S. Smith, February 2, 1788, Malone, *Jefferson and the Rights of Man*, 171.

7. Henry, II:416.

8. Ibid., II:419–420.

9. Ibid., II:421.

10. Ibid., II:422.

11. Ibid.

12. Ibid.

13. Ibid., II:423–425.

14. Henry, III:527–528.

15. Patrick Henry to Mrs. Elizabeth Aylett, November 11, 1788, Henry, II:434.

16. Patrick Henry to Richard Henry Lee, November 15, 1788, ibid., II:428–430.

17. Tobias Lear, January 31, 1789, ibid., II:433.

18. James Madison to Thomas Jefferson, February 15, 1789, *Writings of James Monroe,* I:199.

19. Richard Labunski, *James Madison and the Struggle for the Bill of Rights* (New York: Oxford University Press, 2006), 64.

20. William Grayson to Patrick Henry, June 12, 1789, Henry, II:443.

21. Robert R. Rutland, ed., *The Papers of James Madison* (Charlottesville: University Press of Virginia, 1984–1989, 17 vols.), 12:203.

22. The Tenth Amendment reads: "The powers not delegated to the United States by the constitution, nor prohibited by it to the states, are reserved to the states respectively, or to the people."

23. Patrick Henry to Richard Henry Lee, January 28, 1790, Henry, II:451

24. Edmund Randolph to George Washington, November 22, 1789, ibid., II:449.

25. Henry Lee to President George Washington, August 17, 1794, Tyler, 399.

26. Fitzpatrick, *Writings . . . ,* 33:474–479.

27. Ibid.

28. Meade, *Patrick Henry, Practical Revolutionary*, 397.

29. Henry, II:478–479.

30. Morgan, 387.

31. Spencer Roane to William Wirt, in Morgan, 447.

32. Henry, II:484.

33. Ibid.

34. Wirt, 389–391.

35. Edmund Randolph to George Washington, June 24, 1793, PGW Pres., 13: 137–142.

36. Henry, II:472.

37. Morgan, 386.

38. John Marshall to Rufus King, May 24, 1796, in Jean Edward Smith, *John Marshall: Definer of a Nation* (New York: Henry Holt and Company, 1996), 148.

39. Wirt, 337–338.

40. Henry, II:495.

41. Ibid., II:475.

42. Wirt, 363.

43. Morgan, 433.

44. Mark Couvillon, *Patrick Henry's Virginia* (Brookneal, VA: The Patrick Henry Memorial Foundation, 2001), 87.

45. Henry, II:475.

46. Tyler, 369–370.

47. Henry, II:488.

Chapter 16. The Sun Has Set in All Its Glory

1. Roane memorandum to William Wirt, in Morgan, 439.

2. Beeman, 183.

3. Theodore Bland to Patrick Henry, March 9, 1790, Henry, III:417–420.

4. Patrick Henry to Governor Edward Telfair, October 14, 1790, Henry II:507.

5. Although Henry died in 1799, many Yazoo shareholders sued for compensation. When Georgia ceded the territory to the federal government in 1802, they took their claims to the United States Supreme Court and, in 1810, won their case. Although the court conceded the fraudulent basis of the original contract, it ruled that the fraud committed by participants did not affect the obligations of the contract. In 1814, Congress voted $4 million to settle with the Yazoo investors—eight times their original investment.

6. Henry Lee to James Madison, April 3, 1790, in Beeman, 174.

7. Couvillon, 95.

8. *Kentucky Gazette* (Lexington), April 5, 1794.

9. George Washington to Edmund Pendleton, January 22, 1795, in Fitzpatrick, *Writings . . .* , 34:98–101.

10. Patrick Henry to Elizabeth Aylett, August 30, 1796, in Henry, II:568–571.

11. Edmund Randolph to George Washington, June 24, 1793, PGW Pres., 13:137–142.

12. Patrick Henry to Elizabeth Aylett, August 20, 1796, Henry II:568–571.

13. Patrick Henry to Henry Lee, July 14, 1794, ibid., II:547.

14. Patrick Henry to Edmund Randolph, September 14, 1794, ibid., II:548–549.

15. George Washington to Patrick Henry, October 9, 1795, ibid., II:556–557.

16. Patrick Henry to George Washington, October 16, 1795, ibid., II:558–559.

17. Henry, II:519.

18. Ibid., II:518.

19. Thomas Jefferson to James Monroe, July 10, 1796, cited in Henry, II:572.

20. John Marshall to Rufus King, May 24, 1796, Smith, *John Marshall*, 148n.

21. Patrick Henry to Elizabeth Aylet, August 20, 1796, in Daily, 156.

22. *Virginia Gazette*, September 15, 1796.

23. *Virginia Gazette and General Advertiser*, November 16, 1796.

24. Morris, *Encyclopedia of American History*, 130.

25. John C. Miller, *The Federalist Era, 1789–1801* (New York: Harper & Brothers, 1960), 240–241.

26. Patrick Henry to George Washington, October 16, 1795, Henry, II:558–559.

27. George Washington to Patrick Henry, January 15, 1799, ibid., II:601–604.

28. Henry, II:607–610; Edward Fontaine, "Patrick Henry—A Patrick Henry Essay by Patrick Henry's great-grandson," published by the Patrick Henry Memorial Foundation, 2008.

29. Patrick Henry to George Washington, April 16, 1799, Henry, II:623–624.

30. Ibid., II:625.

31. Ibid., II:610, citing John H. Rice.

Afterword

1. John Locke, *Second Treatise of Government* (1690), as cited in *Bartlett's Familiar Quotations*, 277; Plutarch, *Lives, Life of Solon*, cited in *Bartlett's*, 56; Jonathan Swift, *A Critical Essay upon the Faculties of the Mind* (1707): "Laws are like cobwebs, which may catch small flies, but let wasps and hornets break through." *Bartlett's*, 288.

Appendix A: The Speech

1. As stated earlier, no actual transcript of Henry's speech exists, and the words shown here represent a reconstruction by Henry's first biographer, William Wirt, who extrapolated its contents from recollections—forty years after the event—by those present at St. Paul's, including John Tyler, an intimate of Henry's, Thomas Jefferson, Edmund Randolph, and St. George Tucker, among others. Hardly a friend of Henry, Jefferson did not alter a word in Wirt's reconstruction of the speech and reiterated his

appraisal of Henry as the greatest orator in history. I believe, however, that word-for-word accuracy is less important than what I believe to be an accurate presentation of Henry's meaning, his passion, and his eloquence.

2. Tyler, 140–145, citing Peter Force, ed., *American Archives* (Washington: 1837–1853, 9 vols.), II:167 ff.

Appendix B: Henry on Slavery

1. Patrick Henry to Robert Pleasants, January 18, 1773, in Meade, I:299–300.

Appendix C: Henry's Heirs

1. Morgan, 455, 459.

Bibliography of Principal Sources

Bibliographical Essay

Three principal sources of original Patrick Henry materials that are listed below in the bibliography deserve more complete identification. Henry's grandson, William Wirt Henry (1831–1900), accumulated as much as remained of his grandfather's papers—from more than one hundred of his grandfather's descendants, relatives, and friends. The result was the three-volume epic, *Patrick Henry: Life Correspondence and Speeches* (New York: Charles Scribner's Sons, 1891), which contains the largest trove of original, authenticated manuscripts of Patrick Henry's speeches and correspondence. Although biased in his grandfather's favor, William Wirt Henry was nonetheless a serious scholar and historian. A graduate of the University of Virginia, he passed his bar exams in 1853, served in the Confederate Army during the Civil War, then practiced law in Richmond and served in both houses of the Virginia state legislature. At various times, he was president of the Virginia Bar Association, vice president of the American Bar Association, president of the Virginia Historical Society and the American Historical Association. Besides his biography of Patrick Henry, he was author of *The Trial of Aaron Burr and the Trials of Jefferson Davis*, along with many magazine articles on American history.

Patrick Henry's first biographer actually knew Henry. A prominent attorney and member of Virginia's Tidewater social elite, William Wirt (1772–1834) collected long "memoirs," as they were called, from many of Henry's relatives, in-laws, friends, and political friends and foes. Although he had access to original manuscripts, he let his own patriotic bias—and those of Henry's friends and enemies—color his work, forcing today's researcher to pick carefully among the pages of his 450-plus-page biography to filter factual material from biased interpretations of actual events and documents. Although a valuable resource, Wirt's *Life of Patrick Henry*, which he published in 1817, was but a pastime. He was, above all else, a lawyer, who gained national prominence as a prosecutor in the treason trial of Aaron Burr in 1807. President James Monroe appointed him U.S. attorney general in 1817, a post he retained through Monroe's two terms and President John Quincy Adams's one-term presidency. Thomas Jefferson offered Wirt the presidency of the University of Virginia in 1826, but Wirt declined in favor of remaining attorney general.

Moses Coit Tyler (1835–1900) was a contemporary of William Wirt Henry and one of America's first American history scholars. He was a clergyman as a young man, but his scholarship earned him a professorship in English at the University of Michigan and, later, appointment at Cornell University as America's first professor of history. His 450-page biography, *Patrick Henry,* relies on his own examinations of original manuscripts in the hands of Henry family members—including William Wirt Henry, who cooperated with Tyler. More than William Wirt Henry, however, Tyler often exposed the flaws in the William Wirt biography and tries to separate the actuality of Henry's life from exaggerations, inventions, and biases of his contemporaries. A founder of the American Historical Association, Tyler was author of *A History of American Literature During the Colonial Time, 1607–1765* (1878, 2 vols.), *The Literary History of the American Revolution, 1763–1783* (1897, 2 vols.), and *Three Men of Letters* (1895)—the biographies of George Berkeley, Timothy Dwight, and Joel Barlow.

Few original Henry manuscripts survive. In the first place, he was not a prolific letter writer. Second, he seldom wrote out his speeches, preferring to speak from notes. Thirdly, his wife burned all his letters after his death—a common practice in eighteenth-century America, when widows and widowers routinely remarried after the death of a spouse to ensure continuing care and sustenance for their children. And finally, the few papers that did survive burned in a 1917 fire that leveled the house at Red Hill, his last home. His law office still stands, as does the site of his and Dorothea's graves. The property is now the National Memorial to Patrick Henry and includes reconstructed buildings and an extensive collection of Patrick Henry artifacts.

There never was a manuscript of his famous "liberty or death" speech in St. John's Church. The speech quoted in these pages represents a reconstruction by Henry's first biographer, William Wirt, who extrapolated its contents from recollections—forty years after the event—by those present at St. John's, including Judge John Tyler, an intimate of Henry's, along with Thomas Jefferson, Edmund Randolph, and Judge St. George Tucker, among others.

Bibliography

W. W. Abbot, ed., *The Papers of George Washington, Presidential Series* (Charlottesville: University Press of Virginia, 1987–in progress, 15 vols. to date).

W. W. Abbott and Dorothy Twohig, eds., *The Papers of George Washington, Colonial Series, 1748–August 1755* (Charlottesville: University Press of Virginia, 1983–1995, 10 vols.).

W. W. Abbot and Dorothy Twohig, eds., *The Papers of George Washington, Confederation Series* (Charlottesville: University Press of Virginia, 6 vols.).

W. W. Abbott, Dorothy Twohig, Philander D. Chase, eds., *The Papers of George Washington, Revolutionary War Series, June 1775–April 1778* (Charlottesville: University of Virginia Press, 1984–2004 [in progress], 19 vols.).

Charles F. Adams, ed., *The Works of John Adams, Second President of the United States: With a Life of the Author* (Boston: Little, Brown & Company, 1850–1856, 10 vols.).

John Adams, *Thoughts on Government* (Philadelphia: John Dunlop, 1776).

John R. Alden, *History of the American Revolution* (New York: Alfred A. Knopf, 1969).

James Curtis Ballagh, *The Letters of Richard Henry Lee* (New York, 1911–1914, 2 vols.).

Richard R. Beeman, *Patrick Henry: A Biography* (New York: McGraw-Hill Book Company, 1974).

Charlene Bangs Bickford et al., eds., *Documentary History of the First Federal Congress* (Baltimore: Johns Hopkins University Press, 1992).

Mark May Boatner III, *Encyclopedia of the American Revolution* (New York: David McKay Company, Inc., 1966).

Benson Bobrick, *Angel in the Whirlwind: The Triumph of the American Revolution* (New York: Simon & Schuster, 1997).

Claude G. Bowers, *The Young Jefferson, 1743–1789* (Boston: Houghton Mifflin Company, 1945).

Julian P. Boyd et al., eds., *The Papers of Thomas Jefferson* (Princeton, NJ: Princeton University Press, 1950, 34 vols.).

John Buchanan, *The Road to Guilford Courthouse: The American Revolution in the Carolinas* (New York: John Wiley & Sons, 1997).

Lester J. Cappon, ed., *The Adams-Jefferson Letters: The Complete Correspondence between Thomas Jefferson and Abigail and John Adams* (Chapel Hill: University of North Carolina Press, 1959).

Mark Couvillon, *Patrick Henry's Virginia* (Brookneal, VA: The Patrick Henry Memorial Foundation, 2001).

Lawrence A. Cremin, *American Education: The Colonial Experience, 1607–1783* (New York: Harper & Row, Publishers, 1970).

W. P. Cresson, *James Monroe* (Chapel Hill: University of North Carolina Press, 1946).

George Washington Parke Custis, *Recollections and Private Memoirs of Washington* (New York: Derby & Jackson, 1860).

Patrick Daily, *Patrick Henry: The Last Years, 1789–1799* (Bedford, VA: Patrick Henry Memorial Foundation, 1987).

Henri Doniol, *Histoire de la Participation de la France à l'Établissement des États-Unis d'Amérique* (Paris: Imprimerie Nationale, 1886, 5 vols., quarto).

Alice Morse Earle, *Child Life in Colonial Days* (Stockbridge, MA: Berkshire House Publishers, 1993).

Max Farrand, *The Fathers of the Constitution: A Chronicle of the Establishment of the Union* (New Haven, CT: Yale University Press, 1921).

———, ed., *The Records of the Federal Convention of 1787* (New Haven, CT: Yale University Press, 1911, 4 vols.).

William Findley, *History of the Insurrection in the Four Western Counties of Pennsylvania in the year M.DCC.XCIV* (Philadelphia: Samuel Harrison Smith, 1796).

John C. Fitzpatrick, ed., *The Writings of George Washington, from the Original Manuscript Sources, 1745–1799* (Washington, DC: U.S. Government Printing Office, 1931–1944, 39 vols.).

Paul Leicester Ford, *The Writings of Thomas Jefferson* (New York: G. P. Putnam's Sons, 1892–1899, 10 vols.).

William M. Fowler, Jr., *The Baron of Beacon Hill: A Biography of John Hancock* (Boston: Houghton, Mifflin Company, 1980).

Douglas Southall Freeman, *George Washington*. Completed by John Alexander Carroll and Mary Wells Ashworth. (New York: Charles Scribner's Sons, 1957, 7 vols.).

Henry Lawrence Gipson, *The Coming of the Revolution, 1763–1775* (New York: Harper & Brothers, 1954).

Kevin J. Hayes, *The Mind of a Patriot: Patrick Henry and the World of Ideas* (Charlottesville: University Press of Virginia, 2008).

Burton J. Hendrick, *The Lees of Virginia: Biography of a Family* (Boston: Little Brown, and Company, 1935).

William Wirt Henry, *Patrick Henry: Life, Correspondence and Speeches* (New York: Charles Scribner's Sons, 1891, 3 vols.).

Don Higginbotham, *The War of American Independence: Military Attitudes, Policies, and Practice, 1763–1789* (New York: The Macmillan Company, 1971).

Donald Jackson and Dorothy Twohig, eds., *The Diaries of George Washington* (Charlottesville: University Press of Virginia, 1976–1979, 6 vols.)

Merrill Jensen, *The New Nation: A History of the United States During the Confederation, 1781–1789* (New York: Alfred A. Knopf, 1950).

Merrill Jensen, John P. Kaminski, Gaspare Saladino, Richard Leffler, Charles H. Schoenleber, eds., *The Documentary History of the Ratification of the Constitution* (Madison, WI: State Historical Society of Wisconsin, 1976–[in progress], 22 vols. to date).

John P. Kaminski, *George Clinton: Yeoman Politician of the New Republic* (Madison, WI: Madison House Publishers, Inc., 1993).

———, ed., *The Founders on the Founders: Word Portraits from the American Revolutionary Era* (Charlottesville: University of Virginia Press, 2008).

————, *James Madison, Champion of Liberty and Justice* (Madison, WI: Parallel Press, 2006).

————, ed., *The Quotable Jefferson* (Princeton: Princeton University Press, 2006).

John P. Kaminski and Richard Leffler, eds., *Federalists and Antifederalists: The Debate Over the Ratification of the Constitution* (Madison, WI: Madison House Publishers, Inc., 1998).

Bernhard Knollenberg, *Growth of the American Revolution, 1766–1775* (New York: The Free Press, 1975).

Leonard W. Labaree, et al., *Papers of Benjamin Franklin* (New Haven: Yale University Press, 1959–[in progress], 38 vols. to date).

Richard Labunski, *James Madison and the Struggle for the Bill of Rights* (New York: Oxford University Press, 2006).

George-Washington Lafayette [Gilbert Motier, Marquis de Lafayette], *Mémoires, Correspondence et Manuscrits du Général Lafayette, publiés par sa famille* (Bruxelles: Société Belge de Librairie, Etc., Hauman, Cattoir et Compagnie, 2 vols., 1837).

James Madison, *Notes of Debates in the Federal Convention of 1787 reported by James Madison* (New York: W. W. Norton & Co., Inc., 1987).

————, *The Papers of James Madison*, Robert R. Rutland, ed. (Charlottesville: University Press of Virginia, 1984–1989, 16 vols.).

Dumas Malone, *Jefferson and His Time* (Boston: Little, Brown and Company, 1948–1977, 6 vols.). Individual titles:

Vol. 1. *Jefferson the Virginian* (1948).
Vol. 2. *Jefferson and the Rights of Man* (1951).
Vol. 3. *Jefferson and the Ordeal of Liberty* (1962).
Vol. 4. *Jefferson the President: First Terms, 1901–1805* (1970).
Vol. 5. *Jefferson the President: Second Term, 1805–1809* (1974).
Vol. 6. *Jefferson, the Sage of Monticello* (1977).

Ann Maury, *Memories of a Huguenot Family* (New York, 1872).

Bernard Mayo, *Myths and Men: Patrick Henry, George Washington, Thomas Jefferson* (Athens, GA: University of Georgia Press, 1959).

John J. McCusker, *How Much Is That in Real Money? A Historical Commodity Price Index for Use as a Deflator of Money Values in the Economy of the United States* (Worcester, MA: American Antiquarian Society, 2001, 2d ed.).

Robert Douthat Meade, *Patrick Henry: Patriot in the Making* (Philadelphia: J. B. Lippincott Company, 1957).

————, *Patrick Henry: Practical Revolutionary* (Philadelphia: J. B. Lippincott Company, 1969).

James Monroe, *The Autobiography of James Monroe* (Syracuse, NY: G. P. Putnam's Sons, 1926).

————, *The Writings of James Monroe: Including a Collection of His Public and Private Papers and Correspondence Now for the First Time Printed*, Stanislaus Murray Hamilton, ed. (Washington, DC: Government Printing Branch, U.S. Department of State, 1898, 7 vols.).

George Morgan, *The True Patrick Henry* (Philadelphia: J. B. Lippincott Company, 1907).

Richard B. Morris, *Witnesses at the Creation: Hamilton, Madison, Jay, and the Constitution* (New York: Holt, Rinehart and Winston, 1985).

Daniel Preston, ed., *The Papers of James Monroe* (Westport, CT: Greenwood Press, 2003–2006, 2 vols. [in progress]).

Edmund Randolph, *History of Virginia*. Edited by Arthur H. Shaffer. (Charlottesville: Published for The Virginia Historical Society, The University Press of Virginia, 1970).

Robert R. Rutland, ed., *The Papers of James Madison* (Charlottesville: University Press of Virginia, 1984–1989, 16 vols.).

Carl Sandburg, *The American Songbag* (New York: Harcourt Brace Jovanovich, 1927).

Jean Edward Smith, *John Marshall: Definer of a Nation* (New York: Henry Holt and Company, 1996).

Moses Coit Tyler, *Patrick Henry* (Boston: Houghton Mifflin, 1887).

Harlow Giles Unger, *America's Second Revolution* (Hoboken, NJ: John Wiley & Sons, 2007).

———, *John Hancock: Merchant King and American Patriot* (New York: John Wiley & Sons, 2000).

———, *Lafayette* (Hoboken, NJ: John Wiley & Sons, 2002).

———, *The Last Founding Father: James Monroe and a Nation's Call to Greatness* (Cambridge, MA: Da Capo Press, Perseus Books Group, 2009).

———, *The Unexpected George Washington: His Private Life* (Hoboken, NJ: John Wiley & Sons, 2006).

Carl Van Doren, *The Great Rehearsal: The Story of the Making and Ratifying of the Constitution of the United States* (New York: The Viking Press, 1948).

William Wirt, *The Life of Patrick Henry* (New York: Derby & Jackson, 1860).

Reference Works

John Bartlett, Justin Kaplan, eds., *Familiar Quotations* (Boston: Little, Brown and Company, 16th ed., 1992).

Richard B. Morris, *Encyclopedia of American History* (New York: Harper & Brothers, 1953).

The New Encyclopedia Britannica (Chicago: Encyclopedia Britannica, Inc., 15th ed., 1985).

Ploetz' Dictionary of Dates (New York: Halcyon House, 1925).

Harlow G. Unger, *Encyclopedia of American Education* (New York: Facts On File, Inc., 3rd ed., 2007, 3 vols.).

Webster's American Biographies, Charles Van Doren, ed. (Springfield, MA: Merriam-Webster Inc., 1984).

Index

Adams, Abigail, 86, 89
Adams, John
    Boston Massacre and, 66–68
    on Henry as orator, 3, 88
    independence movement and, 76, 86,
       89, 91–92, 95, 104, 119
    Jefferson letter to, 202
    portrait of, 77
    as president, 269, 276
    Thoughts on Government, 114
    as vice president, 243
Adams, Samuel
    Boston Massacre and, 66–67, 69
    charge of traitor and, 79, 95
    at Continental Congress, 104
    flight from Boston, 100
    Gaspée and, 75–76
    mob and, 44
    opposition to Galloway proposal, 90
    propaganda and, 32, 42, 101–102
    on Virginia's unity with colonies, 81
Alexander, Archibald, 255
Alien Enemies Act, 269–270, 276
American Historical Association, 286
Anglican Church, 5, 7, 9, 11,
    12, 19–24, 27, 30, 53, 54,
    124–125, 167
    parish taxes, 19–20, 30

popular resentment against clergy, 24,
    28, 30
    See also Church of England
Annapolis Convention, 178–179, 181
Antifederalists, 201–205, 208–209, 212,
    233–234, 240, 244, 264, 268–269
Apollo Room, at Raleigh Tavern, 34, 63
Arnold, Benedict, 154
    portrait of, 155
The Articles of Compact, 175
Articles of Confederation, 163
    Annapolis Convention, 178, 181
    revising, 185–186 (*see also*
       Constitutional Convention)
Aylett, Elizabeth Henry, 240
Aylett, Philip, 183

Baptists, 53–54, 167, 242
Battle of Long Island, 118–119
Berkeley, Norborne (Baron de Botetourt),
    61–62, 63, 74
Bernard, Francis, 42
Beverlys, 35
"Bill for Establishing Religious Freedom"
    (Jefferson), 167
Bill of Rights, 233
    The Articles of Compact, 175
    calls for, 197, 202, 205, 209

Bill of Rights *(continued)*
  Henry and, xiv, 2, 234–235, 243–244
  Madison and, 242, 243, 244
  states' rights and, 243–244
Blackstone, William, 17
Blair, John, 34, 62, 186
Bland, Richard, 69
Bland, Theodore, 258
Board of War, 133
Bohun, William, 17
Boston
  boycott of British goods and, 84
  martial law in, 84
  rebellion against Stamp Act, 43–46
  resistance to British rules, 66–69, 78–80
  during Revolutionary War, 104–105
  See also Massachusetts
Boston Evening Post (newspaper), 32
Boston Gazette (newspaper), 42, 66, 75
Boston Independent Chronicle
  (newspaper), 181
Boston Massacre, 66–69
Boston Port Bill, 80, 84
Boston Tea Party, 78–80
Botetourt (Lord), 61–62, 63, 74
Boucher, Jonathan, 69
Bowdoin, James, 67
Boycotts of British goods, 47–49, 59–60,
  61, 63, 65, 83–85
Breed's Hill, 104
British Board of Trade, 78
British colonies, map of (1763), 8
British Debts Case, xiv, 249–255
Bunker's Hill, 105
Burgoyne, John, 130–131, 132
Burke, Edmund, 80, 94
Burr, Aaron, 286
Byron, Lord, 3

Cabell, Dr. George, 272
Canal-building projects, 166–167
Capitol (Williamsburg, Virginia), 29
Carlisle, Lord, 141, 142
Carpenters' Hall, 87
Carrington, Edward, 206
Carters, 35
Chapelle, Alonzo, 56
Charleston, British capture of, 152–153

Cherokees, war with, 129
Christian, Anne Henry, 58, 173, 184
Christian, John Henry, 246, 262
Christian, William, 58, 173
Church and state, separation of, 51,
  53, 167
Church of England, 5, 27, 167
  See Anglican Church
Clark, George Rogers, 124, 137,
  146–147, 148
Clinton, George, 207–209, 229,
  236, 243
Coercive Acts, 80–81, 83
  Continental Congress and resolves
  against, 89–90, 91
Coke, Edward, 15
College of William and Mary, 13, 20, 34,
  35, 36, 62, 108, 189
Colonies
  1763 map of, 8
  protests against Townshend Acts, 59–62
  trade with Britain, 31–33
  travel between, 87
  See also individual colonies
Colonists
  boycotts of British goods, 47–49, 59–60,
  61, 63, 65, 83–85
  opposition to British-imposed taxes,
  30–32, 42–50, 59–64, 65–68
Commentaries on the Laws of England
  (Blackstone), 17
Committee of Safety, 107–108, 109,
  110, 111
Committee on Privileges and Elections, 28
"Committee on Stile," 193
Committees of correspondence, 76–77
The Compleat Chancery-Practiser
  (Jacob), 17
Concord, battle at, 100–101
Confederation Congress, 163, 174, 185
Connecticut, 45, 60, 119–120, 192,
  193, 204
Constitution
  final draft, 194
  Henry and Antifederalist objections to,
  2, 197, 198–200, 203–204, 209–210,
  216–222
  ratification of, 198, 201–213, 233–235

Constitutional Convention, xiv, 186,
    187–195
Continental Army
    establishment of, 104
    Henry's efforts to aid, 121–122, 123,
        127–129, 136–140, 144–145, 153
    shortages and, 143–144
    at Valley Forge, 125, 136–140
Continental Association, 91
Continental Congress
    First, 77, 84–92, 93, 100, 113
    Second, 102, 104, 105
    See also Intercolonial congresses
Conway, Thomas, 133–134, 135
Corbin, Francis, 223–224, 236–239
Cornwallis, Charles, 110, 133, 153, 154,
    156, 157, 158, 159
Creek Indians, 259
Culpeper Minutemen, 108, 110, 111,
    118–119
Custis, Martha Dandridge, 13

Dabneys, 9
Dandridge, Bartholomew, 172
Dandridge, Dorothea, xiii, 130, 132. *See also*
    Henry, Dorothea Dandridge
Dandridge, Nathaniel West, 13, 28–30, 130
Dandridge, Nathaniel West, II, 262
Dartmouth, Lord, 100
Davis, Jefferson, 286
Debt
    American government, 163–164,
        259–260
    British government, 31, 249–255
Declaration of Independence, 117, 119, 194
"Declaration of Rights and Grievances of
    the Colonists in America," 45
"Declaration of the Causes and Necessities
    of Taking Up Arms," 105
Declarations and Pleadings (Bohun), 17
Declaratory Act, 50
Delaware, 60, 93, 177, 178, 204,
    206, 209
Demosthenes, 3
d'Estaing, Charles-Henri Comte, 149, 150
Dickinson, John, 60, 105
Digest of Virginia Acts, 15
Don't Tread on Me motto, 108, 109

Le Droit des gens (The Law of Nations)
    (von Vattel), 251
Dunmore, (Lord) John M., 74, 75, 77, 93,
    95, 102, 103, 107, 110, 111, 189

Earl of Shelburne, 64
East India Company, 78, 80
Economic troubles after Revolution,
    173–174
Eisenhower, Dwight D., 277
Ellsworth, Oliver, 192

Fairfax Independent Company, 93
Farmers
    Continental Army and, 108, 113, 131,
        143–144
    flooding and, 72–74
    Parsons' Cause case and, 5, 20–23
    Piedmont/western, 152, 162, 173–174,
        186–187, 225
    protests after Revolution, 174, 175,
        177–178
    Whiskey Rebellion and, 260, 263
Fauquier, Francis, 42
The Federalist (Madison), 242
Federalists, 201–205, 233–234, 244,
    267–268, 270, 276
    attempts to discredit Henry,
        215–216, 218
    response to Henry's arguments against
        Constitution, 222–227
Federal Republicans, 208–209, 235
First Continental Congress, 77, 93,
    100, 113
*First Part of the Institutes of the Lawes of
    England, or, A Commentarie upon
    Littleton* (Coke), 15
Floods of 1771, 72–73
Fontaine, Edward, 246
Fontaine, John, 71, 72, 73, 93, 151, 246
Fontaine, Martha Henry, 71, 72, 73, 93,
    108, 124, 151, 169, 246, 272
Fontaine, Patrick Henry, 124, 251, 262, 272
Fowey (ship), 103
France
    aid in Revolutionary War from, 149–150,
        158–159
    British declaration of war on, 143

France *(continued)*
    recognition of United States, 132
    treaties with United States, 140, 141
Franklin, Benjamin, 87, 104, 119, 140,
    193, 205
Freedom of religion, 2, 108, 116,
    197, 200
Freeman's Journal (newspaper), 204

Gage, Thomas, 61, 84, 100
Galloway, Joseph, 89
Gardoqui, Diego de, 179
Gaspée (ship), 75
Gates, Horatio, 131, 132, 133–134,
    135, 153
General Court, 55–57
George III, 39, 51, 94
    Coercive Acts and, 79–80
    Olive Branch Petition and, 105, 110
    slave trade and, 75
    Stamp Act and, 40, 49–50
    Townshend Acts and, 60
George Washington University, 177
Georgia, 45, 87, 104, 148, 150, 152, 204,
    258–259
"Gettysburg Address" (Lincoln), 279
Government
    Montesquieu on, 113–114
    Virginia plan of, 114–116, 189–191
Grayson, William, 210, 234, 240, 243, 244
Great Flood of 1771, 72–73
Greene, Nathanael, 139, 153, 154, 156
Grenville, George, 31, 46, 47, 49, 59

Hall, Lyman, 104
Hamilton, Alexander, 145, 181, 259–260,
    262–263, 267
Hampden-Sydney Academy, 124
Hampden-Sydney College, 185, 246, 270,
    285
Hancock, John, 47, 59, 61, 79, 91, 95,
    100, 104, 117, 122
Hanover County Courthouse, 5, 6, 12,
    13, 20
Hanover County (Virginia), 7, 9, 14, 28,
    43, 90
Harrison, Benjamin, 62, 157, 161, 198, 210
Henry, Alexander, 219, 286

Henry, Anne (daughter), 124, 132, 183
Henry, Anne (sister), 58, 124
Henry, Dorothea Dandridge, xiii
    birth of children, 132, 143, 152, 162,
        166, 169, 219, 246, 261, 275
    as hostess, 171
    at Leatherwood, 151
    portrait of, 144
    Red Hill and, 261, 286
    remarriage, 285
Henry, Dorothea (daughter), 143
Henry, Edward (son), 132, 185, 246,
    285, 286
Henry, Edward (son, 2nd), 261, 285, 286
Henry, Elizabeth (Betsey), 124, 130, 132,
    154, 183, 240, 246, 264, 265, 268
Henry, Fayette, 169, 285, 286
Henry, Jane Robertson, 275
Henry, John (father), 6–9, 11, 13
    Parsons' Cause case and, 20–21
Henry, John (son), 12, 108, 124, 130, 285
    disappearance of, 132, 142–143
Henry, John (son, 2nd), 264, 286
Henry, Martha, 12, 43, 71, 72, 73. *See also*
    Fontaine, Martha Henry
Henry, Martha Catherina, 162
Henry, Nathaniel, 285, 286
Henry, Nathaniel West, 246
Henry, Patrick
    address to Continental Congress, 88
    aid to Continental Army, 121–122, 123,
        127–129, 136–140, 144–145, 153
    arguments for perpetuation of
        Confederation, 216–222
    attempt to establish Christian religion in
        Virginia, 167
    attempt to replace Washington and,
        134–135
    Baptists and, 53–54
    Bill of Rights and, xiv, 2, 234–235,
        243–244
    birth of, xiii, 9
    birth of children/growth of family, 12,
        132, 143, 152, 154, 162, 166, 169,
        219, 246, 261, 264, 275
    boyhood, 9–12
    British army attempt to capture, 156–157
    British Debts case and, xiv, 249–255

call for constitutional amendments,
236–237, 239
canal-building projects and, 166–167
chronology, xiii–xiv
as commander of Virginia revolutionary
forces, 107–113
committee of correspondence and, 76–77
Constitutional Convention and,
186–187, 188, 192, 195
Corbin and, 223–224, 236–239
court presentation, 56–58
death of, xiv, 272–273, 275
defense of farmers affected by flooding,
72–74
defense of Williamsburg, 102–103
as delegate to intercolonial congress, 69,
84–85, 86, 91–92
as delegate to Second Continental
Congress, 104
as delegate to Second Virginia
Convention, 95–99
diplomatic relations with France and
Spain and, 142
dress, 14
education of, 11
in Electoral College, 243
entertaining as governor, 171
exhortation for Revolutionary War, 1
family home, 9–10
as farmer, xiii, 12
as father, 70–71, 154, 267
father of, 6–9, 11
Federalist attack on, 215–229
flexing political power, 240–242
freedom of religion and, 2, 108
frontier life and, 3
before General Court, 55–57
"Give me liberty, or give me death
speech," xiii, 97–98, 279–282
as governor, xiii–xiv, 2, 116–118, 169,
170–172, 183–184, 231
as governor during Revolutionary War,
120–125, 127–130, 132, 134–140,
142, 144–145, 46–149, 150–151
heirs, 285–286
in House of Burgesses, xiii, 28–29,
33–41, 35–42, 50–53, 55, 56, 58,
62–63, 69, 74–75, 76–77

in House of Delegates/Assembly, xiv, 29,
83, 103, 147–148, 151, 152,
163–168, 177, 201, 203–204,
236–239, 270–272
intermarriage of whites and Indians and,
xiv, 166, 170
Jay-Gardoqui agreement and, 179, 186,
187, 227–228, 229
as land owner, 257, 286
land purchases/speculation, xiv, 30, 43,
58, 142, 177, 185, 258
law examination, 15–16
law practice, xiv, 17, 53, 54–58,
200–201, 246–249, 261–262
as leader of western block in House of
Burgesses, 50–51
on limitation of federal power, xiv, 1, 2
loan to John Shelton, 31
Madison's attempts to dislodge him,
167–168, 170
malaria and, 123–124, 153, 162
marital advice, 183–184
marriage (first, Sarah), xiii, 12–13,
71–72, 93, 94
marriage (2nd, Dorothea), xiii, 130, 132,
143, 154
mother of, 7–9, 11
as musician, 10, 14–15
natural rights and, 3, 24
need for money, 184–185, 187, 198, 246
objections to Constitution, 2, 197,
198–200, 203–204, 209–210,
216–222
offer of Senate seat, 245–246, 264, 265
offers of political appointments,
265–266, 267–268
Parsons' Cause case, xiii, 5–7, 17, 19–25,
27–28, 30
portraits of, 56, 231, 250
pre-Revolutionary War debt, 250
Presbyterian church and, 11–12
as prophet on federal abuse of power,
260, 263–264, 276–277
Quebec Act and, 81
ratification of Constitution and, 206,
207, 209–213, 229–230, 233–235
Red Hill and, xiv, 261, 262, 272, 275,
285, 286

Henry, Patrick *(continued)*
    religiosity in later life, 173, 267
    religious education, 11–12
    resignation as governor, 184–185
    resolutions on taxation, 62–63
    retirement, 261
    return of Tories and, 165–166
    reversal of political position during war,
      127–128
    Roundabout home, 43, 54
    Scotchtown, xiii, 69–71, 72, 83, 123,
      124, 132, 151, 171
    separation of church and state and,
      51, 53
    Shelton tavern and, 12–13
    as slave-owner, 12, 13, 148, 151, 257
    on slavery, 51–53, 283–284
    slave trade ban, 51–52, 74–75, 148
    Stamp Act debate, 37–42
    Stamp Act speech, xiii, 97–98, 279–282
    state sovereignty and secession, 2
    as storekeeper, xiii, 12, 13
    study of law, xiii, 15–16, 17
    support for boycott in response to
      Coercive Acts, 83–85
    support for revolutionary war, 93–94
    suspicion of federal government power,
      90, 163, 179–180, 264–265
    threat of arrest, 95
    threat of secession over Mississippi River
      navigation rights, xiv
    ties to West, 58, 241
    trade relations with Spain and, 121
    Virginia's new government and,
      113–116
    war in West and, 122–123, 124, 129,
      137, 146–148
    wealth of, 257, 260–261
    Yazoo Land Company and, xiv, 258–259
Henry, Patrick, Jr., 166, 261–262, 285, 286
Henry, Patrick (Rev.), 5, 9, 21, 30, 130
Henry, Sarah, 152
Henry, Sarah Shelton, xiii, 12–13
    death of, xiii, 94
    depression of, xiii, 43, 55, 71–72
    suicide attempt, 93
Henry, Sarah Syme, 7–9, 11
Henry, William (brother), xiii, 9, 12, 172

Henry, William (son), 12, 124, 151, 185,
    218–219, 285–286
Henry, William Wirt, 90, 286
Henry County (Virginia), 125, 142, 151,
    153, 285
Hook, John, 248–249
House of Burgesses, 19–20, 28–29, 45, 84,
    87, 88–89, 181, 185, 213
    dissolution of, 63
    Henry and, xiii, 28–29, 33–41,
      50–53, 55, 56, 58, 62–63, 69, 74–75,
      76–77
    membership, 34–35
    Stamp Act debate in, 37–42
House of Delegates, 29, 99, 125, 127, 148,
    151, 152, 177, 183, 203, 239, 240,
    286. *See also* Virginia Assembly
Howe, Richard, 119
Howe, William, 118, 119, 130, 132–133
Hutchinson, Anne, 44
Hutchinson, Thomas, 44, 46, 67, 76, 84

Illinois, 2, 58, 137, 147–148
Illinois County, 147, 148
Independent Gazetteer (newspaper), 204,
    205, 229
Indiana, 2, 4, 58, 137, 147
Indians (native Americans)
    intermarriage with whites, xiv,
      166, 170
    wars with, 122–123, 129
Intercolonial congresses, 42, 45, 46, 69,
    83, 84–92
Iredell, James, 255

Jacob, Giles, 17
James River Company, 177
Jay, John, 89, 179, 227
Jay-Gardoqui agreement, 179, 186, 187,
    227–228, 229, 240
Jefferson, Thomas, 11, 85, 107
    amendments to Constitution, 276
    British attempt to capture, 156, 157
    committee of correspondence and,
      76–77, 81
    Declaration of Independence and, 117
    as governor, 151, 153, 154
    on Henry and call to revolution, 46

on Henry's increased power during
wartime, 127, 128
on Henry's opposition to national
tax, 164
on Henry's Stamp Act speech, 40
in House of Burgesses, 62
investigation of performance as governor,
157–158, 159–160
as leader in Virginia's House,
124–125
Madison and, 167–168, 267
Maury and, 20
meeting Patrick Henry, 13
as minister in Paris, 198
new capitol building and, 172
as political mentor, 242
portrait of, 159
on Randolph's betrayal of Henry, 213
ratification of Constitution and,
202–203, 204, 206, 234, 236
on Robinson's malfeasance, 36
as vice president, 269
Jones, Willie, 236
Jouett, Jack, 156, 157

Kentucky, 2, 173
call for amendments to Constitution, 241
Kentucky Resolutions, 269, 271, 276
land speculation in, 58, 258
navigation rights on Mississippi River
and, 180
nullification and, 277
ratification of Constitution and, 206,
210, 228, 233
war with Shawnees, 122–123
King, Rufus, 268
Knox, Henry, 175

Lafayette, Marquis de, 135–136, 145,
146, 156
farewell tour, 168–169
Latrobe, Benjamin Henry, 250
The Law of Nature and Nations
(Pufendorf), 17
Lear, Tobias, 241–242
Leatherwood plantation, 143, 150,
151–152, 162, 166, 286
Lee, Charles, 145

Lee, Francis Lightfoot, 34
Lee, Henry (Lighthorse Harry), 254, 260,
268, 277
Federalist attack on Henry and, 215,
216, 225–226
offer of Senate seat to Henry,
244–246, 264
Lee, Richard Henry, 34, 64, 85, 94, 122,
129, 135, 139, 144, 171, 244, 258
Coercive Acts and, 81
committee of correspondence and,
76–77
Constitutional Convention and, 187
death of, 264
as delegate to Continental Congress,
95, 116
as delegate to intercolonial congress,
84, 91
as delegate to Second Virginia
Convention, 95, 96
on Henry's return to governorship, 170
as Henry supporter, 40, 62, 96
on independence from Britain, 141
land purchases, 58
objections to Constitution, 197–198,
201–202
objection to proportionate voting, 89
portrait, 48
proposes American independence, 116
on revising Confederation, 175
as Senate candidate, 240, 241
Westmoreland Protests, 47, 84
Lee, William, 142
Lee family, 34, 35
Legal training in colonies, 17
L'Esprit des lois (The Spirit of Laws)
(Montesquieu), 89
Letters from a Farmer in Pennsylvania
(Dickinson), 60
*Letters of the Federal Farmer to the
Republican,* 201
Lexington, battle at, 100, 101
Liberty or Death motto, 99, 103, 109,
174, 175
"Liberty or Death" speech, xiii, 97–98,
279–282
Liberty (ship), 61
Liberty Tree, 44, 47

The Life and Opinions of Tristam Shandy
    (Sterne), 11
Lincoln, Abraham, 279
Lincoln, Benjamin, 152
Locke, John, 276
London (ship), 78
Long Island (New York), battle of, 118–119
Long Island (Virginia), 254, 261
Louisa County (Virginia), 43, 54

Madison, James, 164, 170, 177, 260
    Alien and Sedition Acts, 269
    Bill of Rights and, 233, 242, 243, 244
    Constitutional Convention and,
        186–187, 188
    on Henry's objections to ratification, 235
    as House candidate, 241–242
    Jefferson and, 167–168
    portrait of, 168
    ratification of Constitution and, 203,
        204, 206, 210
    response to Henry's anti-Constitution
        arguments, 223, 224–225,
        227–229, 230
    as Senate candidate, 240
    Virginia Resolution, 276
Magdalen (ship), 102
Maison Carée, 172
Malaria, Henry and, 123–124, 153, 162
The Manual Exercise, 113
Marshall, John, 108, 166, 167, 180, 250,
    251, 268, 270
Marshall, Thomas, 108
Maryland, 45, 60, 65, 85, 122, 206, 209
    boundary/commerce dispute with
        Virginia, 174–177
    preparation for war, 93, 95, 104
Maryland Gazette (newspaper), 42
Maryland Journal (newspaper), 180
Mason, George, 85, 171, 177, 186
    Constitutional Convention and, 192,
        194–195
    death of, 264
    declaration of rights, 116
    on Henry as hero of the
        Revolution, 160
    on Henry's oratory, 83
    land purchases, 58

objections to Constitution, 198,
    203–204, 206, 209, 210, 212, 235
on Patrick Henry, 3
portrait of, 117
resolutions on taxation, 62
Massachusetts
    boycott of British goods, 60, 65
    creation of first independent government
        in America, 90–91
    population of colony, 34
    in Revolutionary War, 100–101,
        104–105
    Shays's Rebellion, 178
    Tea Party and aftermath, 78–80
    See also Boston
Massachusetts Centinel (newspaper), 204
Maury, James, 20, 21–22, 24–25, 27–28
Mercer, Hugh, 107
Meredith, Jane Henry, 124
Meredith, Samuel, 10, 30, 50, 70–71, 132,
    254, 267
Mifflin, Thomas, 136, 139, 205
Minutemen, 100–101
Mississippi River, navigation rights on,
    xiv, 177, 179–180, 192, 210, 223,
    227, 265
Monmouth Court House, battle near,
    145–146
Monroe, James, 267
    as House candidate, 242
    navigation rights on Mississippi River
        and, 180
    objections to Constitution, 210, 227,
        234, 235
    in Revolutionary War, 108, 129
    as Senator, 264
Montesquieu, 3, 89, 113–114
Monticello, 157
Morgan, Daniel, 131, 154–156
Morris, Gouverneur, 193, 197, 208
"Mount Brilliant," 9
Mount Vernon, 85, 177
Moustier, Comte de, 229
Murray, John, 69

Native Americans. *See* Indians (native
    Americans)
Natural rights, 3, 16, 24, 58, 186, 225

Navigation Acts, 33
Nelson, Thomas, 158
Nelson, William, 55
The New Art of War, 113
New Hampshire, 45, 60, 98, 119, 131,
    174, 193, 206, 207, 235
New Hampshire Gazette (newspaper), 81
New Jersey, 45, 60, 69, 79, 178,
    204, 209
    Revolutionary War in, 122, 125, 128,
        129, 143, 145–146, 149, 173
Newport (Rhode Island), 45, 149, 158
New York
    ratification of Constitution, 207–209,
        236
    Revolutionary War in, 118–120,
        130–131, 135, 149
Nicholas, Robert Carter, 16, 57, 62
Norfolk (Virginia), 110–111, 150
North, (Lord) Frederick, 67
North Carolina, 45, 60, 65, 74, 174,
    241, 257, 258
    declaration of independence from
        Britain, 104
    ratification and, 206, 207, 209,
        236, 244
    Revolutionary War in, 111, 122,
        154, 156
Northwest Ordinance of 1787, 174–178
Nullification, 277
Nymphe (ship), 168

Odyssey, 11
Ohio, 2, 58, 81, 122, 170
Olive Branch Petition, 105, 110
Oliver, Andrew, 44
Otis, James, 32, 45–46
Otto, Louis-Guillaume, 205

Parker, John, 100
Parsons' Cause case, xiii, 5–7, 17, 19–25,
    27–28, 30
*Patrick Henry: Life, Correspondence and
    Speeches* (Henry), 286
Patrick Henry Foundation, 285
Patrick Henry National Memorial, 285
Pendleton, Edmund, 37, 41, 58, 85, 108,
    109, 112, 116, 219–220

Pennsylvania
    ratification of Constitution and,
        205–206, 221
    Revolutionary War in, 133, 136–140
Pennsylvania Chronicle (newspaper), 60
Percy, Hugh, 101
Pickering, Timothy, 272
Piedmont region of North Carolina,
    rebellion in, 73–74
Piedmont region of Virginia, 3, 11, 35
Pinckney, Charles, 191
Pinckney, Charles Cotesworth, 191
Pinckney, Thomas, 269
Pitcairn, John, 100
Pleasant Grove, 185, 247
Pleasants, Robert, 52, 53, 90, 118, 283
Plutarch, 276
Poindexter, Edith C., 285
Polly (ship), 78
Potomac Company, 177, 186
Powder Horn (Williamsburg), 102, 103
Powell, Leven, 268
Presbyterians, 11–12, 20, 167
Preston, Thomas, 66–67, 68
Propaganda, patriot, 32, 101–102
Proportionate representation, 87–89
Pufendorf, Samuel, 17

Quakers, 53
Quebec Act, 80–81
Quincy, Josiah, 67–68

Raleigh Tavern, 34, 38, 63, 76, 84
Randolph, Edmund, 96, 99, 115, 158, 244,
    264, 265
    arguments against Henry, 222–223, 224,
        226–227
    on Henry as young Burgess, 11–12, 35,
        37, 41
    invitation for Henry to attend
        Constitutional Convention, 185–186
    objections to Constitution, 194, 198, 203
    portrait of, 190
    pre-Revolutionary War debt, 250
    ratification of Constitution and, 203,
        210, 234
    support for Union, 212
    Virginia plan of government and, 189

Randolph, John, 16, 34
Randolph, Peyton, 34, 87, 96
Randolphs, 35
Rattlesnake flags, 109
Red Hill, xiv, 261, 272, 275, 285, 286
  sketch of, 262
"Regulators," 74
Religion
  attempt to establish Christianity as
    Virginia's, 167
  freedom of, 2, 108, 116, 197, 200
  separation of church and state, 51, 53,
    116, 167
  See also individual sects
"Repeal Day," 49
Revere, Paul, 67, 68, 69, 79, 90–91, 101
Revolution, calls for, 75–76
Revolutionary War
  cessation of hostilities, 158–159
  early battles, 100–101, 104–105
  in New Jersey, 145–146
  in New York, 118–120, 130–131,
    135, 149
  in North Carolina, 111, 122, 154, 156
  in Pennsylvania, 133, 136–140
  in the South, 150–151, 153–157, 158
  in South Carolina, 110, 118, 119, 148,
    153, 154, 156
  in Virginia, 107–113, 156–157
  in the West, 122–123, 124, 129, 137,
    146–148
Rhode Island, 45, 60, 65, 88, 139, 149,
    158, 188, 193, 206–207, 244
Richmond (Virginia), in Revolutionary War,
    154, 156, 158
*The Rights of the British Colonies Asserted
    and Proved* (Otis), 32
Roane, Spencer, 11, 83, 117–118, 171, 183,
    200–201, 239, 248, 257
Robertson, David, 223
Robinson, John, 34, 35, 36–37, 41, 45, 50,
    51, 69
Rochambeau, 159
Romney (ship), 61
Rush, Benjamin, 135
Rutledge, Edmund, 119
Rutledge, Edward, 89
Rutledge, John, 193

Scotchtown plantation, xiii, 69–71, 72,
    93, 123, 124, 132, 151, 171
Secession threats
  Alien and Sedition Acts and, 270–272
  of "middle confederacy," 229
  in New England, 181
  over Mississippi River navigation
    rights, xiv
  in parts of Virginia, North Carolina and
    Kentucky, 241
  of South, 258, 277
  Southern justification for, 230
  in West, 180–181
Second Continental Congress, 102, 104
Second Virginia Convention, 95–99
Sedition Act, 269–270, 276
Separation of church and state, 51, 53,
    116, 167
Seven Islands plantation, 286
Seven Years' War, 28, 31, 33
Shawnee Indians, war with, 122–123
Shays, Daniel, 178
Shays's Rebellion, 178
Shelby, Evan, 147
Shelton, John, 31
Shelton, Sarah, xiii, 12
Shelton tavern, 13, 14, 30
Shippen, William, 135
Shippen, William, Jr., 85
*A Short Narrative of the Horrid Massacre of
    Boston* (Bowdoin), 67
Simpson, Colonel, 138
Slaves, xiii, 2, 9, 12, 14, 34–35, 51–53,
    73, 74–75, 152, 191, 230
  British freeing during Revolution,
    150, 153
  federal government power to free, 230
  Henry's views on, 51–53, 230,
    283–284
  prohibition on owning, 175
Slave trade, attempts to end, 51–52, 74–75,
    84, 91, 118, 148, 192
Sonnets and Other Poems, 169
Sons of Liberty, 42, 47, 50, 65–66, 78, 79
South Carolina, 45, 60, 191–192, 193, 206,
    272, 277
  Revolutionary War in, 110, 118, 119,
    148, 153, 154, 156

Spain, navigation rights on Mississippi
River and, 177, 179–180, 192, 210,
227, 265
The Spirit of Laws (Montesquieu),
113–114
St. John's Anglican Church, 95, 96, 99
St. Paul's Anglican church, 9
Stamp Act (1765), 2, 30–31, 33
debate in House of Burgesses, 37–42
popular opposition to, 42–50
repeal of, 49–50
Stamp Act speech, xiii, 97–98, 279–282
Stills, tax on, 263
Stuart, Archibald, 232, 248–249
Suffolk Resolves, 89–90
Sullivan, John, 119
Surveying skills, 7
Swift, Jonathan, 276
Syme, John, 7, 113
Syme, John, Jr., 7, 35, 50, 156
Syme, Sarah, 7–9

Tabb, William L., 238
Tarleton, Banastre, 153, 154–156
Taxes
Anglican parish, 19–20, 30
colonial opposition to British-imposed,
30–32, 42–50, 59–64, 65–68
national, 163–164
Stamp Act, 30–31, 33
on stills, 263
tea, 67, 78
Townshend Acts, 59–60
Virginia, 161–162
whiskey, 260, 262–263, 276
Tea
Boston Tea Party, 78–79
tax on, 67, 78
Tenth Amendment, 277
Thomson, Charles, 88
Thoughts on Government (Adams),
77, 114
Tidewater aristocracy, 9, 35, 40, 87, 213
Quebec Act and, 81
Tidewater region of Virginia, 9, 35
Todd, John, 148
Tories, return of, 165–166
Townshend, Charles, 59

Townshend Acts, 59–60, 65
repeal of, 67
tax on tea, 67, 78
Trade
between colonies and Britain, 31–33
lack of central authority over, 173–174
slave, 51–52, 74–75, 84, 91, 118,
148, 192
Treatise of Military Discipline, 113
Treaty of Paris, 28, 250, 252
Tryon, William, 74, 78
Twopenny Act (1758), 19–20, 24, 28
Tyler, John, 29–30, 165, 166

United States, map of (1783), 176

Valley Forge (Pennsylvania), xiv, 134,
136–140
Venable, Richard, 246
Virginia
Alien and Sedition Acts and, 269–270
boundary/commerce dispute with
Maryland, 175–177
as largest colony, 34
martial law in, 111
new capitol, 172
new government, 114–116
Piedmont region, 3, 11, 35
plan of government, 114–116, 189–191
preparation for war, 93–99
response to Coercive Acts, 80, 81, 83–85
response to Quebec Act, 81
response to Townshend Acts, 60, 61–64
in Revolutionary War, 107–113,
156–157
separation of church and state in, 116
1771 floods, 72–73
slave trade in, 51–52, 74–75
taxes proposed after the Revolution,
161–162
Tidewater region, 9, 35
western lands of, 28
Virginia Assembly, xiv, 103, 147–148, 151,
159, 161–163, 168, 177, 203, 236.
See also House of Delegates
Virginia Constitution, 116
Virginia Conventions, 95, 96, 107,
113–118, 124, 208, 234

Virginia currency, 108
Virginia Gazette and General Advertiser
    (newspaper), 268
Virginia Gazette (newspaper), 12, 41, 60,
    65, 84, 112, 114
Virginia Historical Society, 286
Virginia militias, 93, 95, 99, 102, 111
von Vattel, Emmerich, 251
Voting
    Continental Congress and, 87–89
    in Virginia, 115–116

Wallace, George, 277
War, declarations of, 95–96
Ward, Samuel, 88
War debt, 163, 164, 250, 260
Washington, George, 94, 171, 211,
    245, 272
    attempts to replace as commander in
        chief, 133–135
    on boycott of British goods, 48–49, 59
    canal-building project and, 167
    command of Continental Army, 104,
        118–121, 123, 128–129, 133–137,
        138–140, 143, 145–146, 148–149,
        153, 156, 158–159
    command of Virginia militia, 93
    Constitutional Convention and, 186,
        187, 188–189, 190–191, 192–194
    death of, 275
    as delegate to intercolonial congress,
        84–85, 91–92
    as delegate to Second Virginia
        Convention, 95, 96
    farewell tour with Lafayette, 168–169
    on frontier life, 3
    on Henry as commander, 110
    as land owner, 257
    land purchases/speculation, 58, 167, 177
    Locke and, 276
    as member of House of Burgesses, 34, 35
    negotiations over Virginia-Maryland
        boundary/commerce, 175–177

on Patrick Henry, 3
political appointments offered to Henry
    and, 264–266
portrait of, 86
pre-Revolutionary War debt, 250
as president, 190, 243
Quebec Act and, 81
ratification of Constitution and, 198,
    202, 203–204, 234
response to Tea Party, 79
on slavery, 52
search for Henry's son John and,
    142–143
Stamp Act debate and, 40
support for federal government, 163,
    173, 175, 179, 270
Whiskey Rebellion and, 2, 263–264, 276
Yazoo Land Company lands and,
    258–259
Washington, John, 146
Washington, Martha, 85, 161
Washington, William, 129
Wayne, "Mad" Anthony, 145, 146, 157
Weatherford, John, 53
Webster, Noah, 87
Westmoreland Protests, 47, 84
Whiskey Boys, 263–264
Whiskey Rebellion, 2, 263–264, 276
Whiskey tax, 260, 262–263, 276
Whites, intermarriage with Indians, xiv,
    166, 170
Williamsburg (Virginia), in Revolutionary
    War, 102–103
Winston, Edmund, 57, 218, 285
Winston, William, 9, 14
Winstons, 9, 58
Wirt, William, 10, 22, 237, 251, 252
Woodford, William, 107, 109, 110, 111,
    152–153
Wythe, George, 16, 34, 62, 171, 186, 218

Yazoo Land Company scandal, xiv,
    258–259